Social Theory, Psychoanalysis and Racism

Social Theory, Psychoanalysis and Racism

Simon Clarke

First published 2003 by
PALGRAVE MACMILLAN
Houndmills, Basingstoke, Hampshire RG21 6XS and
175 Fifth Avenue, New York, N.Y. 10010
Companies and representatives throughout the world

PALGRAVE MACMILLAN is the global academic imprint of the Palgrave Macmillan division of St. Martin's Press, LLC and of Palgrave Macmillan Ltd. Macmillan® is a registered trademark in the United States, United Kingdom and other countries. Palgrave is a registered trademark in the European Union and other countries.

ISBN 0–333–96117–X hardback
ISBN 0–333–96118–8 paperback

This book is printed on paper suitable for recycling and made from fully managed and sustained forest sources.

A catalogue record for this book is available from the British Library.

A catalog record for this book is available from the Library of Congress.

10   9   8   7   6   5   4   3   2   1
12 11 10 09 08 07 06 05 04 03

Printed in China

Contents

List of Examples

Acknowledgements

Many people have helped in the preparation of this book, both directly and indirectly. Catherine Gray has been a helpful editor and has supported this project at every stage. I'd like to thank my colleagues at the University of the West of England for their support over a number of years. In particular Alison Assiter, John Bird, Anthony Elliott, Jem Thomas and Tamsin Wilton. This book was developed within the vibrant atmosphere of the Centre for Psycho-Social Studies at UWE which has close working links with colleagues around the world and has provided an interdisciplinary base for social research. My special thanks go to Paul Hoggett, Michael Rustin and Robert Young who have all helped enormously with this project in different ways. Finally, I'd like to thank John Solomos and Phil Cohen for their critical reading of the original typescript and their helpful and insightful comments.

SIMON CLARKE

For Karen Wilkin

CHAPTER 1

Sociology, Racism and Psychoanalysis: An Introduction

The more we ourselves are susceptible to such emotional reactions as anxiety, anger, ambition, envy, jealousy, love... and appetites of all sorts, and to the 'irrational' conduct that grows out of them, the more readily we can empathise with them. Even when such emotions are found in a degree of intensity of which the observer himself is completely incapable, he can still have a significant degree of emotional understanding of their meaning and can interpret intellectually their influence on the course of action.

(Max Weber, *Economy and Society*, 1978: 6)

There are two central themes in this book which I want to explore and map out for the reader. First, the relationship between sociological thought and psychoanalytic theory, and, second, how we may use these ideas to gain a better understanding of racism and ethnic hatred. Psychoanalysis has enjoyed a somewhat uneasy position within the sociological community, often rejected because certain key concepts are difficult to demonstrate empirically, not least the epistemological basis of the idea of the unconscious mind. There is a subtext to this book in which I try to make psychoanalytic thinking more accessible for sociologists, social scientists and cultural theorists by positioning psychoanalysis as a hermeneutic interpretative method – a sociology of the imagination. In doing so, I am not positing psychoanalytic sociology as a 'better' explanation of racism and ethnic hatred, rather, I am arguing that the combination of psychoanalysis and sociology gives us a deeper *understanding* of the subject area. I think to *understand* racism and other hatreds is about as good as we can get, or hope for; to explain it fully seems as elusive as stopping racism entirely, and naive to boot; hatred of the other is as old as history itself.

Although primarily written as an introductory text, I feel that the psychoanalytically orientated chapters in this book are detailed enough to interest both the newcomer to this field and those more acquainted with the psychoanalytic literature. Work which focuses on sociological and psychoanalytic theory can often be very abstract and dense for the reader. The idea for this book arose from my own experience of teaching sociological and critical theory and the need for providing an accessible way of demonstrating and applying theory to practice. To these ends I have tried to avoid theorising for the sake of it, but applying the perspective to a very real social problem. The contents of this book, therefore, constantly move between theoretical concepts and concrete practical examples. I draw on three broad theoretical positions to examine the affective and emotional basis of racism and other hatreds. The first is that of sociological and anthropological writers such as Robert Miles, Les Back, Mary Douglas and Zygmunt Bauman who examine the structures of modern society which facilitate racism and define 'otherness'. The second area is that of Freudian psychoanalysis and critical theory, and most notably the work of Theodor Adorno, Eric Fromm and Max Horkheimer who arguably pioneered the use of psychoanalysis within sociological research. I also look at post-Freudian thinkers and thought, particularly the work of Frantz Fanon, Jacques Lacan and Slavoj Zizek. The final perspective is influenced by the work of Melanie Klein and the Object Relations School, including writers and analysts such as Wilfred Bion, Betty Joseph, Thomas Ogden and Robert Hinshelwood. I will provide a chapter-by-chapter outline of the contents of this book at the end of this chapter, but first I want to highlight some of the issues and concerns that have compelled me to write it.

Sociological explanations of racism concentrate on the structures of modern life that facilitate discriminatory practices and hierarchies of inequality. As such, sociology fails to address some of the central issues surrounding racism: first, the ubiquity of forms of discrimination and the affective component of hatred; second, the sheer rapidity, the explosive, almost eruptive quality of ethnic hatred, and the way in which communities which used to coexist together, as in the former Yugoslavia, Rwanda and Sierra Leone come to hate and destroy each other. Third, sociology fails to address the visceral and embodied nature of racism and the content of discrimination. Finally, the psychological structuring of discrimination is ignored in this emphasis on social structure, and thus we are unable to look at the psychological mechanisms that provide the impetus for people to hate each other. In other words, sociologists are very good at explaining *how* discrimination arises, but not *why*, affect is left in the sociological cupboard. I believe that there is a complex interrelationship between socio-structural and psychological factors; both need to be addressed in parallel if we are to *understand* the ubiquity and visceral elements of racism.

The sociological literature on race, ethnicity, racism and discrimination is vast, but until recently we have had to look to social anthropologists and social psychologists if we are to understand motivation. Sociologists are very good at proving that racism exists; by quantifying, interviewing and measuring sociology reveals discrimination in housing, health, welfare and many other areas. We are now in a position that enables us to define concepts such as ethnicity, new ethnicities, racism, new racism and anti-racism to name but a few. We can also talk about combating racism with anti-racist policy or positive-action programmes, but we still seem no further in understanding why people are racist. When sociology has attempted to address this, it is usually couched in terms of a social psychological problem, Allport's (1954) *Nature of Prejudice* is probably the most often cited work. This book sets out to fill the explanatory gap in sociological analysis by examining *why* people are racist, *why* people discriminate and *why* people come to hate others.

Theorists of structure have always used some form of psychological phenomena or psychosocial character to support their argument or thesis. In the *Economic and Philosophical Manuscripts*, Marx (McLelland, 1977) talks of the essence of the worker, his or her 'species being' and the alienation of self:

> The human imagination's own activity, the activity of a man's head and heart, react independently on the individual as an alien activity ... the activity of the worker is not his own spontaneous activity. It belongs to another and is a loss of himself.
>
> (1977: 82)

In the *Protestant Ethic and the Spirit of Capitalism*, Max Weber (1993) argues that the psychological internalisation of a way of thinking, 'worldly asceticism', provides a decisive 'impetus' to the development of the economic and social structure of the Western world. If we look at social anthropology, then the link between structure and psyche becomes firmer and more intrinsic in understanding the nature of phenomena. Mary Douglas (1966) in *Purity and Danger* uses the concept of the 'slimey' to designate the polluting Other. Boundaries of the body are symbolic of societal boundaries; the emphasis on difference sustains order, fear of difference sustains difference. Difference is dirty, difference pollutes, difference is dangerous. Zygmunt Bauman (1990) tells us that some people are particularly prone to prejudice, to see the world in oppositions and difference. This manifests itself in racist attitudes, or more importantly for Bauman – xenophobia (*ibid.*: 49). Again we have an explanation which points to a social psychological solution, but interestingly Bauman also cites the psychoanalytic work of Adorno (1950) in the form of the *Authoritarian Personality*. It is in Bauman's (1990, 1991) concept of the *familiar stranger* that we see the emergence of a psychosocial character. A social construction? I think not, strangers are in Bauman's words neither friends nor enemies, neither/nor; they bring inside out and outside in. They are free to leave but will not go:

> Above all, they are bound to come time and again, uninvited into my field of vision – so that I must watch them at close quarters; whether I want it or not, they sit firmly inside the world which I occupy and in which I act and show no signs of leaving. Were it not for this reason, they would not be strangers, but just nobodies.
>
> (Bauman, 1990: 54)

The stranger, like the slimey, is a psychosocial character who threatens us from within and without, or from the inside out. A psychological manifestation, a projection and internalisation of our fear of difference, of being polluted, of being psychologically invaded by otherness. Who are these strangers, refugees from Kosova? Peoples from the former colonies? They are familiar, not enemies, not friends, but strangers. Bauman's analysis centres on the structure(s) of modernity that facilitate racism and ethnic hatred, yet his thesis, like Douglas' is supported by a psychological element. Motivations can be explored with the help of psychoanalysis that address feelings that in some way are more primitive, basic and preemptive of prejudice.

Several sociologists have suggested that we use psychoanalytic ideas to explain and explore racism. Rustin (1991) draws our attention to the work of Jean-Paul Sartre (1976) and Melanie Klein (1946) locating racism and communal hatred in phantasy and paranoia. Rustin stresses that psychoanalytic interpretations are not sufficient in themselves, but are crucial in examination of the irrational mental processes that uphold social and political structures. Stephen Frosh (1989) provides an interesting comment on how some of the psychoanalytic literature on racism has developed, drawing on the work of Lacan (1977), Adorno (1950) and Billig (1978) to chart social psychological and psychoanalytic explanations of fascism. Interestingly, Frosh highlights psychoanalysis's own association with racist modes of thought and investigation. Frosh attributes racism to fears around the 'safety of the psyche'; otherness, whether it be based in gender or ethnic otherness, is perceived as a danger to the psyche. Thus, for Frosh:

> The racist defence, along with the fantasy of 'masculine' order, is part of the hatred of all that modernity brings – of its terrors and disconnection's, of its promise and its fertile creativity. Racism, consequently, is not just anti-Semitic or anti-black; it is anti-world, anti-desire, anti-modernity itself.
>
> (1989: 243)

Frosh's explanation lays the foundation for a thorough examination of the relationship between psychoanalytic understanding and racism. Elliott (1994), similarly, tries to chart the relevance of psychoanalysis, and particularly Kleinian theory, to contemporary cultural criticism. Elliott argues that the Kleinian view of hate and destructiveness, of human pain, anger and despair is of considerable importance for critical social analysis:

> That envy, hate, and destruction are prime components of modern culture is obvious from the amount of violence generated in social relationships, as well as the fascination with violence throughout the population as a whole.
>
> (1994: 84)

Elliott goes on to highlight our morbid, even perverse interest in high-technology weapons during the 1991 Gulf War, a perverse fascination which for Elliott was encapsulated in the television coverage of the war. The war, Elliott describes as a product of a complex interplay between political and military forces and destructive paranoid phantasy. The contemporary world is a mixture of disintegration and reintegration, construction and destruction – love and hate. If, Elliott argues, we are to successfully confront the implications of violence to the self and to others, an awareness of pain, despair and anger is fundamental to analysis. Psychoanalytic theory provides us with a way of thinking about such things in a way that I believe is commensurable with interpretative sociological analysis.

It is from this position, then, that this book has evolved. I have structured it in a way that enables an examination of the theory, the application of theory, method and practice. I start in Chapter 2 with a discussion of theoretical, conceptual and definitional issues surrounding the term racism. The concepts of 'race' and racism are both highly contentious and contested, each meriting a book in its own right. The analysis I provide is not intended to be a definitive guide, rather a point of reference for working definitions that are used in the book. For example, if we view 'race' as a product of pseudo-scientific enquiry, then can we have racism without the concept of race? What did we have before 'race' and do we have something that is in some way 'post-race'? I conclude this chapter by providing some practical examples of the way in which sociologists identify and point to racism through structural inequalities in employment and education before examining sociological ethnographies and institutional racism.

This leads to a discussion of notions of Other and 'Otherness' in Chapter 3. I argue that the concept of 'race' is a socially constructed container through which we project our 'inner world' onto others. Others are a psychological manifestation of our fear of difference. I suggest that the idea of 'new racism' is anything but new, and is merely a different articulation of older beliefs about 'race' set within a comfortable package of cultural difference. It is argued that both forms of racism are in reality the same thing, and there is merely a shift in the use of language from one form to the other. The author illustrates this shift using the work of writers such as Anna-Marie Smith and Martin Barker, who highlight the discursive nature of cultural difference and its use in the political arena. Ethnicity has replaced 'race' as the preferred term of social scientists, but has it just replaced 'race' as another form of pathological categorisation, is it better to think of Diaspora? I address these questions before going on to suggest a series of tentative working definitions.

In Chapter 4 I explore the way in which contemporary sociology has focused on social structure to explain the way in which modernity has facilitated mass violence and made racism possible. Racism, for Bauman, is unthinkable without the structures of modernity – the nation-state, rational scientific techniques, technology – and as such, racism is a strictly modern product. I examine in some detail the notion of 'race' as social engineering and the way in which romantic and ideological mythologies formed an uncanny relationship with science in the Third Reich, with particular reference to the involvement of the medical profession in the perpetration of atrocities. I go on to argue that Bauman's concept of the *stranger* has a particular quality, that of a psychosocial character. A bridge is drawn for the reader between the socio-structural and the psychological, demonstrating the way in which psychological mechanisms support structures of inequality and discrimination. This chapter is pivotal in that it demonstrates some of the shortcomings in traditional sociological explanation and the need for the sociologist to introduce psychological mechanisms to support structural arguments.

Chapter 5 is an introduction to psychoanalytic thinking and an examination of the way in which Freudian psychoanalytic theory can contribute to our understanding of racism and ethnic conflict. I start with a general discussion of psychoanalytic theory before going on to focus on the theoretical underpinnings of Freud's work in which I discuss his model(s) of mind(s) and thesis on civilisation. The reader is introduced to the concepts of repression, sublimation and, critically, projection. Projection is used as a defence in paranoia through fear of the 'other'. In a discussion of Freud's notion of the 'uncanny' I argue that the concept of projection is central to our understanding of the way in which we perceive and treat others. This chapter lays a theoretical foundation for the following psychoanalytic chapters in this book.

To illustrate in a practical sense the application of Freudian theory, in Chapter 5 I examine the early work of the Frankfurt Institute for Social Research and in particular the work of Eric Fromm, Max Horkheimer and Theodor Adorno. The work of Fromm has long been neglected and highly criticised for what Herbert Marcuse has described as Freudian revisionism. Horkheimer and Adorno have been slated as biological reductionists conducting ethnocentric studies under the auspices of the Institute. Despite these criticisms, few others have tried to explain racism and ethnic conflict in terms of psychoanalytic theory. The Frankfurt

School offer a considerable body of literature from which to illustrate and build a psychosocial explanation of racism and exclusion – a critical base which has been largely neglected in contemporary studies. Horkheimer and Adorno draw heavily on Freud's instinct theory weaving powerful primitive drives and projective mechanisms of defence to explain the pathological nature of anti-Semitism. Fromm, however, attempts to argue a social basis in the shaping of instinctual drives in a historical, social and psychological explanation of conflict.

Thus we have a tension between biological explanations of the motivation of the racist and explanation which is set within the social psychological realm. This serves as both an introduction to the reader of the application of Freudian theory and the problems that surround the area, thus providing a basis for the exploration of the work of contemporary theorists.

Chapter 7 continues the Freudian theme with an exploration of the seminal work of Frantz Fanon (1968) – *Black Skin White Masks*. The strong reference throughout Fanon's work to Jean-Paul Sartre's writings allows us to address the notion of 'Psychoexistentialism' and its impact on the explanation of colonialisation and anti-Semitism. The work of Frantz Fanon is widely accepted as one of most important contributions to postcolonial studies, to the critique of colonial discourse, and is widely used in cultural studies. This has spurred a whole set of secondary literature on Fanon's work including Bulhan's (1985) *Frantz Fanon and the Psychology of Oppression*, Gordon *et al.*'s (1996) *Fanon: A Critical Reader*, McCulloch's (1983) *Black Soul White Artefact*, Sekyi-Otu's (1996) *Fanon's Dialectic of Experience*, and of course David Macey's (2000) *Frantz Fanon: A Life*. Gordon *et al.* (1996) point to the sheer breadth and coverage of Fanon's writings which span the academic disciplines of politics, social science, literature and philosophy. Indeed, such is the interest in Fanon's work that Gordon *et al.* (1996) argue that we now have a distinct area which we can term *Fanon Studies*. I use Fanon's interest in the work of Jacques Lacan to provide a basic introduction to contemporary Lacanian writings on 'race', ethnicity and the construction of black identity. Key authors include Kalpana Seshadri Crooks (2000) and Slavoj Zizek (1991). This chapter provides both a detailed account of Frantz Fanon's work and an easily understood introduction to the work of Lacan, which in itself provides an opening for discussion of the work of Melanie Klein in the following chapter.

Chapter 8 starts with a concise introduction to the work of Melanie Klein and the object relations school(s). In this chapter I suggest ways in which we might start thinking about racism, exclusion and discrimination within a Kleinian interpretative schema and the advantages this may bring to social science enquiry. I introduce the concept of a critical sociological theory of racism, and go on to argue that a Kleinian psychodynamic interpretation of racism can overcome many of the theoretical leaps of Freudian theory, providing us with a critical analysis of the social and psychological dynamics at work in a racist society. The work of Klein provides a new and exciting way of exploring and thinking about issues of 'race' and conflict. It is the communicative aspect of Klein's work which can help us explain the ways in which we think of others, of how we feel about others and, crucially, how we make others feel. This chapter looks in detail at key Kleinian ideas. The concepts of 'positions', 'splitting' and 'phantasy' are discussed and applied in explanations of racism and ethnic hatred. These concepts together with the mechanism of projective identification, I argue, are at the heart of understanding hatred and discrimination.

Projective identification is, for Klein, the prototype of all aggressive object relations and a crucial mechanism of defence. Projection *per se* is a relatively straightforward process in which we attribute our own affective state to others, we project *onto* rather than *into*. Projective identification, however, involves a deep split, a ridding of unpalatable parts of the self into some other, forcing them to feel the way we do, or feel how we feel about them. In Chapter 9 I guide the reader through different interpretations of projective identification, drawing on the work of Klein, Bion, Joseph, Ogden, Hinshelwood and Young to demonstrate the complexity of the idea and the different levels on which it operates. I argue that the mechanism of projective identification is crucial to our understanding of the ubiquity of racism. This idea is reinforced by a series of examples and case studies of racism and ethnic hatred.

I conclude this book by arguing that a synthesis of sociological and psychoanalytic research methodology and theory can provide the social scientist with a new set of tools to use in explanation of social and political phenomena. In a Kleinian re-reading of Freud's concept of the 'uncanny' I argue that as an aesthetic, a quality of feeling, the uncanny is deeply entrenched in phantasy. Phantasy provides a vehicle for the construction of our own identity and that of others. Uncanniness is not produced by the repression of drives, but in the way we relate to our fellow human beings. I suggest that if we take these Kleinian ideas and combine them with socio-structural analysis, then we are better placed to *understand* the eruptive and visceral nature of racial violence and ethnic hatred in a critical sociological theory of racism.

CHAPTER 2

The Concept(s) of Race(s) and Racism(s)

The idea of 'racism without race' is not as revolutionary as one might imagine ... A racism which does not have the pseudo-biological concept of race as its main driving force has always existed.

(Balibar, 1991)

Introduction

In this chapter, and Chapter 3, I want to provide an introduction to some of the theoretical, conceptual and definitional issues surrounding the terms 'race', racism and ethnicity, the concepts of which are highly contentious, each meriting a book in its own right. What I hope to provide, therefore, is not a definitive guide, rather a point of reference from which to provide working definitions of concepts, terms and notions that will be used throughout this book.

The concept of race will be discussed as the basis of racism, how can we have racism without race? This opens up a discussion of notions of 'otherness'. What did we have before 'race', what do we have 'post-race'? I will argue that the notion of race is a socially constructed 'container' through which we project our inner world onto others. Others are a psychological manifestation of our fear of difference. The concepts of both ethnicity and 'new racism' will be examined in detail in the following chapter where I will suggest that new racism is not new, rather it is a way of articulating older beliefs about race by shifting the emphasis of discourse to make cultural comparisons of biological things. I will then go on to argue that the term ethnicity can be just as problematic as notions of race, and in itself can also be used as a form of containment, a category for holding feelings, emotions and fear of difference. I provide in this chapter some examples of how sociologists point to and identify racism in the social fabric of society, before concluding with a discussion of institutional and structural racism in which I argue that it is not enough to view institutional racism as merely the discriminatory aspect of administrative procedures, rather there is a complex interaction between structure and affect.

Race and the other

The notion of race corresponds to or occupies a highly contentious area of academic debate. The word 'race' has been associated with ideas of inferiority and superiority, hierarchy and persecution. Race as a science, race as a pseudo-science, race as a social construct. As Miles (1993) argues, whatever the manner in which the term is used it implies

> an acceptance of the existence of biological differences between human beings, differences which express the existence of distinct, self reproducing groups.
>
> (1993: 2)

Race more than any other term is associated with a dangerous, if not ignorant assumption that implies the world is split into very distinct dichotomies, that there is more than one human race, ignoring the wealth of cultural and ethnic diversity and as Miles (1993) suggests recent scientific knowledge which shows that the 'world's population could not be legitimately categorised in this way' (1993: 3). We have a historical legacy in which scientific enquiry has developed the notion of 'race' or 'races' based, as Fryer (1991) suggests, on a form of enlightenment dualism, of superstition and ignorance in which biological endowment and physical features were thought to have a causal relationship with cultural superiority. Banton (1970) locates the genesis of racism in Knox's *The Races of Men* (1850), Gobineau's *Essai* (1853) and Nott and Gliddon's *Types of Mankind* (1854), arguing that with the demise of slavery 'some people sought new justifications for maintaining the subordination of those who had earlier been exploited by being counted as property' (Banton, 1970: 19). Biological racism was espoused through social Darwinism and other pseudo-scientific theories of race. Darwin's theory of evolution was applied to human society by Herbert Spencer who coined the phrase the 'survival of the fittest'.

The white Anglo-Saxon represented the culmination of the evolutionary process. Scientific racism has two key characteristics. The first, a biologising of race in terms of 'colour' and 'stock'. The second, a ranking of people in hierarchies of race implying gradations of inferior and superior beings. Mason (1995) and Fryer (1991) highlight the interaction between science and politics which led to the use of 'race science' as a justification for slavery:

> nineteenth-century race science was possible in part because it was in tune with wider social developments. Early discussions of racial difference had found a ready audience in those who wished to justify slavery. By the time Social Darwinism emerged, the age of the empire had truly arrived, with the great powers of Europe dividing up Africa between them.
>
> (Mason, 1995: 7)

Miles (1989) also draws attention to the use of pseudo-scientific race discourse to both justify the environmental use of Africans in slavery, and the notion that it would give 'them' (the 'other') a chance to escape from 'savagery'. However, this is a view that Miles argues was not widely legitimated. The notion of the African as being biologically suited to slavery had only a minority status. The importance lies not in the link between race and justifications for both colonisation and slavery, but in the way in which representations of the 'other' were narrowed down and clearly defined by scientific enquiry:

> The sense of difference embodied in European representations of the Other became interpreted as a difference of 'race', that is, primarily *biological* and *natural* difference which was inherent and unalterable. Moreover, the supposed difference was presented as scientific (that is, objective) fact.
>
> (Miles, 1989: 31; emphasis in original)

Race as 'containment'

Clearly, what is important for Miles is not what notions of race were used to justify, but the power of scientific enquiry to define, classify, categorise and perpetuate ideas of inferiority between 'men' through the concept of 'race'. 'Race' itself becomes a product of scientific enquiry. This concept is central to any explanation of racism, hatred and exclusion. Race theory represents a consolidation of hundreds, perhaps thousands of years of hatred and fear of and persecution of those who are different, the 'Other'. There is no doubt that certain structures of modernity make racism more possible; global transportation and communication links, technology and science, but in the same way, the atrocities of Nazi Germany have nullified this consolidation. It is no longer acceptable, with the exception of a few individuals on the periphery of society, to talk of others as being biologically inferior. As Mason (1995) notes: 'The revelation of the horrors of the Holocaust, and the enlistment of science in its perpetration, caused a wave of international revulsion' (1995: 7). In light of this, can we suggest that the concept of 'race' is just one symptom of our fear of difference. An attempt to pinpoint something we are scared of; after all, if we can classify and contain it we can control it. This suggests that there was something before race, something unclassified, and something 'post-race'. 'Race' becomes a container, or more specifically a *containment* of our fear of difference.

If we postulate that the concept of race is about the containment of the Other, then who is the Other? Robert Miles (1995) provides an extended commentary on 'representations of the Other' in his book *Racism*. Miles argues that the very process of representing some Other entails acts of inclusion and exclusion. For example, if we define ourselves by either cosmetic or cultural characteristics, then we automatically exclude Others from our social group. Geographically, we can define ourselves by reference to the Other: They are non-European, therefore we are European. We do not need a (pseudo) scientific explanation of biological difference to exclude or even hate Others.

Mary Douglas (1966) argues in *Purity and Danger* that the boundaries of the body are symbolic of societal boundaries. Black 'otherness', or Jewish 'otherness' emphasises difference to create order, and in doing so excludes others in structures of discrimination.

The Other is a crucial *symbol* in the definition of who 'we' are. If 'race' is about clinical definitions of difference, then the construction of the 'Other' is about both perception and fear of difference, a specific 'otherness' imputed by biological-racial inferiority. Highlighting the significance of pollution in relation to the body, Douglas parallels reactions to dirt with reactions to ambiguity, in some sense representing 'reaction to fear in another guise' (Douglas, 1966: 5). Race is about containment of that fear. In this way, the exaggeration of difference creates a form of order, who we are, or perhaps more precisely who we are not, by the stigmatisation, marginalisation and intolerance of Others. 'Pollution powers' are, for Douglas, an integral part of the structure of ideas:

> I believe that ideas about separating, purifying, demarcating and punishing transgressions have as their main function to impose system on an inherently untidy experience. It is only by exaggerating the difference between within and without, above and below, male and female, with and against, that a semblance of order is created.
>
> (Douglas, 1966: 4)

Pollution powers punish the breaking of things that should be joined and the joining of things that should be separate. Douglas is arguing that the notion of the 'polluting Other' defines the way in which boundaries are constructed. Pollution and dirt are associated with danger which becomes associated with the Other. The Other then becomes dangerous. Representations of polluting Others became rife in colonial Britain with travellers reporting back from their escapades:

> In this river there are great store of savages which we saw, and had conference with them: they were man eaters, and fed altogether upon raw flesh and other filthy food.
>
> (in Hakluyt, 1972: 279)

The power associated with the 'polluting Other' is central to the way in which the structures of society are maintained and protected. The physical crossing of a boundary has two implications: the Other is not only wrong for crossing that boundary, but s/he endangers the lives of others by subjecting them to the danger of difference. If we are to assume that the concept of 'race' is a containment of this Other, scientifically defined, categorised and manageable, or at least seemingly controllable, what is the position of the Other post-Holocaust or post-race? In Chapter 4 I will discuss, using the work of Zygmunt Bauman, the fate of the post-race Other.

So, what is racism?

Racism – a true 'total social phenomenon' – inscribes itself in practices (forms of violence, contempt, intolerance, humiliation and exploita-tion), in discourses and representations which are so many intellectual elaborations of the phantasm of prophylaxis or segregation (the need to purify the social body, to preserve 'one's own' or 'our' identity from all forms of mixing, interbreeding or invasion) which are articulated around stigmata of otherness (name, skin colour, religious practices).

(Balibar and Wallerstein, 1991: 17)

The debate surrounding conceptual and definitional issues of the term 'racism' is both vast and at least as contentious as the notion of 'race'. This area is too large to be covered thoroughly in this text, rather an outline will be provided of various arguments to provide a basis from which to seek reference in the context of this book. Racism, expressed by Balibar and Wallerstein (1991) in the quote above, can manifest itself in practices, discourse and representations of otherness. Racism is a social and psychological phenomena, it is 'intersubjective, ideological and systematic' (Anthias and Yuval-Davis, 1992: 16). The term 'racism', however, is fairly new (Banton, 1970; Solomos and Back, 1996), and was first used by Ruth Benedict in *Race and Racism* (1940) where it referred to a set of ideas which defined groups in terms of biological inferiority or superiority. Similarly Banton (1970) defines racism as

The doctrine that a man's behaviour is determined by stable inherited characteristics deriving from separate racial stocks having distinctive attributes and usually considered to stand to one another in relations of superiority and inferiority.

(1970: 18)

Banton roots his definition of racism in scientific concepts of race whereby people may be discriminated against or excluded from society on the basis of racial doctrines. This led Banton to conclude, as Miles (1989) notes, that racism was dead (Banton, 1970: 18). Miles argues that racism should only be viewed in terms of ideology, suggesting that 'conceptual inflation' serves only to create more problematics. As the term encompasses wider phenomena it starts to lose any explanatory power. Miles uses the term ideology to mean a discourse which (mis)represents human beings in a distorted way (1989: 42). It would seem that what Miles is trying to argue is that by concentrating on specific individuals and institutions we are drawing away from discourse or analysis situated in notions of the 'other'. Explanation becomes highly specific in a social, political and historical context. We then begin to have instances where, for example, Daniel Goldhagen (1996) in *Hitler's Willing Executioners*, focuses on the 'Germaness' of the crime, in relation to the Jewish Holocaust. This, then, has very little explanatory power when looking at other instances of twentieth-century genocide. Thus, Miles argues:

> We are offered definitions and theories of racism that are so specific to the history of overseas colonisation (that is, specific to the domination of 'white' over 'black' as so many writers express it) that they are of little value in explaining any other (non-colonial) context.
>
> (1989: 68)

We therefore have an argument that conceptual definitions of racism are both too specific to be of any explanatory use, but also that it encompasses so many different phenomena that again it has very little explanatory power. Miles (1989) prefers to use the term 'racialization'; 'where social relations between people have been structured by the signification of human biological practices in such a way as to define and construct differentiated social collectivities' (Miles, 1989: 75). Thus, race is a social construct at the centre of the racialisation process, and this becomes racism (ideologically) when there is a negative evaluation.

In Example 2.1, Bauman is referring to racism in terms of a pseudo-scientific construct that forms part of the modernist project, these ideas become embedded in the social structure and practices of modern life. These ideas are not new, Oliver Cox (1948) argues in *Caste, Class and Race* that 'race prejudice' is a direct result of the class structures of capitalism. Similarly, Rex (1970) and Rex and Tomlinson (1979) have argued that 'race' relations between people are shaped by certain structural conditions, and in particular the degree to which minority ethnic groups share the class position of the white working class. Rex and Tomlinson (1979) argue that many minority ethnic groups stand outside the position of their white working-class counterparts and therefore constitute an 'underclass' – a group of people who are systematically disadvantaged. Bauman's explanation goes beyond these traditional structural accounts and concentrates on the structures and practices of the nation-state:

> Racism stands apart by a practice of which it is a part and which it ratio-nalises: a practice that combines strategies of architecture and gardening with that of medicine – in the service of the construction of an artificial

---

Example 2.1   Modernity and racism

In *Modernity and the Holocaust*, Zygmunt Bauman (1989) provides us with what is probably the best example of a structural account of racism and ethnic hatred (I will provide a detailed account of this in Chapter 4). Racism, for Bauman, is unthinkable without the structures of modernity. Rapid changes in the social sphere, urbanisation and dislocation, the triumph of science as a mode of cognition and the growth of bureaucracy have provided the technological and scientific conditions that have made racism possible. As such, 'racism is a strictly modern product' (Bauman, 1989: 61). Modernity not only made racism possible, but created a demand for it; a justification for boundary-drawing and boundary-guarding. For Bauman:

> Modernity made racism possible. It also created a demand for racism; an era that declared achievement to be the only measure of human worth needed a theory of ascription to redeem boundary-drawing and boundary-guarding concerns under new conditions which made boundary-crossing easier than ever before.
>
> (Bauman, 1989: 62)

---

social order, through cutting out the elements of the present reality that neither fit the visualised perfect reality, nor can be changed so that they do.

(Bauman, 1989: 65)

For Bauman, racism is a form of social engineering that is wholly congruent with enlightenment ideas of rationality, of structure, of order, and of the modern state. Bauman's notion of racism provides a counter to Miles' notion of racism as an ideological construct. Bauman is clear about this point: 'Racism is a policy first, ideology second. Like all politics, it needs organisation, managers and experts' (1989: 74). If we return to Miles' ideas: in defining Racism as an ideological construct, Miles plays down what the term means to many people. In other words, structures and practices of discrimination and exclusion based on prejudice and embedded in a process of racial and ethnic categorisation rooted in stereotypy. Anthias and Yuval-Davis (1992) note that the most common forms of racism are not explicit ideologies or discourses of biological inferiorisation, rather they are exclusionary practices that result from not belonging to the dominant culture. The discreditation of 'race' has led to a shift in racist discourse from a stress on biological inferiority to the language of cultural difference. The emphasis is now expressed in terms of what Barker (1981) calls the *New Racism* (see Chapter 3). Difference legitimises acts of inclusion and exclusion. Racism is no longer justified in terms of physicality, but in terms of cultural difference.

Identifying racism: structural inequalities

A point that I make throughout this book is that in advocating a psychoanalytic understanding of racism and ethnic hatred I am in no way criticising sociological analysis. Rather, I am trying to build on the understanding that sociology has already offered us. The huge contribution that sociology has made in the study of racism and ethnic hatred is nowhere better exemplified than in the ability of sociologists to point to and identify racism and structural inequalities. The variables used by sociologists are fairly standard: class; inclusion and exclusion from the labour market; housing; access to health care; and access to and exclusion from the education system. Work in these areas often takes the form of a scientific enquiry using statistical evidence to point to and identify structures of inclusion and exclusion which promote inequality between various groups. To take two of these areas – education and employment, we can see how sociology addresses the structural impediments to social progress.

Modood (1997) argues that racial discrimination in employment has become so routine that it is almost invisible to those who actually practice it. Indeed, for Modood, 'racial disadvantage, then continues to be a fact, even if it does not apply to all ethnic minority groups' (1997: 144). Mason (1995) argues that the fundamental question in any analysis of the labour market position for ethnic minorities is whether or not one has access to employment at all. Mason notes that minority ethnic groups are constantly at risk of higher unemployment than their white counterparts, and this tends to be cyclical. In other words, in times of economic recession the minority ethnic unemployment rate rises rapidly; as the economy grows, the rate falls rapidly. Mason argues that the unemployment rate of minority ethnic men is about twice that of their white peers (Mason, 1995: 49). There are also substantial differences in the unemployment rate between minority ethnic groups (see Modood, 1997). Solomos and Back (1996) draw our attention to the high levels of unemployment amongst ethnic minority youth, citing evidence from a Runnymede statistical survey which concluded that the differential employment rates between black and white youth had reached astronomical proportions (Solomos and Back, 1996: 70).

There is clear evidence, then, that there are huge disparities in the employment prospects of different minority groups. These are taken as an indicator of direct, indirect and subtle forms of discrimination. Thus we have pointed to a fact, that racism and discrimination exist in the labour market, and we can then move on and try to explain this phenomenon from a sociological perspective. Mason (1995) highlights two trends in explaining disadvantage. The first is to blame the victim of discrimination by explaining unemployment in terms of poor language skills and lack of formal educational qualifications. However, this thesis does not hold water for several reasons: (a) although there is some evidence to suggest that those with poor English skills face more difficulties in the labour market, this does not account for the difficulties faced by minority ethnic groups who were born and educated in Britain (Mason, 1995: 57); (b) there is extensive evidence to suggest that minority ethnic workers are more likely to be unemployed than their white peers with the same qualifications (see Modood, 1997; Mason, 1995; Jenkins, 1986); and (c) there is also clear evidence to suggest that discrimination in the education system stands as a barrier to obtaining formal qualifications for a significant number of minority groups (see Clarke and Bird, 2000; Gilborn, 1996).

Although these explanations may account for some of the disadvantages suffered by minority groups in the labour market, Mason draws our attention to a number of studies which point to discrimination as a major factor in unemployment. This second explanation of disadvantage focuses on acts of intentional discrimination which remains a major feature of the labour market (Mason, 1995: 58). Mason notes that the usual method to isolate acts of such discrimination is to submit job applications matched in every way except ethnic origin. Although substantial numbers of employers treated applications in a fair and equal way, equally large numbers did not. The result was a large difference between ethnic groups in terms of positive responses to their applications from employers. As various laws have made it more difficult for this type of practice to take place, research has focused on less overt forms of discrimination.

We have, therefore, some very good examples of sociological studies that point to and identify acts of discrimination and ultimately

---

Example 2.2   Racism and employment

Richard Jenkins' (1986) study of racism and recruitment focuses on the criteria used by employers in the selection process. Jenkins argues that selection is often based on two broad criteria: *suitability* and *acceptability*. Suitability criteria are defined by the requirements of the job itself. So a bus driver must be qualified to drive a bus. Jenkins is not as much interested in suitability, but places a considerable emphasis on acceptability. Selection criteria of acceptability include: appearance, manner and attitude, maturity, a manager's 'gut feeling' and speech style. Twelve criteria in all are listed which Jenkins argues form the basis for discrimination against minority ethnic workers:

> Some of these criteria, such as the ability to 'fit in' or literacy, may, in their application by specific managers, be directly discriminatory in a straight-forward and obviously racist fashion. Less obviously, however, a criterion such as maturity will, given the age and structure of the black population, be indirectly discriminatory in its effects.
>
> (Jenkins, 1986: 79)

Thus, for Jenkins, employers use a set of criteria in the selection process which is ethnocentric and based in a set of stereotypes of workers from different minority groups. Someone may be wholly suitable for a job in terms of qualifications and experience but using these acceptability criteria is discriminated against in the selection process.

---

racism in the labour market and employment practices. If we now turn to the education system, then there seems to be a similar picture. If we take, for example, the exclusion from school of African Caribbean boys then there seems to be some kind of lucana in sociological explanation. Rates of exclusion from school are rising, but these exclusions have remained largely unexplained.

In a society which emphasises the importance of social inclusion, the exclusion of students from compulsory schooling and the fate for those excluded in terms of prospective employment is a major issue. This is particularly the case given that exclusion rates have been rising for a number of years, and the apparent inability of the education system to do anything about this rise (see Gillborn, 1996). Gillborn argues that between 1994 and 1996, permanent exclusions from school have risen from 3000 to just over 10 000 students. African Caribbean students are seven times more likely to be excluded than their white counterparts, and this exclusion is more prevalent in boys.

The most obvious, commonsensical explanation of exclusions is likely to focus on two things: *ability* and *behaviour*. In sociology, for example, there is a long history, starting with Cohen's (1995) studies of working-class gangs, of arguing that working-class boys are unable to succeed in school and see membership of a gang, and the consequent rejection of education, as their only source of social status. Their bad behaviour becomes the reason for exclusion, and that exclusion gives the boys height and status, and therefore makes their return to schooling unlikely. We could suggest that a similar argument would explain the exclusion of African Caribbean boys. First, they are working-class and see no future in education. Second, they are of low ability, often the result of racism within the education system. Third, because of the first two issues they behave badly in school and are therefore excluded. And finally, that exclusion gives them status among their peers.

Again, though, as with the example of employment, there seems to be a certain tendency to blame and label the victim of exclusion. There is overwhelming evidence to suggest that the parents of African Caribbean pupils put a high priority on education (see Smith and Tomlinson, 1989), and there is no consistent evidence that African Caribbean students are of low ability. Indeed, Ofsted (1996) argues that of the group that are most likely to be excluded, the African Caribbean group, is the only group that is *at* or *above* average levels of attainment. Finally, there is no reliable evidence that the behaviour of African Caribbean boys in school is noticeably disruptive in comparison with the behaviour of groups that are not excluded. As Gillborn (1995) argues:

> Some African Caribbean young people are frequently in disciplinary conflict with teachers. Of particular concern is the way that a small minority of teachers express generalised views that depict African Caribbean students (as a group) as a greater threat to their authority. This 'myth' prompted teachers to greater control and criticism of African Caribbeans.
>
> (1995: 183)

For Gillborn, the myth has a number of significant features: challenge to teachers is seen as deep-seated; such a challenge is seen as needing to be tackled early, 'to nip it in the bud'; expressions of African Caribbean ethnicity are seen as part of this challenge; and the challenge is seen as rooted in African Caribbean culture.

In addition, the Afro Caribbean group is distinct in terms of ideas about disruptive behaviour and its origins. This is how Ofsted puts it:

> Although many of them [Afro Caribbean pupils] had been excluded several times, their disruptive behaviour did not usually date from early in their school career, nor was it so obviously associated with deep-seated trauma as with many white children.
>
> (1996: 11)

Again, we have some very good examples of how sociology is able to point to, and identify a problem. Some of the more revealing studies of racism tend to be ethnographies where the researcher has immersed him or herself in the community studied. I am thinking particularly of the work of Les Back (1996) whose excellent insight into urban life gives us many clues about the transmission and persistence of racism. There has been a long tradition of ethnographic research based in an anthropological model, for example Evans-Pritchard's (1965) classic account of the Azande – *Witchcraft, Oracles and Magic Among the Azande,* the work of the Chicago school – I have already mentioned Cohen's work on gangs, and Whyte's (1955) street-corner society. A more recent and contemporary study is Ken Pryce's (1979) study of life in St Pauls, Bristol – *Endless Pressure.* Back's (1996) work, however, seems to give a real taste of life in the urban environment and some of the complex and elaborate forms of exclusion that exist there (see Example 2.3).

Institutional and individual racisms: attitude and action

Racism is embedded in the structure of society: as inequalities in access to housing, employment and education bear testimony. Institutions reflecting this society maintain rules and practices which perpetuate racism, these in turn rebound back to the individual: attitude manifests itself in action which becomes discrimination. We need, however, to understand the relationship between individual and institutional racism in order that we may have some form of understanding of these complex phenomena.

Put quite simply, institutional racism is an attempt to move away from the idea that inequality arises as a result of the attitudes of

---

Example 2.3   Racism and urban life

Les Back (1996) conducted his research over a number of years using participant observation in two postwar housing estates that he describes as situated in south London. Fictitiously named Riverview and Southgate to provide anonymity, the first is a predominantly white working-class area, the latter a multi-ethnic area. Back rented a flat in the area for the duration of the research and worked as a voluntary youth-club worker to gain access to the young people he was studying. What Back produces is a rich ethnography of culture, community and youth identity, which is explored through the analysis of racist name-calling; the creation of a ghetto through mass housing; the exploration of black and white identity; the parodying of racism, and musical culture. Back draws to our attention to how identities and ethnicity (see the following chapter for a discussion of ethnicity) are negotiated. Negotiation takes place on two levels of meaning. First, there is the specific micro context in which negotiation takes place through dialogue in multiracial friendships – 'in the context of these friendship patterns young white and black people construct an alternative public sphere in which truly mixed ethnicities develop' (Back, 1996: 158). The second negotiated meaning is based in the way young people re-fashion publicly-generated definitions of identity. As Back points out, these negotiations are often undermined by racist discourses, but the result in these communities is that young people create a culture which is neither black nor white, which defies the logic of the new racism (see Chapter 3).

I feel that what is particularly useful in Back's work is that rather than merely pointing to and identifying racism, he starts to develop an account of why people are racist. Back notes that white youth use popular racism as a strategic resource (*ibid.*: 242). Although racism is understood to be 'out of order' it is precisely because it is out of order that it is used, to gain advantage in duelling play by white youth over their black peers. In a more predominantly multi-racial area racism was expressed in terms of the experience of institutions, namely education, work and the police force.

---

a few, sad, prejudiced people. Rather, racism is endemic in the structures, rules and practices of institutions and in this context racism becomes self-perpetuating. As Troyna (1992: 85) notes: 'Racism is frequently used as a synonym for institutional racism. This is intended to denote how far it has been naturalised into established attitudes, procedural norms and social patterns'. Institutional racism, therefore, is not overt or open but becomes concealed in practices established as the norm. Equal Opportunities policy is such that employers are unable to openly discriminate against people, but as Cashmore and Troyna (1990) lucidly comment:

> An organisation might have what it considers to be a perfect equal opportunities policy. But, if ethnic minorities don't get recruited in the numbers one might expect, then the end result means that racism is at work.
>
> (1990: 18)

Thus, for example, individual conscious designs may not motivate the exclusion of ethnic minorities from higher education, rather exclusion stems from underlying structural, 'taken-for-granted' practices, the constructed nature of education, and unconscious motives. This view is supported by Miles (1989) who differentiates between racism (ideological), racialisation (identification based on biological collectivity), and institutional racism (practice). Institutional racism for Miles may be the cause of disadvantage for certain groups but may no longer contain explicit racist content:

> racist discourse becomes silent, but is nethertheless embodied (or institutionalised) in the continuation of exclusionary practices or in the use of a new discourse. The continuing practice or the new discourse is expressive of an earlier, racist discourse.
>
> (1989: 85)

In other words, practices that we take for granted, that are not explicitly racist, may have had their origins in racist discourse; exclusion still occurs, but the reasoning behind that exclusion is no longer explicit in present discourse. Hence, as Bird (1996) argues, institutions are not made up of the sum total of the actions of the individuals working in them, and therefore we can have non-racist individuals working in racist organisations. This, of course, can only be a theoretical model; it assumes that people who work in organisations abide by the rules. If we follow Weber's (1978) model of bureaucratic organisations, then we all become faceless office-holders. This thesis ignores individual agency and the power of affect. While the institution may still carry racist discourse within its tenets, arguably this is reinforced by individuals who have been socialised in a racist society, or, in other words, hold prejudices. Prejudice, simply defined is 'thinking ill of others without warrant' (Allport, 1954: 6). Again, put simply, discrimination can be seen as acting on that prejudice. The fact that people hold prejudices is enough to make others feel excluded. Exclusion may not result from any form of overt racism, but from a form of individual and embodied racism within the institution.

The concept of institutional racism is therefore more complex that it first seems. On one level it may be defined as 'the discriminatory impact of administrative procedures' (Braham, Rattansi and Skellington, 1992: 107), on another it is a complex interaction between a silent racist discourse which has become embodied within an institution which is reinforced and interacts with individuals within that institution. In this sense, structure and affect fuel each other and cannot be separated. It is naive to think that inequality and exclusion arise from the attitudes of a handful of racists. We all hold prejudices, these are inscribed in the institutions and structure of society as well as the individual. Exclusion may have become unintentional but has the same effect. I therefore argue that the term institutional racism encompasses emotional and organisational structures which generate both feelings and processes of exclusion within both institutions and the workplace.

Summary

There are very clear structural impediments in the social fabric of society that emanate from a history of colonialisation and racist discourse. These are ingrained in the procedures and practices of institutions which contine to transmit discourses of exclusion. One of the reasons why sociology seems only to offer a partial understanding, albeit a very good one, of racism, is that whilst addressing social structure it fails to explore the ways we relate to each other as individuals, and as a group. There is a distinct lack of attention to emotions, to our hopes and fears, to the ways that we perceive others and the construction of otherness. A good part of this book is dedicated to a psychoanalytic understanding of our internal and external worlds, which I feel complements sociological understanding or *Verstehen*.

The aim of this chapter has been to provide a discussion of the theoretical, conceptual and definitional issues surrounding the terms 'race' and racism. It is not meant to be an exhaustive review, this has been done elsewhere, but should provide the reader with an overview of some of the key debates and issues. I have traced the historical usage of the term 'race' and have argued that the concept is a form of containment, both a symptom of our fear of difference and an attempt to classify, define and therefore contain otherness. If we can contain our fear, then we can control it. There is thus a clear element of power relations in the construction of the concept. We therefore have the notion of 'race' science, which culminated in the atrocities of Nazi Germany.

If the term 'race' is controversial, then defining racism is even harder. Again, I have outlined some of the key debates in this area. Racism manifests itself in practices, discourses and representations of otherness. For Miles (1990), racism should be viewed in terms of ideology – a discourse that (mis)represents human beings in a distorted way. For Bauman (1989, 1991), racism is a product of modernity, a pseudo-scientific construct which becomes embedded in the social fabric and practices of modern life. Antithetically, Anthias and Yuval-Davis (1992) remind us that the most common forms of racism are not explicit ideologies or discourses of biological inferiority, but are exclusionary practices that result from not belonging to the dominant culture. This I believe to be a salient reminder to all of us to get out of our theoretical models and remember that racism hurts, racism is painful, racism is in your face, and racism effects the ordinary person in the street in a concrete way.

I have concluded this chapter with some practical examples of the ways in which sociologists identify and point to racism through structural inequalities in employment and educational access. Using the work of Back (1996), I have shown how sociological ethnographies start to go beyond identification and suggest ways in which we might understand why people are racist. I have also argued that we cannot separate structures of discrimination from the affective and emotional components of institutions. In the next chapter I want to turn to the discussion of ethnicity and the concept of new racism. I also want to posit some tentative working definitions of race and racism, if nothing else to provide the reader with a framework to develop his or her own ideas in this area.

CHAPTER 3

New Racism(s) for Old

New racism(s) for old

Cultural forms of racism, or what has been termed the *New Racism* are not dependent on racial stereotypes or typologies but are rooted in notions of cultural and ethnic difference. These, it could be argued, are nothing new; rather, there is a shift in emphasis. Biological racism uses, as we have seen in the previous chapter, inferiority as a means not only of demonising the subject but also the culture of that subject. Publicly and certainly politically it is unacceptable to talk of people as biologically inferior; the emphasis has therefore switched to a discourse of cultural difference in which the Other becomes demonised, a referent in a late twentieth-century political project. Phil Cohen (1999) has noted that the concept of new racism has provided an intellectual resource for the anti-racist movement allowing an emphasis on subtle forms of stereotyping and discrimination (1999: 4). Within the context of the debate on immigration policy, Mason (1995) and Balibar (1991) draw attention to the political aspects of border retention and policy-making, in that there has been a marked shift in emphasis from biologism to talk of ethnic boundaries and the culture of difference. In answer to the earlier question 'If the Holocaust did indeed put an end to "race" science, as is generally thought, why do we still have racism?' we can retort:

> current racism ... fits into a framework of '*racism without races*' ... It is a racism whose dominant theme is not biological heredity but the insurmountability of cultural differences, a racism which, at first sight, does not postulate the superiority of certain groups or peoples in relation to others but 'only' the harmfulness of abolishing frontiers, the incompatibility of life-styles and traditions.
>
> (Balibar, 1991: 21; emphasis added)

28

Barker (1981) identifies several components of the new racism. Firstly, there is a notion that 'our' political and cultural systems are superior through difference to those of others. This places an emphasis on the cultural aspects of human behaviour – language, beliefs, religions and custom – thus stressing 'ways of life'. Secondly, we have a strong attachment to 'our' way of life which creates an emotional boundary between 'them' and 'us':

> Human nature is such that it is natural to form a bounded community, a nation, aware of its differences from other nations. They are not better or worse. But feelings of antagonism will be aroused if outsiders are admitted.
>
> (Barker, 1981: 21)

Again there is a powerful language of cultural difference, the stress is on *difference* rather than *inferiority*; and difference is a problem particularly when more than one culture lives in the same location. There follows from this a third point: other cultures are seen as pathological in that they cause problems for the dominant culture. This gives rise to the notion of 'genuine fears'. People feel secure with their way of life; genuine fears are about affective attachment. People share common values, beliefs with their 'own', and desire to keep things that way. Fear generates strong feelings of ambivalence towards other cultures:

> The 'rivers of blood' will flow, not because the immigrants are black; not because British society is racist, but because however 'tolerant' the British might be, they can only digest so much 'alienness'.
>
> (Powell, quoted in Lawrence, 1982: 81)

Powellism influenced immigration policy through the 1950s and 1960s, and manifested itself in Thatcherism in the 1980s. Using powerful emotional hooks, racism becomes about difference, about 'genuine fears' about 'us' and 'them'. This brings us to the final point: It is 'common-sense' that people from different cultural backgrounds cannot live together. We have the notion that it is 'natural' for people to live with their 'own kind'; this isn't racist, it is a perfectly natural response and of course 'foreigners' have their *natural* homes, too, 'stopping immigration is being kind to them' (Barker, 1981: 21).

The new racism recasts racial intolerance under the guise of a multifaceted national 'tolerance' where it is quite simply

Example 3.1   New racism and political discourse

Anna Marie Smith (1992) has highlighted how political discourse, and particularly Thatcherite discourse, has played a role in shaping a new 'common-sense' form of racism which has a distinctly moral 'feel', and takes on an anti-union, racist and homophobic character (1992: 28). Smith argues that Thatcherites were responding directly to popular concerns around race and ethnicity in a symbolic discourse of moral exclusion that responded directly to popular concerns. Smith notes that Thatcherites talked about themes that have always been central to Tory tradition, for example nation and family, but recast them to respond to popular anxieties. Smith argues that we have to see this as part of a wider hegemonic project in which outsider figures define the boundaries of social space, or, should we say, are constructed to define the boundaries of social space:

> The outsider figure has to appear to personify some of the greatest threats to social order. The social space has to appear to be deeply threatened by the outsider and yet, thanks to its apparent transhistorical permanence, ultimately recoverable ... Powell and the Thatcherites were able to construct the black immigrant and dangerous queerness such that they operated as credible figures of outsider-ness. These demonisations were central to the legitimating of specific authoritarian measures, such as the intensification of racially defined immigration policies   (1992: 32)

Smith argues that this creation of these demonised groups allowed for political bartering for power in which politicians claimed that the only way they could protect British families ('the British family') was to have more control over local government – in other words, to strengthen the authoritarian hold of central government.

So, when Smith talks of the 'outsider' figure which was essential to the New Right hegemonic project, the 'outsider' became the focus of popular concern and anxiety resulting in a reactionary common-sense. Smith argues that people are quite simply presented with one reality: It claims that there is nothing beyond the boundaries of the hegemonic project except total political chaos. A hegemonic project does not dominate political subjects; it does not reduce political subjects to pure obedience and it does not even require their unequivocal support for its specific demands. It pursues, instead, a far more subtle goal, namely the naturalisation of its specific vision of the social order as the social order itself (Smith, 1992: 37). Thus, demonisation of the Other reframes racial intolerance within a discourse of cultural difference. This discourse re-codes intolerance as a 'legitimate expression of natural beliefs' (*ibid.*: 36). Thus a strategy for dealing with cultural difference develops within a framework of inclusion of 'us' and exclusion of 'them'. Smith's ideas well-illustrate some of the central tenets of the new racism, the idea of a culture of difference, of genuine fears, and the notion that somehow these fears are a common-sense reaction to our natural state of being. As Smith notes: 'The new racists refused to claim that racial "others" were inferior; they were quite simply, different' (*ibid.*: 54).

common-sense that different cultures can only get on with each other to a certain degree. This is the double bind of the new racism. If you want to be with us, be like us (assimilate); but, you can't be like us, so get out and go away. As Errol Lawrence (1982) notes in his analysis of racist ideologies, there is a cannibalistic metaphor that fits in with assumptions of assimilation:

> If blacks could be 'digested' then they would disappear in the mainstream of British society, they would no longer be visible or different, and therefore no longer a problem.
>
> (1982: 66)

But however tolerant the British people are they can only digest so much – the 'double bind', give up your culture and be like 'us' but you can't because you are not the same as 'us'.

Phil Cohen (1999) has noted that 'old' racism seems to show a remarkable capacity to reinvent itself, suggesting caution in holding binary oppositions between old and new racism(s). There would seem to be no new racism as such, rather there are subtle and diverse applications of racism. In the new racism there is a shift in emphasis (from biology to culture), but it would seem to be very much a case of 'new racisms for old'. Barker himself describes the new racism as 'pseudo-biological culturalism':

> Nations are not built out of politics and economics but out of human nature. It is our biology, our instincts, to defend our way of life, traditions, and customs against outsiders, not because they are inferior, but because they are part of a different culture.
>
> (1981: 23)

Rattansi (1994) notes that the new racism is burdened by two different referents: on one hand we have Barker's argument of sociobiological difference between 'our' nation/culture and that of others; on the other, Balibar argues that differentialist racism (cultural difference) supersedes earlier forms of biological racism. Miles (1993) argues that 'scientific racism' (biology) has always maintained an element, or at least a conception, of cultural difference and national character. Similarly, Small (1994) concludes:

> clear evidence is available of biological, cultural and economic rationales feeding into one another in most periods of recent history, as are examples of subtle and indirect racialised ideologies.
>
> (1994: 94)

Characterisation of the new racism is problematic, it revolves around a theory which itself is fragmentary and contradictory: a theory that makes cultural comparisons of biological things. It assumes that an old racism exists with markedly different character-istics and some element of historical sequentialism. Each type of racism, however, incorporates aspects of the other, with a stress on different elements in each. As Mason (1995) comments: The idea of the new racism raises the question as to whether these arguments are any more than a 'rhetorical smoke-screen behind which lurk older beliefs about race' (1995: 10). This argument around notions of cultural rather than biological difference leads us into an examination of the concept of ethnicity.

Ethnic boundaries and the culture of difference

If the meaning of 'race' has been defined, albeit in a fictitious and misled way, as an objective scientific form, then the shift towards the subjective in the concept of ethnicity is something which has been highlighted by Max Weber:

> The belief in group affinity, regardless of whether it has any objective foundation, can have important consequences especially for the forma-tion of a political community. We shall call 'ethnic groups' those human groups that entertain a subjective belief in their common descent because of similarities of physical type or of customs or both.
>
> (1978: 389)

In other words, for Weber, the emphasis lies in the notion of com-mon descent through physical characteristics or a shared culture; this may be real or assumed, so presumably it may also be imagined. Cashmore and Troyna (1990) describe ethnicity as a way in which we try to encapsulate the responses of various different groups.

Members of ethnic groups are 'people who are conscious of themselves as in some way united or at least related because of a common origin and a shared destiny' (1990: 146). Both these interpretations stress the notion of common descent, as well as incorporating some notion of common culture. There has been a tendency more recently for writers to focus on common cultures and belief systems as a basis for ethnicity, and hence there is a focus on cultural difference and the way in which ethnic boundaries are drawn or constructed. The concept of ethnicity is popular among sociologists not only because of the obvious, in that it is rooted in the social (rather than the biological), but also that it is largely ascribed by the social actor. Barth (1969) discusses ethnicity as a process of boundary-creation and maintenance between groups:

> the critical focus of investigation from this point of view becomes the ethnic boundary that defines the group, not the culture stuff that it encloses.
>
> (1969: 10)

Ethnicity is for Barth, about the way in which social groups maintain their identity through interaction with others. This is based on an exclusive territory protected by social boundaries which exclude others and mark difference as a way of identity-maintenance. This leads Mason (1995) to conclude that ethnicity is situational: people have different ethnic identities for different situations, for example someone may identify as Indian, south Asian or British depending on the situational context and the behaviour or reaction of others. Hutchinson and Smith (1996) use the term ethnicity to mean a sense of kinship, group solidarity and common culture. Again, as in notions of 'race' we have many interpretations of what ethnicity is, and loosely it would seem to be an amalgam of strongly-felt shared beliefs that serve as a source of identity-formation and maintenance which set a group apart from others.

The concept of ethnicity raises several problematic points. Firstly it would seem that ethnicity is used to set aside or exclude certain groups as was the case with 'race'. We now have racism based on a discourse of cultural difference as well as biological inferiority. Secondly, the term ethnicity is often used to refer to minority groups who are perceived as somehow different from the indigenous 'norm', suggesting that only minorities have some form of ethnicity which distinguishes 'us' and 'them'. The third point, which encompasses the preceding points, is that ethnicity is culturally constructed and, as Hall (1992) notes, can be particularly closed, exclusive and regressive. The constructed form of 'Englishness' that exists in 'Thatcherism', 'Majorism' and even 'Blairism' is for Hall, one of the core characteristics of racism today. It suggests that ethnicity is a problem, on the margin or periphery, whilst denying ethnicity in 'Englishness' by regressing to notions of 'race' and nation. Mason (1995) illustrates this point:

> The term 'ethnic minority' is widely understood in Britain to denote a category of people whose recent origins lie in the New Commonwealth and Pakistan; in other words, in former British colonies in the Indian sub-continent, the Caribbean, Africa, and, sometimes, the so-called Far East.
>
> (1995: 15)

This excludes other groups of people, for example Italian and Polish communities, who have a distinct culture, who are quite simply not thought of by some people as constituting an ethnic community. The Commission for Racial Equality (1996) would disagree, and as such their definition of minority ethnic groups would include those above. The term 'ethnic minority' still uses as its main referent skin colour, in other words it means non-white. This has led Hall (1992) to suggest that we should perceive ethnicity in a new way by retheorising the concept of difference, as difference is also a double-edged word. In one sense it implies an unreconcilable rift, a separation that cannot be bridged. On another dimension difference is something 'positional, conditional and conjunctural', the latter engaging rather than suppressing ethnicity. Hall argues that we have to decouple ethnicity from its equivalence with racism, nationalism, imperialism and the state, which for Hall sums up 'Britishness', and look at its positive aspects as a non-coercive and diverse concept, in other words, what Hall refers to as *New Ethnicities*:

> a recognition that we all speak from a particular place, out of a particular history, out of a particular experience, a particular culture ... We are all, in that sense, *ethnically* located and our identities are crucial to our subjective sense of who we are. But this is also a recognition that this is not an ethnicity which is doomed to survive, as Englishness was, only by marginalising, dispossessing, displacing and forgetting other ethnicities.
>
> (1992: 258)

The idea of new ethnicities de-pathologises the concept of ethnicity by ascribing ethnicity to all rather than 'troublesome' minorities. Every group or individual with some form of culture and identity has an ethnic basis, thus getting rid of the notion that ethnicity only applies to non-whites and disengaging with ideas of race and nation.

Anthias and Yuval-Davis (1992), however, question this relationship between culture and identity. They argue that culture is just one of many ingredients that characterise ethnic groups – others may include religion, language or 'race'. Ethnicity is not just about identity, it is also about partaking in the 'social conditions of a group, which is positioned in a particular way in terms of the social allocation of resources' (*ibid.*: 9). This is placed with the context of difference in relation to other groups, as well as differences in relation to the division of labour and gender. Indeed, for Anthias and Yuval-Davis:

> the existence of a conscious ethnic identity may not even be a necessary condition for the existence of ethnicity. Ethnicity may be constructed outside the group, by the material conditions it faces, and by its social representation by other groups, or by the state.
>
> (*Ibid.*)

In this sense, as 'race' was ascribed to others as a form of containment, then ethnicity becomes ascribed by both material, social and economic conditions and the representation of groups by others. Thus ethnicity becomes a term of reference that is both subjectively ascribed by the individual social actor (as identity), and a term imputed or ascribed, a label, or more specifically a container, in which we put 'others'. The term ethnicity, is then, at least as contentious as the term race. Within this text it is used in a positive manner, in other words it is meant to signify the plurality of difference that exists within the social world, that is inclusively of all people. We cannot, however, ignore the negative connotations that surround all the terminology that has been discussed. Ethnicity has been used to stress negative (perceived) aspects of cultural difference and positive aspects of whiteness in a way which pathologises minority groups, and as with the New Racism, older notions of race lurk in the background. As Lyon (1997: 204) remarks: 'Ethnicity is a way of imagining peoplehood that ignores everything that makes a people – asserting a boundary that asserts only uniqueness.'

A note on diaspora

Diaspora is, as Anthias (1998) notes, a different way of thinking about transnational migration and ethnic relations to models that rely on the idea of 'race' and ethnicity (see Example 3.2). The term refers to the dispersal of peoples and has been used to describe a commonality that transcends nation-states; in that, for example, black African people have been dispersed throughout the world for a variety of reasons (usually slavery) but still hold some form of attachment or identification with the original homeland. The idea of diaspora is used to describe 'the complex modes of belonging which dispersed communities are in but not of particular social formations' (Solomos and Back, 1996: 141).

Example 3.2   Diaspora: a meeting of postcolonial minds?

Solomos and Back (1996) emphasise Paul Gilroy's (1987, 1993) and Homi Bhabha's (1994) use of diaspora to talk about changing forms of black culture in America and Britain, and in particular the changing cultural dynamics of minority identity. Both writers see black culture as a constantly moving and changing entity, in other words in a constant state of creation. Gilroy gives us a taste of his thesis: black Britain defines itself crucially as part of a diaspora – its unique cultures draw inspiration from those developed by black populations elsewhere. In particular, the culture and politics of black America and the Caribbean have become raw materials for creative processes which redefine what it means to be black, adapting it to distinctively British experiences and meanings. Black culture is actively made and re-made (Gilroy, 1987: 154).

Thus, Gilroy argues that the negotiated cultures of black Britain have developed at both a regional and transnational level, it is impossible to theorise black culture in Britain without rethinking British culture as a whole. An 'intricate web of cultural connections binds blacks here to blacks elsewhere' (Gilroy, 1987: 156). Diaspora is in some sense beyond the nation-state, and perhaps even outside modernity; the cultural matrix that is diaspora transcends national boundaries. A sense of identity and belonging may be produced within a particular country (nation), but the nature of identification goes beyond the state drawing on feelings of commonality and belonging from Africa, the Caribbean and America. Phil Cohen (1999) notes that the notions of diaspora and cultural hybridity have given the idea of 'new ethnicities' a spatial dimension: 'a meeting place of postcolonial minds' (1999: 6).

Floya Anthias (1998) argues that part of the success of the concept of diaspora relates to the perceived failures of the 'race' and ethnicity paradigms (1998: 558). Both these ideas tend to focus on the processes within the nation-state rather than at a transnational or even global level. Anthias identifies two main approaches to the idea of diaspora: diaspora as a typological tool (description), and diaspora as a social condition (process). Using the work of Robin Cohen (1997) on global diaspora, Anthias describes the typological use of the term thus: groups called diasporas have travelled across territories for a variety of different reasons, diasporas continue to identify with their 'homelands' (original); the homeland is metaphoric, it may not be a territory, or the territory may not still exist in the same form. The central idea behind diaspora, for Cohen, is dispersal, the forcible scattering of peoples. Anthias describes Cohen's construct of diasporic communities as having five different forms: victim, labour, trade, imperial and culture. Thus, for example, we have Africans as victims, Indians as labour and British as imperial. The problem with this typology is that it assumes a notion of a homogeneous community, ignoring different social conditions, opportunities and forms of exclusion. This typology is also problematic in that the reasons for dispersal between groups differ so much that there is no room for any form of constructive comparison, as Anthias notes: 'such a typology provides an incommensurable comparative schema' (1998: 563). The second approach to diaspora is that of *condition*, and can be seen in the work of Hall (1990), Gilroy (1993) and Clifford (1994).

Rather than a description of a group, diaspora is the condition of being *from* one place but *of* an another, and identified with sentiments towards a homeland (Anthias, 1998: 565). It is, after Clifford (1994), the idea that a diaspora can think globally but live locally, thus breaking the bonds of territory, boundaries and ethnic ties. Anthias raises some critical points about the concept of diasporas. First, there is still some concept of ethnicity in diaspora which functions to celebrate difference and the maintenance of links with ethnic and national belongingness which neglects the aspects of ethnicity that relate to boundaries of exclusion. Second, the notion of diaspora distracts from the trans-ethnic relations that are informed by power hierarchies, and by gender and class relations. Finally , there is no discussion of the ways in which diasporas may actually reinforce absolutist notions of 'origin' and 'true belonging'. There is a danger that we may return to the notion of a pure 'race'.

In some sense the argument seems to have come full circle, an idea that is meant to avoid reductionism and celebrate difference is in danger, if it does not address these issues, of becoming yet another racial theory.

In the final section of this chapter I want to bring together all the concepts that we have looked at in this and the preceding chapter and offer a tentative series of working definitions that I think may be useful, firstly throughout the reading of this book, and secondly in the practical research environment.

Summary and working definitions

In this summary I want to provide some working definitions of the terms that have been addressed in the last two chapters. I call them working definitions as they attempt to address many of the different interpretations in a relatively straightforward way. I have kept linguistic gymnastics to a minimum while trying to cover the basic feel that I have for the terminology, but at the same time I have tried not to detract from this highly contentious academic debate. In other words, I have attempted to make the terms usable.

The word 'race' has been, and still is, associated with ideas of inferiority, superiority, hierarchy and persecution. 'Race' evolved out of pseudo-scientific Darwinist theories in the nineteenth century stressing that biological and natural difference was inherent and unalterable. It has been argued that race theory was a consolidation of hundreds of years of hatred and fear of and persecution of those who are different, the 'Other'. 'Race' is a product of scientific enquiry, a fictitious construction, a category projected onto 'others' in order to classify and therefore control. 'Race' is therefore a *container* or more specifically a *containment* of our fear of difference, of a particular kind, or specific 'other'. The Other is a crucial symbol in the definition of who 'we' are. Otherness emphasises difference to create order; exaggeration of difference both creates who 'we' are and who 'we' are not by the marginalisation, stigmatisation and intolerance of other people. Biological notions of race are expressed in symbolic representations of otherness.

It is clear that there are no such things as 'races', but many people still think and behave as if there are. We still have racism without races which leads to the question: what is racism? Racism is both a social and a psychological phenomenon. It is inscribed in both practices: violence, humiliation, exclusion from and denial of equality of opportunity, and discourse: notions of purification of the social body, the preservation of 'our' identity and 'way of life'. Psychological figures of otherness support racist discourse and ideology. As Miles (1989) notes, racism as an ideology (mis)represents people in a distorted way. The discreditation of 'race' has shifted the way in which racism is articulated; from *inferiority* to *difference*. Emphasis is now expressed in what Barker (1981) terms the New Racism. Cultural forms of racism are not dependent on racial stereotypes but are rooted in notions of cultural or ethnic difference. Exclusion is justified in terms of insurmountable difference and incompatibility of lifestyle. I have argued that there is no new racism as such, just a shift in emphasis from biology to culture, in a fragmentary and contradictory theory, a theory that makes cultural comparisons of biological things. As such, each type of racism incorporates elements of the other, with a stress on different aspects in each. Can we not argue that new racism is simply another way of articulating older beliefs about race. Kovel (1995) describes racism as the maltreatment of people because of their 'otherness'. This I adopt as my preferred definition in this book, as otherness may be defined biologically or culturally with much the same outcome; maltreatment, either physical or psychological, exclusion and denial of equality of opportunity.

Ethnicity has replaced 'race' as the preferred terminology of social scientists. Ethnicity is rooted in social processes and largely ascribed by the social actor; in other words we can define our own ethnicity and in turn define our self by our ethnicity. Ethnicity incorporates notions of common descent, common culture and belief systems. Ethnicity has also been described as a way in which social groups maintain their identity through interaction with others, a process of boundary creation and maintenance between groups. Kinship and solidarity are also associated with ethnicity, and again we can see a multiplicity of interpretations of the same term. I have suggested that the term ethnicity refers to an amalgam of strongly felt *shared beliefs* that serve as a source of identity-formation and reinforcement which sets one group apart from others.

There are several problems with the use of the term ethnicity. Firstly, it is used to set aside or exclude certain groups as was/is the case with 'race'. Racism currently focuses on cultural or ethnic groups, groups which as Anthias (1998) notes are often seen as homogeneous, which ignores diversity within the group. Secondly, ethnicity is often used to refer to minority groups who are perceived as pathological, or at the very least somehow different from the indigenous norm. Thirdly, this suggests that only minority groups have an ethnicity that distinguishes 'us' from 'them'; thus ethnicity becomes particularly closed, exclusive and regressive. In other words ethnicity becomes perceived as negative or as a problem. This has led Hall (1992) to suggest that we should perceive ethnicity in a new way, to decouple its equivalence with racism and nationalism, and to recognise that we all speak from a particular place, we are all ethnically located. This de-pathologises the concept of ethnicity by ascribing ethnicity to all rather than a few minority groups. Again, this is problematic in two senses: firstly, popular conceptions of the term still persist, and secondly ethnicity may be constructed outside a group by both material conditions and social representations by other groups. In this way, just as 'race' was/is ascribed by others, then ethnicity becomes ascribed by both material social conditions and by social representation from other groups. Thus ethnicity becomes a term of reference that is no longer ascribed by the individual actor, but is a form of *containing* fear of difference. Ethnicity, therefore, has as many negative connotations as the term 'race' and has been used to stress negative aspects of cultural difference in a way which pathologises minority groups.

Racism is embedded in the structure of society, and is clearly demonstrated by inequalities in access to housing, education and employment. Institutions that reflect (and reproduce) society maintain rules and practices which perpetuate racism; this is broadly described as institutional racism. Racism has become naturalised into established attitudes, procedural norms and social patterns in underlying and covert practices which are or are perceived as, the 'norm'. The point is, practices that we take for granted, that are not explicitly racist, may have their origins in racist discourse; the reason behind structural and psychological exclusion is no longer explicit in present discourse. Although institutional racism has been seen as a move away from the idea that racism arises from a few individuals and is endemic in the structure of society, I have argued that the two cannot be separated. While an institution may carry racist discourse within its tenets, this is reinforced by individuals who have been socialised in a racist society; in other words for individuals who hold *prejudices*, acting on this prejudice is *discrimination*. To hold a prejudice is arguably enough to make someone feel excluded, to create an 'atmosphere', or to make others feel out of place. This is not explicit or overt, but results from a form of individual and embodied racism within an institution. It is not enough to view institutional racism as the discriminatory impact of administrative procedures.

The definitions detailed in the following summary of key terms are by no means exhaustive, but provide a basis from which to work and a point of reference for the reader. It is becoming apparent as this book unfolds that structural accounts of racism leave an incomplete picture of how racism and exclusionary practices are produced and perpetuated. I have defined racism as both the *physical* and *psychological* maltreatment of people because of their otherness, and hinted at certain psychological mechanisms such as *containment* and *projection* which may give us a better understanding of racism and exclusion. In the following short chapter I want to concentrate on the relationship between modernity and racism, and in particular the work of Zygmunt Bauman. Whilst giving us an account of racism that is based in the structures of modern life, Bauman also introduces a psychosocial character, the *Stranger*. This, provides us with a bridge between sociological and psychological accounts of racism and other hatreds.

Summary of key terms

Race is a socially constructed container through which we project our inner world onto others. Others are the psychological manifestation of our fear of difference.

Racism is the physical or psychological maltreatment of people because of their *specific* 'otherness'. Otherness may be defined in biological or cultural terms and expressed in inferiorisation or insurmountable difference, or both.

New racism denotes a shift from biological typologies and racial stereotypes that stress inferiority, to an emphasis on a discourse of cultural difference in which the Other becomes demonised. There is a strong language which stresses 'ways of life', common-sense, attachments, and the notion of 'genuine fears'. New racism recasts intolerance under the guise of national tolerance.

Ethnicity is an amalgam of strongly felt shared beliefs, common culture, and a sense of belonging, either real or imaginary, that serve as a source of identity-formation and solidarity which sets one group apart from others.

Institutional racism is a complex interaction between a silent racist discourse, administrative procedures, social patterns and established attitudes which are reinforced by, and interact with, individual prejudice within an institution. They are both structural/organisational and emotional mechanisms which generate feelings and processes of exclusion within institutions and the workplace.

Diaspora is the condition of being *from* one place but *of* another, and having identified sentiments towards a homeland. The homeland in itself may be real, imagined or simply no longer exist. A diaspora can think globally and live locally, transgressing the boundaries of time and space.

CHAPTER 4

Sociology, Racism and Modernity

Introduction

What is the relationship, if any, between modernity and racism? Has sociology reached its limits in the explanation of racism and ethnic hatred? How can we bridge the gap between sociological theory and psychoanalysis? These are some of the questions which I address in this chapter. The Holocaust represents the culmination of race science, of eugenics and of social engineering. It is almost unthinkable to talk of inferior or superior 'races' after the terror and evil of Nazi Germany, so what has replaced the concept of 'race'. Academically, we have seen the adoption of ethnicity and new ethnicities, but is there a post-race other? I suggest in this chapter that Zygmunt Bauman's concept of the *stranger* provides us with a sociological model, a psycho-social character that bridges the gap between sociological analysis and psychoanalytic theory. In other words, we have notions of both social structure, that is the nation-state, bureaucracies and technologies of modernity, and some recognition of the role of our imagination and of our 'inner' world encapsulated in this model.

In an examination of the idea of racism as social engineering, I explore the way in which romantic and ideological mythologies share an uncanny relationship with science in the Third Reich and discuss the role that the medical profession played in diagnosing 'life unworthy of life'. How can we explain the terrible treatments meted out by Nazi doctors and the flagrant abuse of the Hippocratic oath? I conclude this chapter by arguing that a fusion of sociological and psychoanalytic theory may give us a greater purchase or understanding of racism and ethnic hatred by combining analysis of both socio-structural factors, and of our 'inner' world, in a sociology of the imagination.

Modernity and the Holocaust

Zygmunt Bauman's (1989) book *Modernity and the Holocaust* has become one of the leading sociological texts on the Jewish Holocaust. It uses in some sense, although this is not always apparent, a radically different explanatory schema in which Bauman explores the structures of modernity which make/made genocide not only possible but eminently reasonable. Bauman rejects the notion that the 'Germanness' of the crime is unique by showing us how the genocidal project is heavily rooted in the idea of the nation-state, of medicalised killing, and the perfect picture of the rational bureaucratic modern garden state. Bauman's thesis is, in itself, anti-modernity. The rationality of the modern social world and, in particular, the rationalisation process is essentially bad for human beings. This is because the instruments of rationality, namely the bureaucratic organisation and structures of bureaucratic office, work most efficiently, and after all that is their goal as part of a centralised power system – a central command unit. Centralised power systems tend to be totalitarian and terrorising, or at the very least oppressive and alienating.

There are two ways, for Bauman, to belittle the significance of the Holocaust for sociological analysis. The first is to think of it as something that happened to the Jews as an event in Jewish history. The second is to think of it as some barbaric and loathsome event or practice that modernity will eventually overcome (Bauman, 1989: 1). No, says Bauman, far from overcoming barbarism, modernity is inextricably linked. The Holocaust, the Shoah, is deeply entrenched in the nature of modernity, in the rapid social change that modernity produced – in industrialisation, urbanisation, changes in political philosophy, dislocation, mobility and the growth of nationalism. In the triumph of science as a mode of cognition, and in the development of race and scientifically legitimated racism, there was no need for Nazis to impose views on scientists and doctors, it was already there, part of scientific and moral philosophy. The sheer scale of the destructive process would not have been possible if it were not for the scientific and technological advancements of modernity. Finally, the administrative procedures and practices of the nation-state as exemplified by the bureaucratic organisation provided an efficient vehicle for both the logistical intricacies of extermination, and also of moral absolvement of responsibility. Indeed for Bauman:

> The most shattering of lessons deriving from the analysis of the 'twisted road to Auschwitz' is that – in the last resort – *the choice of physical extermination as the right means to the task of* Entfernung *was a product of routine bureaucratic procedures*: means–end calculus, budget balancing, universal rule application … At no point of its long and tortuous execution did the Holocaust come into conflict with the principles of rationality. The 'Final Solution' did not clash at any stage with the rational pursuit of efficient, optimal goal implementation. On the contrary, *it arose out of a genuinely rational concern, and it was generated by bureaucracy true to its form and purpose.*
> (1989: 17)

Bauman is not arguing that the Holocaust was determined by bureaucracy or the culture of instrumental reason, rather he is suggesting that, first, instrumental reason is not able to stop such a phenomena. Second, that the bureaucratic culture which objectifies society as something to be catergorised, mastered and controlled is the very atmosphere in which something like the Holocaust can be conceived. Finally, Bauman suggests that the culture or 'spirit' of instrumental rationality not only made the Holocaust possible, but eminently 'reasonable' (1989: 18).

The 'gardening' state

The 'gardening state' is a metaphor that Bauman uses aptly to describe the modernist project of the twentieth century. A combination of designed and planned order, social engineering, and legislative reason mark the transformation into an 'orderly society':

> The modern state was a gardening state. Its stance was a gardening stance. It deligitimised the present (wild, uncultivated) condition of the population and dismantled the extant mechanisms of reproduction and self-balancing. It put in there place purposely built mechanisms meant to point the change in the direction of a rational design. The design, presumed to be dictated by the supreme and unquestionable authority of reason, supplied the criteria to evaluate present day reality. These criteria split the population into useful plants to be encouraged and tenderly propagated, and weeds – to be removed or rooted out.
> (Bauman, 1991: 20)

Bauman (1991) argues that in Nazi Germany the ambitions of the state were firmly set on eradicating all the dangerous and uncontrollable elements of society through a joining of both the gardening and medical metaphor. Scientists were guided by the vision of a 'good' society, one in which man dominated nature through the taming of the chaotic elements by the use of a systematic, rational scientific plan. Bauman argues that it was the Jew that stood as the weed in the carefully designed garden of the future. There were other weeds as well, the mentally ill, the congenitally diseased and the bodily deformed (*ibid.*: 29). Some plants turned into weeds because reason dictated that the space they occupied should be someone else's garden.

Thus, for Bauman, modern genocide is different. It is genocide with a purpose, what Max Weber (1977) would describe as formal, purposeful rationality. Genocide becomes means–ends; calculative and therefore modern genocide, for Bauman, is an element of the gardening state and of social engineering which is meant to bring about 'a social order conforming to the design of a perfect society' (Bauman, 1989: 91). The gardener's vision is that one can create a society, an ideal world, that is *objectively* (where science objectifies) better than the one that exists. In some sense, for Bauman, this is the product of the civilising process gone wrong. Instead of outlawing violence and celebrating difference, modernity is characterised by a gardening culture:

> It defines itself as the design for an ideal life and a perfect arrangement of human conditions. It constructs its own identity out of a distrust of nature. In fact, it defines itself and nature, and the distinction between them, through its endemic mistrust of spontaneity and its longing for a better, and necessarily artificial order.
>
> (*Ibid.*: 92)

Bauman argues that modern genocide is but one of the chores of the gardening state. If rational plans define gardens, then there will be weeds, and weeds have to be exterminated. As Bauman notes, Stalin and Hitler's victims were not killed to capture territory or material things, they were killed because they did not fit the design of a perfect society. Killing was not an act of destruction, but of creation, and this is wholly commensurable with the idea of the therapeutic imperative which I discuss in the following sections of this chapter. Indeed, for Bauman, modern genocide did not betray the spirit of modernity or depart from the trajectory of the civilising process. Modern genocides 'were the most consistent uninhibited expression of that spirit' (*ibid.*: 93).

There are several ways in which Bauman can be misinterpreted. First, when Bauman argues that racism is a strictly modern product he does not mean that hatred, ethnic and group conflicts did not exist premodernity, rather that science defined race, and modern technology and state power made racism possible, and as such modernity not only made racism possible but created a demand for it. Second, and following on from the first point, Bauman is not arguing that there is a direct causal relationship between modernity and the Holocaust, rather modern civilisation was a necessary condition in that it provided the administrative and technological tools and the ethos of scientific progress. Finally, Bauman draws our attention to the fact that he does not mean that we all live by 'Auschwitz principles' (*ibid.*). Just because the Holocaust is modern does not mean, or he does not mean to imply, that modernity is a Holocaust. The Holocaust is a byproduct of the endless drive for control and design of the modern world, it is when the modernist dream is accompanied by absolute power devoid of social controls and countervailing forces that genocide follows. In the following section I want to examine in more detail the idea of racism as social engineering and the way in which romantic and ideological mythologies shared an uncanny partnership with science in the Third Reich. A meeting of modern and premodern ideals.

Racism as social engineering

Social engineering in Nazi Germany was the terrible culmination of race as a science, of social Darwinism, and of racial theories of inferiority and superiority between 'man' in the guise of the Aryan myth. The biologising of German society, the idea of racial superiority, was an intrinsic part of Nazi ideology; the ideology that paved the road to Auschwitz and the systematic annihilation of Jews, Slavs, Gypsies, homosexuals and many other minorities in Europe. The nature of the Aryan myth was imbued with romanticism, with eroticism, and with a strong emphasis on blood, soil, of bonding with fellow man and nature. The highly irrational romantic symbols that were used to generate the myth contrast sharply with the highly rational, calculative, scientific methods of implementation of Hitler's plans for race purity and the notion of the '*Volksgemeinschaft*', the racial or national community.

Anti-Semitism in Germany was nihilistic with intent; the will to destroy the beliefs and values of others, the Jews, as a prelude to the creation of a new Reich. The Jewish community in Europe, and in particular in Germany, existed at the pleasure of 'kings, lords and barons' until the end of the nineteenth century (Gordon, 1984: 97). The Jew transversed the boundaries of the emerging nation-states, and in doing so they became rejected as outsiders, as not belonging to one nationalism. Sarah Gordon argues that the stereotype of the nomadic Jew emerged in the middle ages:

> *Völkisch* anti-Semites perpetuated stereotypes of Jews as rootless, soulless, materialistic ... unassimilable, shallow, conspiratorial, evil ... and most of all alien.
>
> (1984: 25)

The Jewish community in Germany constituted less than 1 per cent of the population between 1870 and 1933, and the German Jews tended to be less noticeable than their Russian counterparts who arrived from the East escaping Russian persecution. The Jewish population of Germany had been discriminated against for centuries before Hitler came to power, and anti-Semitism, dislike and suspicion were deepened and extenuated by Nazi propaganda and Hitler's paranoid hatred of Jews. Hitler, in *Mein Kampf*, talks of the 'naked egoism' of the Jew. He saw the Jewish community as a 'living organism' which transposed state boundaries, swallowing up other cultures, lacking any culture itself; 'For what sham culture the Jew today possesses is the property of other peoples, and for the most part is ruined in his hands' (*Mein Kampf*, 1973: 275). The Jew, for Hitler, lacked any creative qualities; what they did accomplish was either a 'patchwork' of other cultures, or 'intellectual theft'. The Jew, possessing no territory and no culture becomes a parasite, feeding on the body of nations and states: 'He is ... the typical parasite, a sponger who like a noxious bacillus keeps spreading as soon as a favourable medium invites him' (*ibid.*: 277).

The Jew therefore represented the 'mightiest counterpart' to the Aryan race. In contrast to the Jew, the Aryan was the epitome of culture, and Hitler laid the foundations of the Aryan myth in *Mein Kampf*. Those of Aryan blood, stock and breeding were quite simply the 'master race'; the Aryan created all human culture, art, science and technology, and the cultural foundations of Germany were at risk from the parasitic activities of Judaism. Intrinsically linked with the idea of race purity is nationalism, and Nazism took on an extreme form of nationalism and racial ideology (Hayes, 1973: 161). Culture and the natural environment were linked with a strong emphasis on breeding and male bonding, and blood and race became romanticised, as Glaser notes:

> The myth of blood is the pendant to the Germanic myth; what distinguishes the Aryan above all is the specific nature of his blood.
>
> (1978: 151)

The production of a mythical representation of the Aryan race, of blood, bonding and comradeship was effectively used by Hitler and his propaganda machine. Reference was made to an imaginary past which was untainted by the bacillus, the parasite, the Jew. Propaganda posters represented a mixed imagery of eroticism, genitalia, military weapons and warfare. A romantic, chivalrous, male-dominated past was projected through the art of propaganda.

In this we can see the construction of strong symbolic representations of national identity; the construction of an imagined community and a mythical race. David Welch notes: 'A considerable degree of mysticism was involved (in the transformation of feelings) of belonging to a pure community or *Volk*' (1993: 53). Hitler and the Nazi party constantly referred to the word '*Volk*', a word that became associated with race and Aryan superiority. The *Volksgemeinschaft*, the national community, was to secure the eternal generic body of the German race; in one empire, one people, one leader (Hayes, 1973: 148). Nazism promoted the notion of a bonding of people in a racial community, a sacrificing of the 'self' for the sake of the 'whole'. In the analysis of the ideological myth-making tenets of Nazism we can see a biologising of society; an appeal to irrationalism through the creation of affective bonds and the lure of a sense of belonging. The strong emphasis on nature, one people united with their natural environment, reinforces the notion of a pure race from a pure soil. This creates a solidarity, an identity for members of the in-group.

The myth is perpetuated and reliant on folklore and legend; Nazism permeated culture to give a sense of belonging, of what it was to be German. The strong sense of communal solidarity identified superiority with 'us', the *Volk*, the German people, the *Volksgemeinschaft*; and 'evil' with 'them', the non Aryans, the parasites, the racial enemies, the '*Ausgrenzung*'. Blood and violence symbolised the ideology of the Third Reich. Indeed for Glaser: 'A religion of blood was created and practised, including definite rites and symbols' (1978: 152).

Violence became an integral part of culture. Violence or threats of violence were used to impose views, glorify war and instil a sense of being on a 'historic mission'. The militarised cultural symbols of Nazism stress blood, sexuality and inheritance, and Klaus Theweleit (1989: 63) notes that this culture of violence emanated from a history of male dominance and militarism in which uniforms and military regalia take on a symbolic meaning. Violence is used to homogenise the *Volk* and to maintain the mythical status of the Third Reich. This romanticised and eroticised culture of violence systemised and rationalised the use of violence, 'creating not just killing fields, but killing factories' (Griffin, 1991: 111).

The basis of the identification of Aryan 'stock' and both the persecution and the process of *Ausgrenzung* was science: *social engineering* on a grand scale. A shift from religious to scientific theodicies went largely unchallenged in the twentieth century, and Nazi society became medicalised and scientised. Peukert (1989) argues: 'The sciences were now promoted into the role of supplying the key concepts in the repository of everyday constructions of meaning' (1989: 284). By scientifically defining what it was to be a German, an Aryan science designed and planned the future of the *Volksgemeinschaft.* It did so by the separation of the healthy German *Volk* from their racial and biological inferiors. If science in itself was not enough to legitimate this new order, then the scientists themselves were. Christian Pross (1994) notes that the scientists involved in the euthanasia programmes and eventually the construction of the concentration camps were not 'black sheep'; these scientists were the cream of German medicine, university professors, internationally acclaimed scientists and researchers.

Science could not explain suffering and death in the individual; in trying to construct some meaning, to give a rational explanation for death, science fails. Peukert argues that a 'logodicy' drives science into the realms of the irrational. Irrational because it is seeking an answer that does not exist. Thus science becomes obsessed with the gradual elimination of death while the individual dies. The answer for the Nazis was genetic. Peukert (1989) notes:

> The obvious escape from the dilemma is to split the target of scientific endeavour into the merely ephemeral body of the individual and the potentially immortal body of the *Volk.*

(1989: 284)

In this sense, not only does the individual gain eternal life through the genetic body of the *Völkskorper*, but science exonerates itself from its irrational dilemma. The practical embodiment of racial policy was administered through several bureaucratic organisations; The National Hygiene department of the Ministry of the Interior and the Bureau for Enlightenment on Population Policy and Racial Welfare. The euthanasia programme in Nazi Germany murdered more than 200 000 psychiatric patients under the code-name operation T-4. Throughout the 1930s psychiatric patients were used for experimentation, to develop techniques in extermination. An extreme form of social Darwinism emerged that used 'ideological tools for a biological solution to a social problem' (Gotz *et al.*, 1994: 1). The sphere of those encompassed in racial policy extended from those deemed 'life unworthy of life', psychiatric patients, to those considered to be 'aliens of the community'. Bauman notes that the focus of the management of populations did not end with the eventual termination of the euthanasia programmes: 'Its focus, together with the gassing technologies that the euthanasia campaign had helped to develop merely shifted to a different target: The Jews' (1989: 67).

Normality or norm formation seem to be key concepts in the analysis of German society. What we see as a terrible crime, as irrational and incomprehensible, became a part of everyday life in Nazi Germany. As society was medicalised, racial hygiene was routinised. The Jew is singled out as the largest group of victims, one of many enemies of the *Völkskorper*. The Jew became symbolic in a culture of symbolism, the Jew represented a perceived threat to the eternal genetic body of the *Volk* and a threat to the individual in a religion of blood. Nazi science provided the theodicy of good fortune for the *Volk*, and in doing so legitimated the suffering of millions. The goal of the Nazi movement was to secure the immortality of the *Völkskorper*, but in reality it systemised mass annihilation. The question remains, however, as to how doctors and medical workers could reconcile their activities with the ethos of their profession – that of preserving life.

I defined racism in the previous chapter as the maltreatment of people because of their specific 'otherness'. There is no better example of the limits that people are moved to by the internalisation of biological racist ideologies than the story of Nazi doctors. The repugnant and quite often unbelievable activities of the medical profession in Nazi Germany can be explained partially by

Example 4.1   Nazi doctors: the 'therapeutic imperative'

I will use treatment to help the sick according to my ability and judge-
ment, but never with a view to injury and wrongdoing. I will keep pure
and holy both my life and my art. In whatsoever houses I enter, I will enter
to help the sick, and I will abstain from all intentional wrongdoing and
harm

Oath of Hippocrates (in Lifton, 1986: frontispiece)

Robert Jay Lifton (1986) argues that the role of the medical profession has to
be viewed in the context of the visionary motivation associated with ideology which I have discussed at length in the previous section, and the individual psychological mechanisms that enable people to kill. For Lifton, the
notion of 'medicalised' killing addresses both motivational principles and
psychological mechanisms that underlie the work of the Nazi doctors.
Medicalised killing can be seen to encompass two wider perspectives. First,
the 'surgical' method: killing large numbers of people through the use of
controlled technology; and second, the 'therapeutic imperative'. The
motivation behind killing as a therapeutic imperative is clearly illustrated in
the following few lines from Lifton's book in the words of a Nazi doctor
quoted by the distinguished survivor physician Dr Ella Lingens-Reiner.
Pointing to the chimneys in the distance, she asked a Nazi doctor, Fritz Klein,
'How can you reconcile that with your (Hippocratic) oath as a doctor?' His
answer was, 'Of course I am a doctor and I want to preserve life. And out of
respect for human life, I would remove a gangrenous appendix from
a diseased body. The Jew is the gangrenous appendix in the body of
mankind' (Lifton, 1986: 15).

Thus we have eminent scientists and doctors practising an ideologically-
driven policy of extermination which is set against a backdrop of social
engineering; notions of racial purity, deadly racial diseases and scientific
racism. For Lifton, this process went beyond social Darwinism to a vision of
absolute control over the evolutionary process, and over the biological
future of humankind (*ibid.*: 17). The point for Lifton is that the combination
and fusion of anthropological, eugenic and social thought and the resulting
social biology made vicious forms of anti-Semitism appear respectable to
professional people. As Lifton notes, although doctors did not actually run
Auschwitz, they did lend it some perverse medical aura, of a medical
operation and of 'a final common pathway of the Nazi vision of therapy via
mass murder' (*ibid.*: 18).

Thus far we have seen how Lifton has used notions of ideological infusion
and the technology of modernity to explain both the process and motivation behind scientific racism and killing. This motivation also extends to what
Lifton describes as the 'Faustian bargain', the trade-off between the doctors'
own murderous contribution to the killing process and the individual
benefits claimed in terms of the advancement of research and the individual's own career. The key to understanding, for Lifton, how Nazi doctors
were able to work in an environment antithetical to their training is the

notion of doubling: 'the division of the self into two functioning wholes, so that a part-self acts as an entire self. An Auschwitz doctor could, through doubling, not only kill and contribute to killing but organise silently, on behalf of that evil project, an entire self-structure (or self-process) encompassing virtually all aspects of his behaviour' (*ibid.*: 418).

Lifton lists five characteristics of doubling which include a dialectic between the selves, both in terms of autonomy and connection, which succeeds because there is a holistic principle, in other words the self is inclusive and does not connect with the entire environment. This is reinforced by a life–death element in which the Auschwitz self is seen as a form of psychological survival – quite literally the killing self is created on behalf of one's own healing. There is an avoidance of guilt – the second self does all the dirty work and much of this takes place in an unconscious dimension. So, doubling is an active psychological process, a means of adaptation to extremity. This explanation is not about dual personality, it is for Lifton a psychological mechanism of defence which exists in all of us to a certain degree, this perverse and destructive version which Lifton calls 'victimisers' doubling'.

the role of bureaucratic structure and routinisation, but these are not sufficient explanations in themselves. I have used Lifton's work (see Example 4.1) because I feel that it demonstrates a fusion between psychological and structural factors in the explanation of racism. It also illustrates some of the major factors that we can attribute as coming from the modernist project which have facilitated racism and ethnic hatred. In particular, the vision of the modern rational order, the advancement of science and its dominance as a mode of cognition and the use of technologies of oppression and killing. To paraphrase Max Horkheimer and Theodore Adorno (1994): the fully enlightened earth radiates disaster triumphant. In other words, the enlightenment and modernist project contains the seeds of its own destruction and this is nowhere better illustrated than in the atrocities of Nazi Germany, in the Jewish Holocaust. As Zygmunt Bauman notes:

> The Holocaust has dwarfed all remembered and inherited images of evil. With that, it inverted all established explanations of evil deeds. It suddenly transpired that the most horrifying evil in human memory did not result from the dissipation of order, but from an impeccable, fault-less and unchallengable rule of order.
>
> (1989: 151)

In the final section of this chapter I want to look at post-race, post-Holocaust racism and the construction of symbolic and psychological otherness in opposition to the biological discredited model of scientific racism, the notion of the *stranger*. If, indeed, it is unthinkable to talk of 'race' science after the Holocaust, then what is the post-race Other?

Strangers: the post-race 'Other'?

If the Holocaust did indeed put an end to 'race' science, as is generally thought, why do we still have racism ? Have we moved from representations of otherness, through notions of race to arrive at a post-race Other? Mason (1995) argues that although notions of biological races may have disappeared from the natural sciences 'this does not mean however, that biological notions disappeared either from political discourse or from popular conceptualisations of human variation' (1995: 7).

In this section I want to introduce Zygmunt Bauman's concept of the *stranger*. The idea of the stranger has a particular quality, it is a psycho-social character which is partly fictive, partly real and partly a figment of our imagination. I feel this idea is important as it bridges in some sense the gap between traditional sociology and what I would call the *sociology of the imagination*. That is, sociology that goes beyond the bounds of social structure, of function, of cause and effect and starts to address our inner world, a world of love and hate, of terror, fear and human frailty. Bauman's work is such that implicit in his theory(ies) are not only a recognition of the fragility of human existence, but of the complexity of our inner world. I am not talking about some form of cognitive science, rather I am trying to express a way in which sociology can start to think about human emotion and the workings of mind in an interpretative, subjective and hermeneutic way. Psychoanalysis, or certainly some forms of it, are wholly conducive to sociological analysis, or should I say a sociology of the imagination. Bauman's work forms this bridge for me, and has enabled me to start thinking how we may look at racism psychoanalytically and how useful psychoanalytic sociology, or psycho-social studies are in the social sciences. Quite simply, for Bauman, the 'universal stranger' is the Jew. How can this relate to the post-race, post-Holocaust world? In Bauman's words: 'There are friends and enemies. And there are strangers' (1991: 53).

Strangers are not *unfamiliar* people, but they cross or break the dividing line of dualism, they are neither 'us' nor 'them'. There is a clear definition of the social and physical boundaries between 'us' and 'them', 'friends' and 'enemies', both are subject to the same structures and ideas, they define good and bad, true and false, they stand in polarity creating an illusion of order and symmetry. The stranger violates this structure and order; to paraphrase Bauman, 'they [the stranger] bring the "outside" "inside" and poison the comfort of order with the suspicion of chaos' (*ibid.*: 56). The stranger is someone we know things about, who sits in 'our' world uninvited. The stranger has the characteristics of an enemy, but unlike the enemy is not kept at a safe distance. Neither 'us' nor 'them', friend nor foe, the stranger undermines order by straddling the boundary, causing confusion and anxiety, becoming a target of hatred:

> By their sheer presence, which does not fit easily into any of the established categories, the strangers deny the very validity of the accepted oppositions. They belie the oppositions' 'natural' character, expose their arbitrariness, lay bare their fragility. They show the divisions for what they indeed are: imaginary lines that can be crossed or redrawn.
>
> (Bauman, 1990: 54)

Arguably, the concept of the stranger fills in the space vacated by the discreditation of race. There is quite a distinct difference, however, between the two phenomena. 'Race', as we have seen, has been formalised into a specific category that can be pointed to and identified through a series of pseudo-sciences. In other words, race has been qualified and quantified through scientific discovery. The Other, the stranger, is more ambiguous. The stranger in some sense plays into our fears, our imagination, our concerns, into the irrational elements of our psyche. The stranger is at once estranged whilst wholly familiar; the stranger is inside us all. This may seem like a bold, even odd claim, but as the psychoanalytic ideas unfurl in this book we will get some purchase on how things, objects and people that appear repellently alien are in fact all too familiar. The stranger is dangerous, known but unknown; in the same way that the concept of race exaggerates difference, the concept of stranger draws attention to the perception of what might be, rather than what is known. The stranger is Other, but lives around us, within our community (within us). The stranger is a symbol of Other. Other is

---

Example 4.2   The stranger as trader

In his classic essay (1950) on the stranger and strangerdom, Georg Simmel gives an example from the sphere of economics where the trader appears as stranger. If an economy is self-sufficient, then there is no 'middleman'. The trader is only required when products are imported from outside the group or economy, or, if members of a group go elsewhere to buy goods, they themselves then become the transient stranger. In economic terms then the trader is stranger, and the stranger stands out more when he settles in a particular spatial locality. Notice that the stranger may become geographically fixated for some time, but is never the owner of either the physical or symbolic space that he occupies. This, for Simmel, gives the stranger the characteristics of mobility which embrace nearness and distance within a closed group.

Simmel's trader is therefore someone we know something about. We may purchase goods from them or barter, we see them often, but often we do not. The important factor for me is that we have to *imagine* who the stranger is; lots of important information is left for us to literally make up. We are in the same position if we become a trader ourselves, people imagine who we are and it is at this point that we may start to mis-recognise, stereotype or perceive individuals in either an idealised or denigrated form. The big question is how do we move from the fairly harmless state of the stranger as trader, to the stranger as Jew who brings the outside inside and poisons the comfort of order with suspicion of chaos? To answer this I feel that we need to turn to psychoanalysis, and in Chapter 5 I will present an example of how indigenous peoples quite literally become strangers in their own homelands.

---

symbolic of what we believe we are not, what we were, and what we long to be.

Biological notions of race are now expressed in symbolic representations of Otherness. We have done away with 'race' but we still persecute, discriminate and fear those who are different. The discourse of race still finds an outlet in another guise, in popular conceptualisations of human variation tied in with a commonsense discourse of cultural difference. The notion of race is in some ways an attempt to structure and justify feelings of hatred for Others, which is why structural explanations of racism don't quite hit the mark. To structure and create hierarchy is to exonerate individuals and societies, not only from bouts of genocide, ethnic hatred and discrimination against others, but to also reconcile the inner tension we feel as a result of our actions; our actions being a result of both our interests and our fears, our fear of difference. This is why

I have spent quite a large proportion of this book talking about new and cultural forms of racism which specifically tap into our fears and anxieties around difference, but also our concerns around stability and change. This is a double fear, first of a threat to stability in our own physical environment, and second a fear of disruption and chaos in our inner world. Imagination, if you like, feeds imagination, which taps into our own primitive anxieties around the construction and maintenance of our own 'self'. This is why I feel that psychoanalysis is so important if we are to understand racism. It addresses our irrational fears and concerns, our psychic stability, the ways in which we perceive others and, more importantly, why we perceive others in the way that we do.

Summary

Zygmunt Bauman's sociological theory provides us with a very clear analysis of the relationship between modernity – the modernist project – and racism. Bauman demonstrates how social structure facilitates and indeed provides the necessary conditions for both the cultivation of scientific racism and genocide. Through a rereading of Milgram's (1974) studies of obedience, Bauman rejects the Germaness of the crime, arguing that genocidal projects are heavily rooted in the values of modernity and the structure of modern power relations. Thus, the nation-state actually cultivates a need for racism. It is a totalising central power unit which oppresses and alienates individuals in a system of rational planning and the bureaucratic implementation of grand designs. At no time did the Final Solution clash with the rational pursuit of efficient goal implementation – the Holocaust was wholly commensurable with the principles of instrumental rationality. To reiterate, Bauman is not arguing that the Holocaust was determined by bureaucracy and instrumental culture, rather that the bureaucratic atmosphere is unable to stop such phenomena and, indeed, instrumental culture made the Holocaust seem eminently reasonable. Thus, for Bauman, we have the gardening metaphor, the gardening state in which man dominates nature by the systematic application of a planned order – the vision of a 'good society'. The eradication of weeds and the cultivation of the carefully designed garden is at the heart of the nation-state and encompasses all the ideals of the modernist project. The Holocaust is a byproduct of the endless desire for man to conquer nature, to tame the chaotic, and it is when this modernist dream is accompanied by absolute power that genocide follows.

I have examined in some detail the idea of racism as social engineering and the way in which romantic and ideological mythologies shared an uncanny partnership with science in the Third Reich. It is perhaps the involvement of the medical profession that is often most shocking. The flagrant abuse of the Hippocratic oath and the ease with which people were deemed 'life unworthy of life' illustrates well the extreme limits that people are moved to by the internalisation of biological racist ideologies. The notion of the *therapeutic imperative* casts a medical metaphor on the body of society; society is no longer made of the sum of its individual members, society is a living organism to be treated, medicalised and cured. Eugenic practices would secure forever the eternal genetic makeup of the Germanic races.

I have argued that Bauman's concept of the *stranger* has a particular quality, that of a psycho-social character. The stranger takes sociological theory beyond social structure and into the realms of our imagination. The stranger in some sense represents the post-race Other, and arguably fills the gap left by the discreditation of 'race'. Biological notions of race are now expressed as symbolic representations of otherness. The stranger exists in both our inner world and the external world of reality. Psychoanalytically, there is an intense process of projection and introjection of our fears and anxieties. The stranger is paradoxical in that it is a symbolic representation of what we believe we are not, what we were, and what we long to be.

In the following chapters I want to both outline some basic psychoanalytic ideas from Freud through to Klein and the post-Kleinians, and start to think how we may use psychoanalytic theory to further our understanding of racism and ethnic conflict. Racism cannot be understood in terms of structural explanations alone without reference to our inner fears and anxieties. I do not feel that sociology or psychoanalysis can offer a sufficient explanation individually, but together they may give us a greater understanding of the social psychodynamics of hatred.

CHAPTER 5

Freud, Racism and Psychoanalysis

It is always possible to bind together a considerable number of people in love, so long as there are other people left over to receive the manifestations of their aggressiveness.

(Freud, 1930: 114)

Introduction

What does Freud mean by this statement? Although strikingly poignant, how can psychoanalysis help us understand racism? This chapter is an exploration and interpretation of the way in which Freudian psychoanalytic theory can contribute to our understanding of conflict which may result in racism and exclusionary practices. I start with a general discussion of psychoanalytic theory before going on to focus on the theoretical underpinnings of Freud's work in which I discuss his models of mind, the mechanisms of defence – *sublimation, repression* and *projection* – and finally Freud as both interpreter and philosopher. Freud has come under tremendous criticism for developing a pseudo-science, for not being scientific enough and indeed claiming that psychoanalysis is a science. This often distracts from Freud's other qualities, as a thinker, as an interpreter of society and as a philosopher of mind. Using Freud's monograph *das Unheimlich*, I will show this other side of Freud, whilst charting the development of a central concept in psychoanalytic thinking – projection. I argue that the 'uncanny' is central to our understanding of projection and the way in which we both perceive and treat others. To paraphrase Freud, 'what appears repellently alien is in fact all too familiar'.

Freud was born in 1856 in Frieberg, Moravia, now part of the Czech Republic, and is perhaps one of the most influential thinkers of the twentieth century. Freud's life is extremely well-documented (see Jones, 1953; Clarke, 1980; Gay, 1988) from his childhood in Leipzig and Vienna to his death in London in 1939 at the age of 83.

Freud entered university in Vienna in 1873 (see Gay, 1988), graduating as a doctor of medicine in 1881. In the period between 1876 and 1882 he conducted research on the central nervous system in the Physiological Institute of Ernst Brücke before moving on in 1885 to Jean-Martin Charcot's clinic at the Salpêtrière Hospital in Paris (Schwartz, 2000). Charcot's teachings on hysteria, as Storr (1989) notes, awakened Freud's interest in the problems of neuroses in opposition to the organic diseases of the nervous system. Freud's work with Joseph Breuer led to the publication of *Studies in Hysteria* in 1895, and, as Schwartz (2000) notes, the creation of the analytic hour:

> Breuer's and Freud's method of treating the ancient medical syndrome of hysteria stands out as a turning point in the long history of attempts to understand human psychology. Analogous to Galileo's use of the telescope to explore previously unknown structures in the night sky, the development of the analytic hour created an instrument that opened up an entirely new way to explore previously unknown structures in the human inner world.
>
> (2000: 40)

In the period 1895 to 1900, Freud worked on many of the ideas that would be incorporated in the theory and practice of psychoanalysis, publishing the *Interpretation of Dreams* in 1899. He continued to write and practice in Vienna until 1938 when he was forced, as a Jew, to flee to London because of the threatened Nazi occupation of Austria. Freud is now famous as the creator of psychoanalysis, and Freudian theory is the bedrock from which other schools of psychoanalysis, whether they be Lacanian or Kleinian, have developed their practice. This chapter addresses Freud in his many guises, from Freud the neurophysiologist to Freud the philosopher and interpreter of emotion.

Why psychoanalysis?

It would seem the obvious starting point in any study of racism to try and isolate both how and why racism occurs, yet, despite many years of research, explanations of the ubiquity of racism remains unclear. As we have seen in the introductory chapter, sociological explanation has failed to address some of the central issues surrounding racism. First the affective component of hatred; second the rapidity, as in the case of the former Yugoslavia, with which communities that used to co-exist together can come to hate and destroy each other; third the embodied and visceral content of much of the discrimination; and, finally, that traditional explanations ignore any psychological structuring of discrimination. Rather than go into a long protracted argument about why theories which concentrate on structure have been unsuccessful in explanation, I will start with a discussion about what psychoanalysis has to offer in explanations of racism, hatred and exclusion.

Psychoanalysis addresses the relationship between the inner world of the psyche and the outer world of society or reality(ies). Indeed, for such a specialist area, terminology has crept into all spheres of social life. We talk of 'projecting' our fears onto others, repressing our feelings both conscious and unconscious. Often you hear someone with no specialist knowledge referring to their ego, or some other person's, in short, despite ambivalence toward psychoanalysis from the general public and academics alike, many psychoanalytic concepts created in the formative years of the discipline are used to describe situations, feelings and emotions in everyday life – thus both a recognition and denial of the power of the unconscious.

In addressing racism, we have to recognise that social forces which exclude on a structural plane are supported and perpetuated by the subjective experiences of individuals, in other words by affective emotional mechanisms which operate on both a conscious and unconscious plane. As Frosh (1989) remarks:

> The specific point is that racism, which is the most vicious and dangerous form of social oppression, achieves part of its power by being inscribed deeply in individual psychology.
>
> (1989: 229)

As I have indicated in the previous chapters, institutional racism is inscribed in the structure of society, thus at a macro societal level structure perpetuates racism as a social phenomenon. This is supported at an individual affective level by psychological mechanisms, and therefore racism is also a psychological phenomenon. Both are inseparable and bound together, psychoanalysis is one of the few disciplines which can address both in tandem. We can look in parallel at how changing structures in society evoke certain emotions and anxieties or fuel motivation, shaping the ways in which we perceive others; the tension between structure or society, the 'outer' world, and the psyche, the 'inner' world. Thus social and political structures of oppression are upheld by individual mental processes, as Rustin (1991) argues:

> The point is rather that a crucial means by which structures are upheld is through irrational mental processes, and that this dimension needs to be recognised and confronted as such.
>
> (1991: 71)

Psychoanalysis deals with the irrational (emotive or sentimental), or at least the seemingly irrational – love, hate, envy – forces that shape motivation in everyday existence. Using the term 'irrational' is not without problems, in that irrational means many things to different people. In this book I use irrational to mean emotional, of the sentiments, often imaginary and sometimes self-destructive as well as a source of creativity. It is this 'crazy' side of human life, the peculiar and frightening world of affective forces which influence and shape social structures and institutions. Racism, as Rustin (1991) notes, is grounded in beliefs that are amongst the most irrational that people hold, attributes that are both universal and latent parts of the mentality. Psychoanalysis therefore introduces a further level of explanation into the analysis of conflict in the social world, highlighting the massive substantive irrationality that has accompanied the development of modern society where powerful affective forces fuel racist discourse, producing exclusionary practices and together leading to the maltreatment of people because of their 'otherness'.

What follows is an introduction to some of the basic psychoanalytic concepts through the work of Sigmund Freud and an analysis of some initial attempts to apply psychoanalytic theory to racism in the work of the Frankfurt School.

Freud, language and interpretation: the talking cure

Freud more than anything claimed to be a scientist and psychoanalysis, the system he invented, may be described as the science of the irrational. For Freud it was to be a system that incorporated a field of investigation, a method of enquiry and a psychotherapeutic practice. As Elliott (1994) notes, Freud termed this practice the 'talking cure', 'in order to describe the magical power of language in exploring unconscious life' (1994: 9). It is, however, the hermeneutic interpretive aspect of psychoanalysis that will be of interest to the sociologist. In some sense this may seem to be an attempt at splitting theory from practice, but psychoanalysis cannot be viewed as merely a science or technical practice, as Storr (1989) argues:

> Very early in its history, psycho-analysis left the narrow confines of the consulting room and made incursions into anthropology, sociology, religion, literature, art and the occult. It became, if not a philosophical system, at least a *Weltanschauung*.
>
> (1989: 9)

Freud called his invention a science, but many have argued that it is not, a point argued at length by Popper (1962), Gellner (1993) and Grunbaum (1984, 1993). These theorists claim that psychoanalysis lacks any form of systematic universal laws, any form of prediction, or empirical facts that are open to proof. Arguably, then, what Freud developed was a systematic hermeneutic method for analysing the human condition. In the latter part of this chapter I will examine some of the philosophical ideas in Freud's work which indicate Freud as a hermeneutic interpreter, a philosopher of human nature rather than a biological neurophysiologist.

Psychoanalysis becomes a theory of human nature that can be used both as a tool of investigation (as an academic subject) and as a technical practice (the talking cure). This again is a contentious area of debate and, as Bateman and Holmes (1995) suggest, should be taken in context:

> since we inhabit a society which values (and funds!) science above all else, and takes the 'hard' physical sciences as benchmarks against which 'soft' subjects like psychoanalysis are measured and found wanting.
>
> (1995: 20)

From this we can see the need to view psychoanalysis within a wider picture in which hard science may be used to devalue the contributions made by the discipline. This, of course, is of no consequence if we view psychoanalysis as an interpretive hermeneutic method, which is the stance taken in this book. Perhaps an equally contentious area in Freud's work, as we shall see later, is its reliance on basic biological forces or 'drives', again an area which forms a rift between social scientists because of the suggestion of innate human characteristics rather than learnt (socialised) behaviour. Gellner (1985) is particularly scathing:

> This kind of intuitive, metaphorical, and quite untestable psycho-hydraulics or, if you like, hydro-hermeneutics, is somehow married to the naive acceptance of our habitual introspective characterisation of human motivation, feeling and association.
>
> (1993: 106)

Describing Freud's theory of the unconscious as a form of pseudo-psycho-hydraulics, Gellner suggests that psychoanalysis is more than a theory, indeed it is a secular religion (*ibid.*: xiii). Similarly, Bateman and Holmes (1995: 25) highlight Auden's obituary poem in which he wrote, 'Freud is no more a person now but a whole climate of opinion.' Thus psychoanalysis in its Freudian form has been seen as a science, a pseudo-science, the talking cure, a hermeneutic method, a religion and even a way of life. It has moved out of the consultation room into other academic disciplines, spread into everyday language and, if Gellner is to be believed, it has become a secular religion. In the next section of this chapter I will outline this theory that has caused so much controversy before looking at the elements of psychoanalysis that may help us explain racism.

Freud's mind(s)

Freud was probably the first person to analyse in depth the concept of the unconscious mind, an idea central to psychoanalytic theory:

> The division of the psychical in conscious and what is unconscious is the fundamental premis of psycho-analysis; and it alone makes it possible for psycho-analysis to understand the pathological processes in mental life.
>
> (Freud, *SE XIX*: 13)

Central to the concept of the unconscious is the notion of repression. Unpalatable thoughts, phantasies, unacceptable memories, ideas and wishes are pushed back into the unconscious, or repressed along with their associated emotions. These may emerge in everyday life as dreams or slips of the tongue. In what Sandler *et al.* (1972) and Bateman and Holmes (1995) describe as the 'topographical model', Freud identifies three spatial divisions of the mind: unconscious, preconscious and conscious:

> we have two kinds of unconscious – the one which is latent but capable of becoming conscious, and the one which is repressed and which is not, in itself and without more ado, capable of becoming conscious ... The latent, which is unconscious only descriptively, not in the dynamic sense, we call *preconscious*; we restrict the term *unconscious* to the dynamically unconscious repressed; so that now we have three terms, conscious, preconscious, and unconscious, whose sense is no longer purely descriptive.
>
> (Freud, *SE XIX*: 15)

By integrating the idea of the preconscious into his model, Freud acknowledged that things may be unconscious in a descriptive sense, in other words we may be unaware of certain thoughts, but they are easily brought to mind. Thus this turns from a largely descriptive to a dynamic model of mind. Thoughts may move from consciousness to the preconscious mind and back when needed. The unconscious mind is similarly dynamic in that it is a source of motivation but, as Gardner (1991) notes, the dynamic unconscious is of interest to psychoanalysts because of specific motivations which may cause mental conflict. The topographical model represented a shift of emphasis from external reality and its impact on the mind (affect–trauma model), to stressing the significance of the internal world which for Freud represents man's lifelong struggle with instincts or drives:

> The fateful question for the human species seems to me to be whether and to what extent their cultural development will succeed in mastering the disturbance of their communal life by the human instinct of aggression and self-destruction.
>
> (*SE XXI*: 145)

Freud's instinct theory is a way of explaining human motivation. In it we can see the tension between psychological and biological notions that have been at the centre of the argument surrounding psychoanalysis as a science. These instincts, for Freud, are innate behaviour patterns and responses which have an aim to 'discharge'.

Freud identified two basic classes of instinct: the sexual instinct, *eros*, and the aggressive or destructive instinct, the death instinct, *thanatos*:

> the individual was at the mercy of these drives, or instinctual wishes, with adult symptoms arising from the psychological defenses mobilised to deal with their infantile demands. Each instinctual wish forms a component of the system unconscious and has an innate need for 'discharge'.
>
> (Bateman and Holmes, 1995: 33)

Freud believed aggression to be a result of the death instinct being directed at the external world. In other words, a feeling which is generated entirely from within. Some theorists (Glymour, 1992; Storr, 1989) have argued that this takes no account of aggression being a response to threat, either real or imaginary. There is no room for morals, values and ideals which emanate from the external environment and act upon the inner world, thus there is no sense of the social in Freud's early work. Thus as Glymour (1992), Storr (1996) and Bateman and Holmes (1995) indicate, Freud was forced to consider the interaction between the internal world and external events in what has become known as his 'structural model'.

Structuring the mind: id, ego and superego

Freud's notion of id, ego and superego represent the structural model of the mental apparatus. Rather than seeing these as structures, however, it is more helpful to see each as a function of the mind. The id is the oldest part of the mind from which other functions are derived:

> It contains everything that is inherited, that is present at birth, that is laid down in the constitution-above all, therefore, the instincts, which originate from the somatic organisation and which find a first psychical expression here (in the id) in forms unknown to us.
>
> (Freud, *SE XXIII*: 145)

The id therefore refers to innate unconscious drives and impulses; it is illogical (or at least has a different logic), primitive and emotional, and for Freud is the most important part of the psychical apparatus throughout life:

> It is the dark, inaccessible part of our personality... We call it chaos, a
> cauldron full of seething excitations... it has no organisation, produces
> no collective will, but only a striving to bring about the satisfaction of
> instinctive needs.
>
> (*SE XXII*: 73)

If the id is about everything emotive and impulsive, then the ego
can be viewed as the more rational side of personality, conscious,
controlling and reality-orientated. The task of the ego is to control
the instinctual impulses of the id and adapt them to outer reality.
In other words the ego has the task of self-preservation:

> it performs that task by becoming aware of stimuli, by storing up expe-
> riences about them (in the memory), by avoiding excessively strong stim-
> uli (through flight), by dealing with moderate stimuli (through
> adaptation) and finally by learning to bring about expedient changes in
> the external world to its own advantage (through activity).
>
> (*SE XXIII*: 145)

The ego therefore operates in two domains; in the external world it
responds to stimuli, in the internal world it acts as a control on the
demands of the instincts. Freud used a horse-and-rider analogy to
describe this relationship, whereby the ego is the rider wrestling
with the power of the horse, and often the rider has to guide the
horse if he wants to stay on it. In other words, the rider transforms
the id's will into action 'as if it were its own' (Freud, *SE XIX*: 25).
Freud argues that the ego serves three 'masters'; the id, reality and
the superego. The superego develops in response to authority and
cultural influences in early childhood and can be best described as
the unconscious conscience – an internal judge, responsible for the
repression of unpalatable thoughts, wishes and desires which are
pushed back into the unconscious mind. Gay (1988) illustrates:

> Whether conscious or unconscious, it harbours the individuals ethical
> values on the one hand, and on the other, observes, judges, approves, or
> punishes conduct. In obsessional neurotics and melancholiacs, the
> resulting guilt feelings rise to awareness, but for most others they can
> only be inferred.
>
> (1988: 414)

The relationship between the ego, id and superego becomes
clearer, particularly by example, but it must be stressed that Freud

made a sharp distinction between what he termed primary and secondary mental processes. The id uses primary mental processes and is governed by the most primitive of mental dynamics; the avoidance of un-pleasure, or, put another way, the maximisation of pleasure. The ego uses secondary mental processes, it is the 'performer', it mediates between the id and the external world in order to find the best and least dangerous way of obtaining satisfaction. The superego has as its main task the limitation of satisfactions. Thus we have a model of the human psyche that includes a notion of innate biological drives and instincts that strive for pleasure in the id. The performer, so to speak, is the ego, a mediator between external and internal worlds, with the superego, the result of an introjection of early childhood experiences, as an internal judge. In order to understand how this model may help explain human aggression and destructiveness, Freud's thesis on civilisation will be examined together with the concepts of sublimation, repression and projection.

Mechanisms of defence

> The ego makes use of various procedures for fulfilling its task, which, to put it in general terms, is to avoid danger, anxiety and unpleasure. We call these procedures 'mechanisms of defence'.
>
> (Freud, *SE XXIII*: 235)

Freud refers to defence mechanisms as vicissitudes of the instincts, primarily concerned with dangerous instincts being carried through into external reality without modification. As Laplanche (1973) notes, they are a set of operations concerned with both elimination and, or, reduction of any change that is likely to threaten the individual psyche. The mechanisms of projection and repression will be examined in detail as they would seem the most fruitful concepts in the examination of racism and exclusion; repression because Freud saw it as the most dangerous mechanism of all and the basis of civilisation, and projection as an introduction to defence in paranoia and fear of the other.

Although belonging to the ego, the defence mechanisms are largely unconscious. In terms of the structure of the psyche, we have learnt that the superego does the repressing but the ego also mediates by filtering and modifying unpalatable instincts. Repression stems from anxiety, anxiety from separation and loss, the individual fearing annihilation. Hence, as Frosh (1987) notes:

> Anxiety is both the cause of symptoms and of defenses: the purpose of the mechanisms of defence is to ward off dangers; the particular defenses that are characteristically chosen by any individual determining the symptomatology that s/he is likely to show.
>
> (1987: 64)

Thus it is hard to differentiate between a defence mechanism and a symptom, both functioning to avert danger. The symptom expresses both the repressed idea and the repressing agency. Repression, therefore, has multiple meanings – it can be simply a process by which unconscious material is prevented from appearing in the conscious; on another level it is intrinsic to survival, a mechanism which protects the psyche both from internal and external threats of danger and annihilation; and finally, as we have seen, repression rests at the heart of Freud's theory of the unconscious mind. In this we have the notion of conflict within the self; there is an instinctual emotion, affect, trying to discharge, which is blocked by the superego finding it repellent and unpalatable, and it is returned to the unconscious. Bateman and Holmes (1995) simplify:

> *Repression*, the pushing back of unacceptable wishes from consciousness, is the classical primary mechanism of defence. Repression ensures that wishes which are incompatible with reality, superego demands, or other impulses, remain unconscious or disguised.
>
> (1995: 77)

Repression, therefore, is a process by which unpalatable or repellent thoughts which emanate from instinctual drives are pushed back into the unconscious mind only to reemerge in slips of the tongue, dreams and jokes. Freud argues that repression of instincts makes culture and civilisation possible. The energy associated with our instinctual drives is sublimated or channelled into other activities, it finds a discharge or expression in creativity, through art and literature:

> Sublimation of the instinct is an especially conspicuous feature of civilization; it is what makes it possible for higher psychical activities, scientific, artistic or ideological, to play such an important part in civilized life.
>
> (*SE XXI*: 97)

As Gay (1988) notes, Freud's theory of civilisation views life in society as a compromise that is essentially insoluble. The very things that make society or civilisation possible are the things that lead to discontent. Freud paints a very pessimistic view for the future; 'man' cannot live without civilisation, but is unhappy within it. Eros is sublimated in culture whilst the death instinct finds an outlet in the control and domination of nature. Thanatos, the destructive instinct, with nature tamed, finds an outlet in aggressiveness to others. For Freud, the inclination towards aggression is an instinctual disposition in man which constitutes the greatest impediment to civilisation; the meaning of civilisation is thus:

> the struggle between Eros and Death, between the instinct of life and the instinct of destruction, as it works itself out in the human species. This struggle is what all life essentially consists of, and the evolution of civilization may be simply described as the struggle for the life of the human species.
>
> (*SE XXI*: 122)

Freud never used the term 'racism', but destruction, a discharge of the death instinct, he describes as constant feuding and ridiculing of others. With the inclination towards aggressiveness discharged on others, cohesion between members of a community is made easier. Yet, as Freud points out, the massacres of Jewish people in the Middle Ages did little to make the period more peaceful or secure; destructive instincts will always find another target. This led Freud to conclude *Civilization and its Discontents* with the following lines:

> Men have gained control over the forces of nature to such an extent that with their help they would have no difficulty in exterminating one another to the last man. They know this, and hence comes a large part of their current unrest, their unhappiness and their mood of anxiety.
>
> (*SE XXI*: 145)

Das unheimlich: Freud, philosophy and projection

> 'Unheimlich' is the name for everything that ought to have remained ... secret and hidden but has come to light (Schelling).
>
> (Freud, *SE XVII*: 224)

The dismissal of psychoanalysis as a science, as Ian Craib (1998) notes, 'is the usual ground for the philosophical dismissal of Freud', and this dismissal is based in positivistic notions of science. Freud, as we have seen, proposed a new theory and practice – 'the talking cure' – very much based in an interpretive and hermeneutic understanding of the human psyche. Freud, however, claimed throughout his life that psychoanalysis was very much a science, and in doing so left himself open to constant criticism from medical, philosophical and sociological traditions.

The debate on whether psychoanalysis is a science, as expressed in the views of Popper (1962), Gellner (1993) and particularly Grunbaum (1984), exploded in 1993 when the *New York Review of Books* published Frederick Crews' (1993) essay 'The Unknown Freud', a damning report on psychoanalysis and Freud's theory in which Crews describes psychoanalysis as an explanatory worthless hobbyhorse. The problem with taking this as a definitive, is that it detracts from what Freud does give us in terms of interpretation, and it detracts from other less scientific interpretations of Freud's work in terms of its hermeneutic and philosophical quality.

Craib (1998) argues that a hermeneutic reading of Freud opens up many new possibilities. Citing the work of Paul Ricoeur (1970) and Jürgen Habermas (1971), Craib argues that philosophers can learn from Freud rather than trying to teach him – 'they do not destroy psychoanalysis but take it beyond itself' (Craib, 1998: 133). Habermas uses psychoanalysis as a way of maintaining a hermeneutic approach to his philosophical sociology, pointing to forms of ideological domination. Ricoeur uses Freud's ideas to point to the unconscious distortion of meanings in tandem with a more traditional hermeneutic approach to conscious interpretations and meaning.

As Anthony Elliott (1999) notes, despite the recent round of Freud-bashing and the debate around psychoanalysis as a science, Freud's intellectual and cultural influence remains profound. It is Freud the philosopher that is often forgotten in lieu of Freud the biologist, but there are many more interpretations of Freud's work than mere biology. These range from the philosophical discussions mentioned above, to Lacan's reconstruction of Freud with his emphasis on language, to the writings of so-called third-wave feminists, for example Juliet Mitchell's (1974) book *Psychoanalysis and Feminism* and the works of Julia Kristeva (1989, 1991) and Luce Irigaray (1985). As Alvesson and Skoldberg (2000) note, after

Ricoeur (1970), the entities that Freud discovered in the psyche –
the id, ego and superego – are not entities at all, but interpretations –
'the unconscious becomes something that does not really exist, but
is an ascribed meaning' (Alvesson and Skoldberg, 2000: 94).
Alvesson and Skoldberg argue that the concept of hermeneutics has
undergone a fundamental change:

> Psychoanalysis can be seen as belonging to the *hermeneutics of suspicion*
> which, apart from Freud, is also represented by Marx and Nietzsche. All
> three have probed behind what they conceived as an illusory self con-
> sciousness to a deeper-lying, more unpleasant or 'shameful' one. In
> Freud the latter appears as the libido, in Marx as the economic interest,
> and in Nietzsche the will to power.
>
> (2000: 95)

Alvesson and Skoldberg argue that the history of hermeneutics has
been a history devoid of such suspicion, and that psychoanalysis
adds another dimension on the periphery of the hermeneutic
tradition seeking the irrational elements behind societal phenomena. If we return to Freud, perhaps one of the papers which
demonstrates, more than most, Freud's philosophic, imaginative
and interpretive thinking is *das Unheimlich* (1919). Freud not only
addresses aesthetics in this paper, but also traces his own thoughts
in his development of one of the central concepts of psychoanalytic
thinking and practice – projection.

   In the monograph *das Unheimlich*, Freud dons his philosophical
cap to investigate the subject of aesthetics, something he indicates
that a psychoanalyst rarely gets a chance, or feels impelled, to do.
Aesthetics, Freud argues, generally concern themselves with questions of beauty, of that which is attractive, of the sublime. In other
words, things, ideas and feelings of a positive nature. Freud,
however, is not concerned with a theory of beauty, but a theory of
the quality of feelings and particularly the quality of feelings that
belong within the field of 'what is frightening':

> The subject of the 'uncanny' is a province of this kind. It is undoubtedly
> related to what is frightening – to what arouses dread and horror.
>
> (Freud, *SE XVII*: 219)

Freud embarks on an investigation of the linguistic usage of the
term *das Unheimlich*, as well as considering the experiences and situations which arouse in people a sense of the uncanny. Two courses

of investigation, Freud argues, lead to the same conclusion: 'the uncanny is that class of frightening which leads back to what is known of old and long familiar' (*SE XVII*: 220). Thus we have a feeling, the quality of which is both familiar, old and frightening. We may not always be able to identify where this feeling comes from, which suggests that it emanates from something repressed, something in the unconscious mind, something triggered by certain symbols or events.

Freud uses the example of the Sandman from *Eight Tales of Hoffman*. The Sandman is roughly equivalent to the 'bogeyman', the fear of which keeps children in their beds at night. In a linguistic sense the writer creates something uncanny which plays on our unconscious fears and phantasies. In the same way, religion has created gods and demons. These we feel we have surmounted, particularly with the spread of secularisation and the demise of religious practice, but we still have uncanny feelings of supernatural powers that are frightening. Freud thus gives us two forms of the uncanny. First, feelings that are triggered by infantile complexes, and second the uncanny which proceeds from actual experience, from animistic beliefs that have been surmounted. Thus, for Freud:

> animism, magic and sorcery, the omnipotence of thoughts, man's attitude to death, involuntary repetition and the castration complex comprise practically all the factors which turn something frightening into something uncanny.
>
> (*SE XVII*: 243)

Freud draws our attention to themes in uncanniness that are prominent. In literature there is often a 'doubling' of characters, identical people who look alike, joined in some sort of telepathic union such that experiences and feelings become common. Freud also suggests that these characters represent or are marked by the fact that the subject identifies himself in some other. There is a 'doubling, dividing and interchanging of the self' (*ibid.*: 234). Robert Jay Lifton (1986) has made much of this concept in explanation of actions of Nazi doctors. Freud was less convinced:

> having considered the manifest motivation of the figure of a 'double', we have to admit that none of this helps us to understand the extraordinary strong feelings of something uncanny.
>
> (*SE XVII*: 236)

Nothing in the concept of doubling, Freud argues, can account for the urge to project outwards parts of the ego as something foreign; uncanniness in the 'double' stems from our archaic inheritance. Another theme is that of repetition. Freud gives an example of walking on a summer day in a small town in Italy. Despite taking different routes Freud found himself back in the same location; on his return to the same place for the third time, via yet another route, he experienced a sense of uncanniness. I have experienced the same kind of feeling in the souks of North Africa, every attempt at finding a way out results in a return to a familiar landmark, which creates a sense of helplessness, a feeling of the uncanny.

Freud argues that the uncanny fulfils the condition of 'touching' the residues of our animistic mental activity and bringing them to expression. How do we find a discharge for these frightening thoughts, thoughts that evoke a feeling of uncanniness, uneasiness, even repellence? Freud is clear, we project them onto others. Projection is a mechanism of defence in which material is projected outwards as if it is something foreign to the self:

> In the properly psycho-analytic sense: operation whereby qualities, feelings, wishes or even 'objects', which the subject refuses to recognise or rejects in himself, are expelled from the self and located in another person or thing.
>
> (Laplanche and Pontalis, 1973: 349)

Projection for Freud is symptomatic of paranoia. Distorted feelings of persecution are expelled from the internal world onto some other. Internal perception is distorted and suppressed, and in the case of persecution what should have been felt internally as love is perceived externally as hate. Paranoia is a general Freudian term that covers systematic delusions, of grandeur, persecution, jealousy; it is a mechanism of defence. Projection is part of a process of recovery in which thoughts and desires that have been suppressed internally are projected outwards. Laplanche and Pontalis (1973) elucidate:

> Projection was first discovered in paranoia ... a primary defence which misuses a normal mechanism, namely, the search for an external source for an unpleasurable experience. The paranoic projects his intolerable ideas outwards, whence they return in the shape of reproaches.
>
> (1973: 351)

Example 5.1 The Australian aborigine as uncanny stranger

What is it about Aborigines, and their claims, that makes them uncanny strangers for settler Australians, and how is this tied in with the particularity of Australian nationhood? If we move away from these general claims about the psychological dimensions of racism to consider what is specific in the psychodynamic between settler and indigenous populations in Australia, then I would argue that strangerdom is at the heart of the dynamic (see also Moran, 2002). The Aborigine somehow unsettles the settler in the experience of his or her national identity, and therefore in terms of his or her experience of home. This is intrinsic to the settler/indigenous relation, and is exacerbated by the importance of home as enclosure and familiarity. Such an unsettlement is traumatic and disorientating. From its beginning as a penal settler colony to its development into an Australian nation, settler society has displaced the indigenous. Even as they and their lands were exploited and expropriated, the indigenous were largely external and peripheral to the colonising and later nation-building projects. In its initial formulation as 'white Australia' Australian national identity had no place for the Aborigines. However, unlike other groupings excluded from 'white Australia', Aborigines could not be kept out of Australian territories.

If we refer back to Bauman's (and Simmel's) argument we can characterise the colonial situation as follows. From the perspective of the indigenous, the settlers were the 'strangers' entering their land and society. However, because of immense power disparities, and the peculiarities of colonialism, the 'guests' did not take up the position of questioning stranger, but instead turned the situation around, viewing the indigenous as strange – *as those who would enter, or collide with, the sphere of civilisation*. Aborigines were thus treated as the strangers – sometimes hostile, sometimes benign. This is the very reverse of the situation of the immigrant coming into the host society as described by Simmel and Bauman. To occupy the same homely space, and yet to not know the other; to feel that the other is both familiar but at the same time unknowable; this characterises the colonial situation.

What settlers have split off and placed in the indigenous other comes back to haunt them. The 'uncanny', to remind ourselves, is 'that class of the frightening which leads back to what is known of old and long familiar' (Freud, 1919: 220). What we have projected into others, and have repressed within ourselves, comes back to haunt us. This is the essence of the uncanny, and of the psychodynamic dimension of strangeness. One of the most important misconceptions of the settler imagination about the indigenous was that they did not own the land, that they simply foraged over it like animals, a projection perhaps, as Horkheimer and Adorno (1994) might suggest, of our longing to return to a pre-social state of nature. Within this structure it was claimed that the Aborigines were not dispossessed by settlers for, after all, one cannot take what someone does not have. And yet, was there a kernel of truth about the settlers' own situation within this scenario?

Settlers had, in a sense, lost connection with their own ethnic spaces: they had given up (or had been forced to give up) their own landscapes as they came into those of others.

The indigenous themselves inspire *dread* in contemporary Australians. Repressed from colonial memory, they returned with a vengeance in the latter half of the twentieth century – 'something which ought to have remained hidden...has come to light' as Freud (1919: 241, after Schelling) would say. The outback Aboriginal settlements take settler Australians back to the original dispossession and point to the fact that it is still with them, and ongoing. It reminds settler Australia of its own less than glorious beginnings as both a penal colony where violence and desperation reigned, and as a harsh and unforgiving society where poverty and social collapse were ever-threatening.

Thus someone who is racist will project his own faults on to another group which has the effect of disowning that which is unpalatable and recognising this in some other.

Summary

This chapter has introduced some of the key concepts in Freudian psychoanalytic theory and practice. It has identified both topological and structural models of mind and introduced the reader to the concepts of *projection, repression* and *sublimation*. It has also charted a course from the biological Freud to the philosophical Freud – the thinker, interpreter of society and philosopher of mind and emotion. The concept of projection is central to psychoanalytic practice and a clear understanding of it is essential if we are to come close to understanding the motivation behind racism and discriminatory practices. To clarify Freud's position. The uncanny belongs to a set of feelings that have a frightening quality, and the frightening element emanates from a feeling that has been repressed. The recurrence of this feeling causes uncanniness. It matters little if what is uncanny was originally frightening. The uncanny is neither new nor alien, but something old and familiar which has become repressed in the mind. In the following chapter I will examine Horkheimer and Adorno's explanation of anti-Semitism in which they argue that 'those blinded by civilization' experience their own archaic and repressed feelings in others. Certain individuals and groups remind us uncannily of our repressed prehistory. We project our phantasy into others, attacking and experiencing our own aggression as that of the other. Freud's original philosophical piece has been overly biologised by some subsequent interpretations, most notably those of the Frankfurt School. As Robert Young (2000) has recently and succinctly noted when differentiating between Freudian and Kleinian models of human nature: 'One is a world of animals as scientific objects reacting to stimuli, the other is a world of subjects haunted by demons' (Young, 2000).

In this instance, Freud's original work is written in the spirit of the latter rather than the former. The idea of the 'uncanny' is central to our understanding of projection and the way in which we perceive others; it demonstrates Freud's thinking at its most philosophic and imaginative, in other words interpretive, and is a far cry from Freud the scientist. Freud's philosophical ideas, terms and concepts are illustrated in the work of Max Horkheimer, Theodor Adorno, Eric Fromm and Herbert Marcuse and in the formulation of critical theory and the critical social research of the Frankfurt School.

Summary of key terms

Models of mind

Affect–trauma. Trauma leads to painful affect (feelings); the release of dammed up feelings threatens the psyche providing the motivational backdrop to pathological reactions.

Topographical. This model represents a shift in emphasis from external reality and its impact on the mind (affect–trauma), to a stress on the internal world. Dynamic spatial model: the *unconscious, preconscious* and *conscious*.

Structural. This model stresses the interaction between the internal world and external events. It is helpful to see the id, ego and superego as functions of the mind rather than structures.

The id represents the oldest part of the mind from which other functions are derived. It refers to innate unconscious drives and impulses, primitive and emotional, striving to bring about the satisfaction of instinctive needs.

The ego represents the rational side of the personality, conscious, controlling and reality-orientated. It controls the instinctual impulses of the id and adapts them to outer reality.

The superego develops in response to authority and cultural impulses in early childhood – the unconscious conscience, an internal judge responsible for the repression of unpalatable thoughts, wishes and desires which are pushed back into the unconscious mind.

Mechanisms of defence

Freud refers to defence mechanisms as vicissitudes of the instincts and they are primarily concerned with dangerous instincts being carried through into external reality without modification.

Repression is a process by which unpalatable or repellent thoughts which emanate from instinctual drives are pushed back into the unconscious mind only to reemerge in slips of the tongue, dreams and jokes.

Sublimation occurs when the energy associated with our instinctual drives is sublimated or channelled into other activities; it finds a discharge or expression, for example, in creativity, through art and literature.

Projection describes the process in which qualities, feelings or wishes that the subject does not recognise as his own, and finds unpalatable or repellent, are expelled from the self and located in some other person or thing.

CHAPTER 6

The Frankfurt School: Paranoid Projection and the Persecuted Other

The blind murderer has always seen his victim as a persecutor against whom he must defend himself, and the strongest and wealthiest individuals have always thought their weakest neighbours to be an intolerable threat before they fell upon them to destroy them.

(Horkheimer and Adorno, 1994: 187)

Introduction

How can we explain racism using Freudian concepts? What are the implications and problems, if any, of using this type of analysis? Can psychoanalysis help answer the central concern of the Frankfurt School, 'Why is mankind, instead of entering into a truly humane condition, sinking into new forms of barbarism?'

The work of Eric Fromm has been both long-neglected and highly criticised for what Marcuse (1972) describes as Freudian revisionism and the elimination of the explosive elements of psychoanalysis. Max Horkheimer and Theodor Adorno have been described as biological reductionists (see Bahr, 1994), conducting ethnocentric studies under the auspices of the Frankfurt Institute of Social Research. Few others, however, have attempted to explain racism in terms of psychoanalytic theory. In other words, the Frankfurt School offers us a considerable body of literature from which to illustrate and build a psychosocial explanation of racism and exclusion, a critical base which has been largely neglected in contemporary studies. This chapter will focus on the early work of the Frankfurt School and in particular the tension between the theoretical standpoint of Fromm and that of Horkheimer and Adorno who seek to explain Fascism, Nazism and anti-Semitism through a critical fusion of the works of Marx, Weber and Freud.

The Institute for Social Research (Institute für Sozialforschung) was founded with the help of Felix Weil in 1923. Carl Grünberg was appointed the first director of the Institute and made his inaugural speech in the hall of Frankfurt University in June 1924 in which he stressed the deeply empirical nature of the Institute's research grounded in economics and historical materialism. As David Held (1990) notes, Grünberg's Institute and his form of Marxism sought to combine concrete historical studies with theoretical analysis. It is, however, perhaps the names of Max Horkheimer and Theodor Adorno which are most closely associated with the Institute, and with the idea of critical theory.

Max Horkheimer was appointed director of the Institute in 1930. Within three years Horkheimer, together with many of his colleagues, were forced to flee Germany as a result of the Nazi persecution of Jews and seek asylum in the United States. Horkheimer's vision for the Institute was markedly different from that of his predecessor Grünberg. Social philosophy became a leading point of discussion within the school, as did an interest in psychoanalytic thinking and the relationship between science, 'man' and nature. Marcuse became a member of the school in 1932 and, following an association of several years, Adorno joined in 1938. Many of the school's most important, and certainly well-known, work was written in the period of exile between 1933 and 1950 including *Dialectic of Enlightenment* and *Studies in Prejudice* (for a full Bibliography see Held, 1990; Wiggershaus, 1994).

Horkheimer and Adorno returned to Germany in the early 1950s and the Institute was reestablished in Frankfurt with Adorno as co-Director. Marcuse, Fromm and others stayed in the United States to pursue their own projects. The work of the Frankfurt School has been diverse, ranging from economics, history, philosophy and social psychology, to critiques of mass consumption and the culture industry. What follows is an examination of the contribution the School has made to the psychoanalytic understanding of racism and ethnic hatred. The writings of the School at the time must be understood within the historical context and background of the theorists in question; the mass persecution of Jewish peoples; social dislocation, war, fragmentation and a certain rage against what Hannah Arendt (1962) would later describe as the banality of evil.

Dialectic of Enlightenment

Dialectic of Enlightenment is a critique of positivism, of science and of the 'culture industry'. The principle concern of the thesis is the self-destructive nature of enlightenment ideals and can be summarised in the often quoted phrase from the introduction to the book:

> In the most general sense of progressive thought, the Enlightenment has always aimed at liberating men from fear and establishing their sovereignty. Yet the fully enlightened earth radiates disaster triumphant.
>
> (Horkheimer and Adorno, 1994: 3)

The Enlightenment, rather than freeing people, has created a totalitarian regime through the principles of control, order and domination, and this is nowhere better demonstrated than in the culture industry which for Horkheimer and Adorno is a passive form of social control.

It is the final chapter of *Dialectic of Enlightenment* – 'Elements of Anti-Semitism' – that we can see a real synthesis of psychoanalytic and sociological ideas. Horkheimer and Adorno draw heavily on Freud's instinct theory, weaving together powerful primitive drives and projective mechanisms of defence to explain the pathological nature of anti-Semitism. Horkheimer and Adorno argue that mimesis, a powerful instinctual mechanism, a form of self-protection in the natural world, has become perverted in the modern world. In our natural environment we mimic in order to camouflage and blend in; quite simply this may mean freezing if we sense danger, and this is part of our biological pre-history:

> When men try to become like nature they harden themselves against it. Protection as fear is a form of mimicry. The reflexes of stiffening and numbness in humans are archaic schemata of the urge to survive.
>
> (Horkheimer and Adorno, 1994: 180)

As with Freud's thesis on civilisation, Horkheimer and Adorno argue that civilisation, the modern world, has slowly and methodically prohibited instinctual behaviour. Initially this came about by the organisation of mimesis in the magical phase, through ceremony and rite. Religious practice outlaws the instinctual; rational practice banishes the display of emotions. People are taught behavioural norms in the school and workplace, and children are no longer allowed to behave like children. Mimesis now takes a form in which society threatens nature; control equals self-preservation and dominance over nature. We no longer make our 'self' like nature to survive, but attempt to make nature like us:

> Society continues threatening nature as the lasting organised compulsion which is reproduced in individuals as rational self preservation and rebounds on nature as social dominance over it.
>
> (*Ibid.*: 181)

In other words, the instinctual mechanism of mimesis becomes sublimated in the practice of the rational control of the modern environment. Jay (1994), summing up the theoretical stance of the Frankfurt School, notes that anti-Semitism, racism and other functional equivalents are characterised by a 'rage' against difference, against the 'non-identical' that is part of the 'totalistic dominating impulse of western civilisation' (Jay, 1994: 243). In this critical fusion of Weber's theory of the rationalisation process, our relationship with nature, and Freudian instinct theory, Horkheimer and Adorno are arguing that any 'other', any minority that refuses to assimilate, becomes a target of hatred, of exclusion and ultimately of extermination.

The application of the Freudian notion of projection is pivotal in Horkheimer and Adorno's theory of Fascism. It is, For Horkheimer and Adorno, a 'perverted' form of mimesis which leads to the urge to make the natural world fit our purposes which develops into an urge to dominate and control others through paranoid fantasy. We project onto the world experiences and qualities that are part of ourselves as if they are part of someone else. When the feeling involved is bad, the projection becomes paranoid: 'they cannot stand the Jews yet imitate them' (Horkheimer and Adorno, 1994: 183); again, what appears repellently alien is in fact all too familiar.

Horkheimer and Adorno develop psychoanalytic theory from an individual to a societal level. As the individual psyche collapses, we imagine this is happening to some other group. This 'collapse' is politicised in the modern world; certain individuals and groups remind us of our repressed prehistory, and it matters little if these groups actually have these mimetic features, these urges are unpalatable so we project them:

> Impulses which the subject will not admit as his own even though they are most assuredly so, are attributed to the object – the prospective victim … in Fascism this behaviour is made political; the object of the illness is deemed true to reality; and the mad system becomes the reasonable norm in the world and deviation from it a neurosis.
>
> (*Ibid.*: 187)

Anti-Semitism is based, for Horkheimer and Adorno, on 'false' projection. The mimetic attempts to reconcile difference by blending in with the environment, by making the inner world like the outer world, accepting difference, assimilating, a form of sociability and self-preservation. False projection, however, attempts to change the environment, to make it like its 'self'. In a confusion of inner and outer worlds, the other is no longer familiarised, but becomes dangerous, frightening and threatening. Intimate experiences are seen as hostile, in the production of a psychological boundary that must not be crossed:

> Mimesis imitates the environment, but false projection makes the environment like itself. For mimesis the outside world is a model which the inner world must try to conform to: the alien must become familiar; but false projection confuses the inner and outer world and defines the most intimate experiences as hostile.
>
> (*Ibid.*: 187)

The product of false projection is the stereotype, the transference of socially unpalatable thoughts from subject to object. This is particularly interesting in the study of racism, in that stereotypical constructions of otherness form the basis of both direct and indirect discrimination and exclusion from equality of opportunity. This is also particularly alarming if, as Horkheimer and Adorno argue, the paranoiac cannot help or accept his own instincts. In doing so he attacks others, experiencing his aggression as that of the 'other', a classic case of projection. This has two implications. Firstly the 'other' reminds us of the peace and happiness that we cannot have, persecuted minorities form a receptacle for the betrayed of modern society. We cannot have it so we will destroy it, an envious attack. Secondly, the 'other' stands as a direct reminder, either real or imaginary, of our repressed longings to return to a pre-social state of nature, to satisfy socially banished instinctual needs; we accuse outgroups of behaving like animals because we long to behave like animals. In this way, Horkheimer and Adorno argue, the Jew became the persecuted other. Horkheimer and Adorno describe the anti-Semite:

> since he cannot allow himself the pleasure of following his own instincts, he attacks other individuals in envy or persecution just as the repressed bestialist hunts or torments an animal.
>
> (*Ibid.*: 192)

Horkheimer and Adorno's explanation of anti-Semitism provides a theoretical basis for the explanation of racism, hatred and exclusionary practices by using a critical fusion of both structural and psychological factors. It also serves as an introduction to the application and limitations of Freudian thought in an examination of the massive substantive irrationality that has accompanied the development of modern society. By placing an emphasis on affective forces, they produce a more complete picture of the ways in which psychological mechanisms support and perpetuate structural forms of racism. Jay (1994) notes that Horkheimer and Adorno go beyond a purely psychoanalytic account of paranoid false projection, adding an epistemological dimension. Projection *per se* is not a problematic, we all use it in our everyday lives. A healthy projection preserves the tension between subject and object. Reflection on the dialogue between subject and object creates understanding, it is (after Kant) the key to enlightenment. The morbid aspect of anti-Semitism for Horkheimer and Adorno is not projection but lack of self-reflection:

> When the subject is no longer able to return to the object what he has received from it, he becomes poorer rather than richer. He loses the reflection in both directions: since he no longer reflects the object, he ceases to reflect upon himself, and loses the ability to differentiate.
>
> (*Ibid.*: 189)

Horkheimer and Adorno's thesis is often ignored by theorists and critics alike, and this is particularly true of the section on paranoia and projection. Bahr (1994) is particularly scathing:

> To make projection understandable as well as the manner in which it is deformed into false projection – a process regarded as part of the essence of false anti-Semitism – the authors employed a rather naively realistic physiological theory of perception.
>
> (1994: 233)

Bahr goes on to describe Horkheimer and Adorno's work as a far-fetched theory pertaining to biological prehistory. In his criticism, Bahr is noticeably uncritical. There is no doubt that some of the theoretical contributions made in *Dialectic of Enlightenment* are unclear and need developing. Bahr fails to notice some huge theoretical leaps; for example, it is not clear how the urge to control and dominate nature turns into the urge to control and dominate others, and this tends to cloud some of the more useful components of the research. Bahr, however, questions the link between the instinctual and its condemnation in the modern world, ultimately challenging the Institute's view of nature. Horkheimer and Adorno are clear about their position: 'The domination of nature represents a particular type of relationship; nature has utility, in so far as it is instrumental to human purposes' (in Held, 1980: 154). There seems little doubt that the public display of emotion is something that has been seen as increasingly inappropriate (see Elias, 1978), although, interestingly, the public display of grief for celebrities seems an exception to this condemnation in the modern world.

Ultimately, the most severe criticism of Horkheimer and Adorno's work stems from the biological nature of Freud's instinct theory. It is quite simply the nature–nurture debate with an acidic twist. In situating explanation of racism within the context of a biologically derived theoretical framework, Horkheimer and Adorno argue that the racist or anti-Semite is biologically predisposed to a certain type of inferior behaviour – the case against the racist becomes racist, or at the least ethnocentric, as Horkheimer and Adorno reduce explanation to particular dispositions in the German personality. What we can take from *Dialectic of Enlightenment* is the social psychological process of projection and some basis for the application of psychoanalytic theory from an individual to a societal level. If we dispense with the biological determinism, we are left to look at the psychodynamic processes between individuals and groups that are rooted in (un)sociability. As Fred Alford notes:

> *Dialectic of Enlightenment* is not the last word on anything. It does, however, grasp the way in which the irrational stealthily intrudes upon the rational.
>
> (1997: 725)

Eric Fromm: *Fear of Freedom*

Eric Fromm (1942) in the *Fear of Freedom* tried to address the problematics associated with Freud's instinct theory by arguing for a social basis in the shaping of instinctual drives. Fromm examined the structure of modern society, addressing the relationship between the social and psychological, attempting a revision of Freudian theory in a critical Marxist social psychology. Fromm is interested in the individuality and uniqueness of personality: we are not all biological clones, rather we are shaped by historical and social factors in which psychological conditions are in turn based. More specifically, Fromm focused on what he described as the social crisis of our day: 'The meaning of freedom for modern man' (1942: xi).

For Freud, man's lifelong struggle is that between the discharge and satisfaction of instincts and their transformation into civilised behaviour. In society, man's biological instincts are either repressed or sublimated, channelled into other activities; there is a constant tension between repression and sublimation – the greater the repression, the greater the culture, but at a price – unhappiness. Fromm describes this as a static position between man and society. The individual remains essentially the same and only becomes changed in the sense that his/her instincts are either satisfied or sacrificed. Fromm takes issue with Freud's position:

> This book differs from Freud's inasmuch as it emphatically disagrees with his interpretation of history as the result of psychological forces that in themselves are not socially conditioned. It disagrees as emphatically with those theories which neglect the role of the human factor as one of the dynamic elements in the social process.
>
> (1942: 10)

Fromm argues that Freud is wrong to assume that man's position in relation to society is fixed. We cannot separate biological instincts, drives and desires as something that are impeded, frustrated or satisfied by society. This dichotomous relationship between the social and biological is, for Fromm, quite simply unrealistic. Although acknowledging that there are certain biological functions that are common to all men, for example thirst, Fromm argues that man's nature, passions, are a cultural product:

> Those drives which make for the *differences* in men's characters, like love and hatred, the lust for power and the yearning for submission, the enjoyment of sensuous pleasure and the fear of it, are all products of the social process.
>
> (1942: 10)

Fromm is arguing that society, although having a repressive function also has a creative function; in full Marxist rhetoric he argues that man is the creation of human effort, the record of which we call history. Fromm's work in this context becomes fundamental to the way in which we can understand racism as a learned behaviour. Racism for Freud emanates from a biological striving for self-protection, particularly in times of anxiety. In Fromm's work we can start analysing racism in terms of a socially learnt behaviour which develops into personality characteristics as society evolves. In other words, drives are not fixed biologically but are moulded by the social, by society, in a continuous process which we call history. These personality characteristics are learnt in early childhood through interaction within the family unit.

How can this help us explain racism? Implicit in this theory is the need of the individual to have some 'other' from which to define him/her self. This is not particularly new or different from the social constructionist viewpoint. Goffman (1978), Garfinkel (1967) and Harré (1986) have shown that the self is constructed in relation to others, and indeed what we believe to be instinctual or emotive can be the product of the cognitive state of how we read situations rather than a bodily state that determines the feeling. What Fromm appears to provide is a midway link between biological instinct theory and social constructionism. Human drives adapt to socio-economic conditions and the product of this process is what Fromm describes as the 'social character', and this character determines attitudes and ideals in society.

In trying to explain Fascism, Nazism and ultimately racism, Fromm focuses on the dynamic factors in the character structure of modern man. Why are people increasingly being manipulated by their emotions, blindly following political cultures which seem to be against their rational self-interest (by giving up their personal freedom), and why, despite being free, do people seem so unhappy. Fromm situates explanation in 'the very essence of the human mode and the practice of life: the need to be related to the world outside oneself, the need to avoid aloneness' (1942: 15). Fromm argues that the need to belong is essential to the very essence of being and self-consciousness, without it we could simply not live at all, it's basic and in some sense not social. Belonging is a form of defence from others (which requires others), from nature and ultimately from ourselves.

Medieval society was characterised by a lack of individual freedom; people were tied in feudalism, but they were not alone and isolated. With the collapse of feudalism and the onset of capitalism people became free(er) but experienced an increase in feelings of isolation and aloneness. Protestantism provided the answer to the 'human needs of the frightened, uprooted and isolated individual' (*ibid*.: 87). In secular modern society the sense of belonging that Protestantism provided has disappeared. Freedom has a double edge: in one sense it is a release from the traditional bonds of medieval society, in another the individual becomes alone and isolated, filled with doubt and anxiety. Modern man cannot bear the burden of freedom and therefore has to escape; escape from aloneness, powerlessness and isolation.

Fromm identifies three mechanisms of escape that have a direct influence on the ways in which we perceive and treat others. *Authoritarianism* is the tendency to give up one's individual self and fuse with somebody or something else. Fromm argues that the greater part of the lower middle class in Europe and in particular Germany exhibits sado-masochistic personality characteristics: the authoritarian personality is characterised by a striving for domination and submission:

> He admires authority and tends to submit to it but at the same time he wants to be an authority himself and have others submit to him.
>
> (1942: 141)

Fromm does not mean that the individual wants to inflict pain on others when he talks of sadism. Rather, it is the desire to make some other the subject of our power. The extreme would be the infliction of pain; pleasure is, however, derived from control. The masochistic tendency is to give up one's self, to escape from aloneness. The root of both these tendencies for Fromm is a weak ego, and the aim is symbiosis: 'the union of one's individual self with another self' (1942: 136). Both become dependent on each other. As we have noted, this leads to a particular personality type characterised by a striving for both submission and domination. This would seem a perfect match for the appeal of Nazism, Fascism and totalitarian regimes; the individual becomes situated within a dense and complex hierarchy. Hitler, an extreme authoritarian, appealed to others of the same personality structure. The authoritarian becomes submerged in the masses at the expense of the self, hating life and feeling envy for those who enjoy it.

The second form of escape, *destructiveness*, is linked to authoritarianism through envy. Envy, as Klein (1988) notes, is entirely destructive, seeking to destroy the whole of the good. Fromm fails to make this link but identifies two forms of destructiveness: the first reactive – a reaction against attack or a threat to life; the second irrational:

> a constantly lingering tendency within a person which so to speak waits only for an opportunity to be expressed ... the destructive impulses are a passion within a person, and they always succeed in finding an object.
>
> (1942: 155)

In an attempt to alleviate feelings of powerlessness, the subject destroys the object – the world. Fromm again is vague about the particular circumstances that may bring about this type of destructiveness, ascribing an expression of this once again in the European lower middle class. We can see, however, a parallel with Freud: the repression of instinctual drives enables society to function in a civilised way, but in some sense these drives need to find an outlet, the more they are repressed the stronger and more destructive they become. The 'other' becomes an outlet for the expression of destructiveness.

Destructiveness, however, is not what the majority of normal people use as a mechanism of escape; *automaton conformity*, Fromm's third mechanism, is for him of the greatest social significance:

> This particular mechanism is the solution that the majority of individuals find in modern society. To put it briefly, the individual ceases to be himself; he adopts entirely the kind of personality offered to him by cultural patterns; and he therefore becomes exactly as all others are and as they expect him to be.
>
> (1942: 161)

The individual loses himself in society, in the mass. Fromm likens this to the protective colouring that some animals use, and there are similarities with Horkheimer and Adorno's notion of mimesis. The individual, although believing s/he is free, has surrendered their self to society. But freedom is illusory; what emerges is a pseudo-self, ways of thinking and feeling that are part of the group rather than the individual. This split causes anxiety and panic, and the only way to alleviate these feelings is to conform. The combination of authoritarianism and automaton conformity are of course trying to explain the allure and attraction of Nazism and the seemingly mindless following of a charismatic leader.

Racism is an integral part of the ideological tenets of Nazism. The process of the persecution and maltreatment of people because of their 'otherness' takes several forms. Firstly, the other is perceived as a threat to the Darwinian scheme of race purity – dirty, polluting and necessarily pervasive. Secondly, the other is demonised. In a process of paranoid projection outgroups are accused of actions and aims that are really those of the persecutor: the drive for mastery, self-preservation, power. The individual conforms to the paranoid wishes of the authoritarian father figure in a wish both to escape from freedom (through submission and domination) and to alleviate the anxiety caused by the automaton psychological split.

There are several problems with Fromm's thesis, particularly if we were to use it as a basis for the explanation of racism and exclusion. Fromm is vague about the circumstances that bring about destructiveness in the individual, ascribing this as a characteristic of lower middle-class Europeans and Germans in particular. This is not helpful as we live in a racist world; situating analysis in a particular class and ethnic category exonerates individuals outside these categories producing an exercise in finger-pointing or ethnocentrism. It is clear that Fromm situates explanation within the family to counter his critics, as Rickert (1994) observes: 'Psychoanalysis argues that character is essentially formed in early childhood when contact with society is minimal' (1994: 278).

Fromm argues, however, that the child's instincts are not moulded by society but by the family, whose values, attitudes and character traits are shaped by social influences. Thus personality traits are handed down from generation to generation and not biologically fixed; in other words, human drives are dynamic and adapt to socioeconomic conditions. If this is the case, surely something can and would have been done to address the question of racism. Fromm also fails to link some elements of his own theory. For example, when discussing mechanisms of defence the least likely to be used is that of outright or total destructiveness. Yet there is a clear link between envy, destruction and authoritarianism. There also seems to be a tenuous link between automaton conformity and authoritarianism. Surely the anxiety brought about by the production of a pseudo-self is tantamount to resistance to authority and strict hierarchy. In other words, the split between the real self and the pseudo-self may be an important site of resistance, contesting the authoritarian regime and demonstrating that people can never really become total automatons. In the same way that Weber's thesis on bureaucracy is flawed, in that it does not allow for human interaction and the power of affect, Fromm's thesis relies on a rigid stereotype of a particular personality type.

Despite these criticisms there are several important issues we can gather from the work of Eric Fromm. Firstly, Fromm highlights the interaction between the social and the psychological in the manipulation of drives. Although this is within the context of a Marxist class analysis, it forms the basis for both a critique of Freudian instinct theory and a basis for viewing drives as potentiality shaped by the social. Fromm also suggests, or hints at, the destructive nature of envy which will be discussed in Chapter 8 in relation to the work of Melanie Klein. Fromm explores the construction of a group ego lifting psychoanalysis away from the individual and setting explanation in a societal form. In terms of racism this can help us understand how other people are demonised, persecuted and excluded from society. And, perhaps as importantly, it allows us to explore the links between the racist and the group. In the next section of this chapter I want to look at how Adorno *et al.* have built on Fromm's ideas in *Studies in Prejudice.*

Example 6.1 Narcissistic libido transfer: Adorno on Fascist propaganda

In his analysis of Fascist propaganda, Adorno (1991) gives a very clear example of the application of Freudian theory in the explanation of a social and political phenomenon. Adorno argues that Fascist propaganda is characterised by two distinct features. First, its material is not particularly concerned with concrete political issues; statements are directed *ad hominen.* They are based in psychological calculations rather than any rational statement of rational aims. These psychological calculations are quite simply aimed at 'rabble-rousing' – promoting an atmosphere of irrational emotional aggressiveness. It is, argues Adorno, the aim of would be 'Hitlers' to transform people into crowds bent on violent action.

The second characteristic is that the agitators' approach is truly systematic, following a pattern of clear-cut devices. Speeches are monotonous, repetitive and constantly reiterate simple messages. Indeed, for Adorno:

> Moreover, the speeches themselves are so monotonous that one meets with endless repetitions as soon as one is acquainted with the very limited number of stock devices. As a matter of fact, constant reiteration and scarcity of ideas are indispensable ingredients of the entire technique.
>
> (1991: 115)

Fascist propaganda is therefore a form of conditioning which uses a psycho-dynamic element to reach its audience. Turning to Freud's theories of group psychology, Adorno notes that the bond which integrates individuals into the mass is of a libidinal nature. After Freud, Adorno argues that what is peculiar to the masses is not so much a new quality, but an awakening, a manifestation of old qualities that have been hidden.

Adorno compares the process involved in Nazi propaganda to that of the hypnotist. The individual is guided back to their childhood, an archaic inheritance is awakened – the compliance to the will of parents and in particular the individual's father. What is awakened is a dangerous personality to whom one's will has to be surrendered: this is the relationship between the individual member of the primal horde and the primal father. This awakening is facilitated by the formation of imagery and symbols which transcend the individual father and develop into a group ego – the pseudo-self. Hitler shunned the traditional role of the loving father figure and replaced it with threatening authority. This gratifies the followers' wish to both submit to and wield authority. The primal father is on the one hand authoritarian, sexually magnetic; on the other a form of big brother who will care for us and will lead us against threats.

There is an intense process of identification and projection involved in the psychodynamic between leader and follower, a form of narcissistic libido transfer in which 'I' see features of 'myself' in another, and love them. In this process of identification the leader figure becomes both father and brother, but also 'me'. There is, therefore, for Adorno:

> The partial transfer of narcissistic libido to the object. This, again, falls in line with semblance of the leader image to an enlargement of the subject: by making the leader his ideal he loves himself, as it were, but gets rid of the strains of frustration and discontent which mar his picture of his own empirical self.
>
> (*Ibid.*: 121)

In obeying Hitler, I am obeying myself. Conversely, unpalatable feelings such as sexual lust, cruelty, dirt are projected outward onto the other – the projection of rage where the other is perceived as dangerous and frightening. The libidinal nature of the bond between group and leader creates a shared sense of guilt and a shared fear of punishment; in other words, the primal crime. Thus Adorno uses Freudian psychoanalytic ideas to explain what he describes as the collectivisation of the hypnotic spell. The psychodynamic processes of projection, identification and idealisation underlie the Nazi battle cry of 'Germany Awake', which hides its very opposite in an untruth, and regression to a pseudo group self.

Studies in prejudice

The Authoritarian Personality (Adorno *et al.*, 1950) is probably the most universally known and oft-cited work of the Institute, yet it forms part of a larger project directed by Max Horkheimer and was published in five volumes as *Studies in Prejudice* (Horkheimer and Flowerman, 1950). The studies included Leo Lowenthal and Norbert Gutterman's research on the parallels between the use of emotional mechanisms by American and Nazi rabble-rousers; Bettlehiem and Janowitz's work with veterans; Ackerman and Jahoda's research into anti-Semitism as an emotional disorder; and finally Paul Massing's work on anti-Semitism as a political tool. The studies were conducted whilst the school was in exile in America.

The Authoritarian Personality is an odd book, a pastiche of interpretive psychoanalytically informed methodology and practice which has been combined with large-scale quantitative data analysis. The book itself is co-authored by Adorno, Else Frenkel-Brunswik, Daniel Levinson and R. Nevitt Sanford. Max Horkheimer in writing the preface describes the central theme of the work:

> This is a book about social discrimination. But its purpose it not simply to add a few more empirical findings to an already extensive body of information. The central theme of the work is a relatively new concept – the rise of an 'anthropological' species we call the authoritarian type of man. He is at the same time enlightened and superstitious, proud to be an individualist and in constant fear of not being like all the others, jealous of his independence and inclined to submit blindly to power and authority.
>
> (Adorno *et al.*, 1950: xi)

At the heart of the project, and therefore the book, are two quite complex tasks. The first is to define or map out the character structure of people who are prone to anti-Semitic tendencies. In other words, to be able to point to and define the anti-Semitic character. The second task was to develop tools for measuring tendencies towards anti-Semitism, the results of which produced the now famous F-scale. Over 2000 questionnaires were distributed to differing groups of people, the majority of whom were either students or members of the middle classes, and about one-tenth were interviewed (Held, 1990). The questionnaires contained questions which related to three scales. The E-scale, the ethnocentrism scale which related to anti-Semitism; the PEC-scale, which was designed to measure levels of political and economic conservatism; and finally, the F-scale, designed to address levels of potential fascism. These questionnaires were supported by in-depth clinical interviews.

The interviews were conducted using a psychoanalytically-orientated interview schema: 'and the equally psychoanalytically orientated catalogue of fifty six categories, divided according to high and low variants, used to interpret the interview material' (Wiggershaus, 1994: 415). These interviews included questions on family background, school, social relations, sexuality and childhood. The questions were designed to provide insights into socialisation and psychic structures and, in particular, addressed and noted the occurrence of parents who were prone to domination and submission within the relationships, and who in turn themselves demanded blind obedience from their children. Both these interviews and the questionnaires were carefully drawn up in a way that facilitated contrast and comparison on the one hand, and stereotypy on the other. The results yielded an outline of a syndrome, of the potential Fascist character – the authoritarian personality. This character type was marked by nine personality traits:

- **Authoritarian submission**: a tendency to submit to leader figures and adopt an uncritical attitude towards the authority of the in-group.
- **Authoritarian aggression**: to condemn others who do not fall into the conventional norm of this character type, to actively seek out and punish those who are different.
- **Sex**: this personality type shows an exaggerated interest in sexual matters.
- **Conventialism**: a rigid and inflexible adherence to middle-class values and attitudes.
- **Anti-intraception**: a stance against signs of tenderness (which become weakness) and against the imaginative and emotionally-caring individual.
- **Projectivity**: the tendency to project unpalatable and unbearable parts of the psyche onto others.
- **Stereotypy and superstition**: to hold rigid stereotypes of and in the world, whilst believing the individual's fate lies within the realm of some mystical power.

- **Power and toughness**: the tendency to identify and become preoccupied with dichotomies; weak–strong; dominance and submission; leader and follower; good and bad. This is supported by an exaggerated and idealised notion of self-strength and toughness.
- **Destructiveness and cynicism**: hostility and hatred of life and humanity. Nilism. (Adorno *et al.*, 1950: 228)

Thus we have the authoritarian personality, described in Eric Fromm's (1942) work, empirically demonstrated in the studies and exemplified in Adorno's (1991) writings on Fascist propaganda. The authoritarian strives for a position of both submission and control, whilst hating those who are different and projecting his or her unpalatable feelings onto outgroups in the form of racist stereotypes. The authoritarian idealises his or her parents, and submits without question to family authority and particularly the authority of the father. This syndrome is characterised by a weak ego and the propensity to blindly comply to, or obey authority in the absence of a strong sense of self. Both relief and pleasure are gained from obedience and hatred of otherness and weakness which represent qualities that the authoritarian finds unbearable in his or her own self. For Adorno and his colleagues, this syndrome is nowhere better typified than in the characteristics of the European lower middle class (Adorno *et al.*, 1950: 759).

There are, of course, several problems with this study; at its very worst it produced yet another typology of stereotypical character traits based in conjecture rather than evidence. Wiggershaus (1994) draws our attention to several more subtle problems with the study. First, the F-scale was never seriously tested. Second, the rigid and stereotypical nature of the questions used in the surveys left little room for complex answers or explanations. Third, the effort to produce quantitative results defied in some sense the object of using in-depth qualitative interviews, the qualitative data became quantified in an rigid system of responses. Finally, and perhaps most damning, Adorno who was trying to exploit the richness of the psychoanalytic encounter and of the live interview, never actually took part in the interviews himself. The people he was attempting to use to demonstrate a link between ideology and personality structure were completely alien to him, as was the environment of the respondents.

Despite these criticisms, Adorno's empirical work in *The Authoritarian Personality* offers the reader a wealth of ideas and concepts from which we can start thinking about a psychodynamic explanation of racism and ethnic hatred. As Held (1990) notes, we should not read this study out of context, rather we should view it as part of an ongoing research programme in which Horkheimer and Adorno were simultaneously writing *Dialectic of Enlightenment.* As Wiggershaus (1994) argues:

> When they returned to Frankfurt, it was as the authors of Dialectic of Enlightenment and of Studies in Prejudice, as philosophers of history and critics of culture, as social psychologists and experts in modern sociological research technique; as established academics who seemed willing to pass on their achievements, and as a team.
>
> (1994: 430)

Conclusion: towards a psychoanalytic explanation of racism

The work of the Frankfurt School has left us with a considerable legacy from which to start thinking about psychoanalytic explanations of racism. There are substantial problems with some of the studies conducted under the auspices of the Institute, not least is the problem that Horkheimer and Adorno have in convincing others to accept the validity of Freud's work. What the work of the Institute does provide us with, however, is a very clear and detailed account of how we combine both sociological and psychoanalytic theory in the practical application of a research programme.

Psychoanalytic explanations of Nazism, Fascism and anti-Semitism focus on both structural and psychological facilitants in a critical fusion of the work of several theorists. Horkheimer and Adorno's work places an emphasis on the massive substantive irrationality that has accompanied the development of modern society. By focusing on the affective dimension, they produce a more complete picture of the ways in which psychological mechanisms support and perpetuate structural forms of racism, hostility and hatred than traditional sociological accounts. There are several problems with their work which have been discussed at length, perhaps the most worrying is the biological determinism emanating from the use of Freud's instinct theory.

This problem is addressed in Fromm's work who argues that there is a social basis in the development of drives. Turning Freud's theory on its head in an analysis of personality and individuality, Fromm argues that our instincts are shaped by historical and social factors in which psychological conditions in turn are based. In other words, instincts and drives are not fixed, they are dynamic, and there is a dynamic between the psychological and social or structural.

Adorno's Freudian analysis of Fascist propaganda attempts to take psychoanalytic observation and explanation from an individual to a group level. It sets the basis of political manipulation on an emotional and affective plain in the portrayal of the collapse of the individual psyche and the development of the group or pseudo-self. It draws on Fromm's (1942) original work in *Fear of Freedom*, and Adorno's own work in *The Authoritarian Personality*, to demonstrate the complex pychodynamics of projection and identi-fication. The value of this work is in the way that it combines theory with concrete example of social structure and purposeful psycho-logical manipulation. There is a tendency, however, to hinge these ideas on the notion of an authoritarian syndrome, and this is one of the areas that the School has come in for considerable criticism.

Studies in Prejudice and its most oft quoted book, *The Authoritarian Personality*, represent a massive undertaking of empirical social science research by a group of scholars in exile, and to certain degree in alienation to use Horkheimer and Adorno's own words, from their natural environment. The criticisms of *The Authoritarian Personality* have been well-rehearsed many times, and range from accusations of stereotypy and ethnocentrism to doubts about the validity and reliability of the research methodology. *The Authoritarian Personality* should, however, be read in the context of the Institute's wider research programme, and certainly in tandem with *Dialectic of Enlightenment*. What the Frankfurt School have given us is a wealth of ideas from which we can start to think about our own psychoanalytic research to address the problem of racism and ethnic hatred. These ideas have served as an introduction to the practical application of Freudian thought. The following chapter will build on these ideas in an exploration of the work of Jacques Lacan and Jean-Paul Sartre and their influence on Frantz Fanon's psychodynamic critique of postcolonialism.

Summary of key terms

Mimesis. A powerful instinctual mechanism, a form of self-protection in the natural world which has become perverted in the modern world.

Natural or mimesis proper. In our natural environment we mimic in order to camouflage and blend in; quite simply this may mean freezing if we sense danger, and this is part of our biological prehistory. We make ourselves like nature.

Magical mimesis is the gradual prohibition of instinctual behaviour. Initially this came about by the organisation of mimesis in the magical phase, through ceremony and rite. For example, there is still an element of mimesis in the rituals of indigenous peoples – imitating animals, wearing bearskins.

Modern or rational mimesis. People are taught behavioural norms in the school and workplace; children are no longer allowed to behave like children. Mimesis now takes a form in which society threatens nature; control equals self preservation and dominance over nature. We no longer make our 'self' like nature to survive, but attempt to make nature like us. In other words, the instinctual mechanism of mimesis becomes sublimated in the practice of the rational control of the modern environment.

Projection. We project onto the world experiences and qualities that are part of ourselves as if they are part of someone else. When the feeling involved is bad, the projection becomes paranoid.

False projection is an attempt to change the environment, to make it like one's own self. In a confusion of inner and outer worlds, the other is no longer familiarised but becomes dangerous, frightening and threatening. Intimate experiences are seen as hostile.

Mechanisms of escape

Authoritarianism is the tendency to give up one's individual self and fuse with somebody or something else. The authoritarian personality is characterised by a striving for domination and submission.

Destructiveness. In an attempt to alleviate feelings of powerlessness, the subject destroys the object – the world.

Automaton conformity. The individual loses himself in society, in the mass. Fromm likens this to the protective colouring that some animals use, and there are similarities with Horkheimer and Adorno's notion of mimesis. The individual, although believing s/he is free, has surrendered their self to society. Freedom is illusory. What emerges is a pseudo-self, ways of thinking and feeling that are part of the group rather than the individual. This split causes anxiety and panic, and the only way to alleviate these feelings is to conform.

CHAPTER 7

Colonial Identity and Ethnic Hatred: Fanon, Lacan and Zizek

Introduction

How can psychoanalysis help us understand the construction of colonial identity? Why choose to hate? Why do we fear the theft of our enjoyment? In this chapter I examine some of the philosophical and theoretical developments in the area of racism, hatred and colonial identity-formation through the lens of the work of Frantz Fanon, Jean-Paul Sartre, Jacques Lacan and Slavoj Zizek. In some sense this chapter provides a bridge between Freudian, post-Freudian and object-relations schools in the practical application of psychoanalytic theory.

Frantz Fanon, as Joel Kovel (1970) has noted, is in some respects the most powerful voice to have articulated the emerging con-sciousness of black peoples across the world (see Kovel, 1970: 65). In *Black Skin White Masks,* Fanon draws on the psychological work of Sigmund Freud, Jacques Lacan and Jean-Paul Sartre to explain the position of the 'black man in the dominant white world'. Fanon suggests that it would be interesting to investigate how the image of the white person develops in relation to the black person with ref-erence to Lacan's notion of the mirror stage. I start this chapter by examining Fanon's work and in particular the influence of Jean-Paul Sartre's existential philosophy in the development of the concept of 'Negrophobia'. Using, as Fanon suggests, Lacan's notion of the mirror stage I highlight the way in which colonial black identity is constructed in relation to 'whiteness', before going on to argue that the mirror has a double edge; the black person is persecuted as 'other' and oppressed as 'I'. I also provide a brief introduction to Slavoj Zizek's Lacanian philosophical commentaries on ethnic and intergroup hatred. Zizek's work is an exemplar of the synthesis of psychoanalytic and sociological theory used in practical explanation of social phenomena. Although I provide a critique of Lacan's work, I do not want to dwell on it, and prefer to use Lacanian notions of identity construction to serve as a platform from which to develop a Kleinian perspective on the construction of black identity, and to further our understanding of racism. I argue in the following chapters that Klein's notions of phantasy and projective identification are crucial to our understanding of the construction of 'otherness', and central to our understanding of racism and ethnic hatred. In doing so, I attempt to show how we can learn from the experience of a series of writers in a synthesis of ideas which enables us to confront the problem of racism.

Fanon and the critique of colonial discourse

Perhaps the two key thinkers in the development of Fanon's ideas are Jean-Paul Sartre and Jacques Lacan. Jean-Paul Sartre was born in Paris in 1905 and read philosophy at the prestigious École Normale Superieure. During the Second World War Sartre was captured and held as a prisoner of war, and after his escape he became active in the resistance movement. Sartre's existential philosophy was influenced by the writings of Nietzsche and Heidegger, indeed Sartre's (1943) *Being and Nothingness* was conceived as a companion volume to Martin Heidegger's (1927) work *Sein und Zeit* (Being and Time). At the heart of existential philosophy is an emphasis on the supreme importance of the individual and his or her choices. Existence, for Sartre, precedes essence; life is a series of choices, as there is no God; man cannot escape choosing, and thus life is no more than the sum of past commitments. For Sartre we are all free, but being conscious of this fact brings much anguish and pain. We thus try to avoid consciousness of our freedom, a self-deception that Sartre describes as 'bad faith'. We are, therefore, for Sartre, ultimately responsible for our own actions. Sartre's philosophy was one of active resistance and action. In 1958 he participated in protests against the Algerian war which no doubt had a great influence on Fanon's own thought. Sartre wrote the introduction to Fanon's

(1961) book and comment on the Algerian struggle, *The Wretched of the Earth.*

Frantz Fanon was born in 1925 in the French colony of Martinique. After fighting with the Free French in the Second World War, he studied medicine and psychiatry in France where he was greatly influenced by the existential philosophy of Sartre. Fanon wrote his first and probably best-known work, *Black Skin White Masks* (1952, 1968), whilst still practising psychiatry in France. In the 1950s Fanon moved to become head of psychiatry in an Algerian hospital, and whilst there the Algerian war for independence broke out. Fanon resigned his post in repugnance at French Imperialism and the brutal torture of individuals both by French and Algerian forces. A graphic and emotionally disturbing account of this can be found in Fanon's final work *The Wretched of the Earth* (1961, 1990) which contains the most powerfully damning indictment of colonialism in written words. Fanon died of leukaemia at the age of 36.

Fanon's work has become almost compulsory reading in cultural studies and in the critique of colonial discourse. Writers such as Bulhan (1985), Gordon *et al.* (1996), McCulloch (1983) and Sekyi-Otu (1996) contribute to a large and still growing secondary literature on Fanon's work. In the introduction to *Fanon: A Critical Reader* Gordon *et al.* (1996) point to the enormous breadth and quality of Fanon's work which crosses the academic disciplines of philosophy, social science, politics and literary studies. Indeed, the interest in Fanon's work has been so great that Gordon *et al.* argue that we now have a distinct area which we can term Fanon Studies, which encompasses four stages. The first represents applications and reactions to Fanon's writings, the second is largely biographical, the third encompasses Fanon's ideas within political theory, and the fourth and by no means last stage is the incorporation of Fanon's work within postmodern cultural studies as represented by writers such as Edward Said (1993) and Homi Bhabha (1986). Gordon *et al.* (1996: 7) intimate that there is a fifth stage which consists 'of engagements with the thought of Fanon for the development of original work across the entire sphere of human studies'; they argue that its 'purpose is neither to glorify nor denigrate Fanon but instead to explore ways in which he is a useful thinker'. It is from this perspective that Fanon is a useful and enlightening thinker for the student of psychoanalytic studies. What follows in this chapter is not an exhaustive review of Fanon's work, this has been done elsewhere, rather it is an exploration of Fanon as a psychoanalytic thinker. As Fanon suggests himself in the introduction to *Black Skin White Masks*: 'Only a psychoanalytic interpretation of the black man can lay bare the anomalies of affect that are responsible for the structure of the (inferiority) complex' (1968: 10).

Fanon, Sartre and psychoexistentialism

In *Black Skin White Masks*, Fanon argues that the black person is both objectified and denigrated at a bodily level, and psychologically blinded or alienated from his or her black consciousness and identity by the effects of colonialisation and of racist culture and society. This is the premise of much of Fanon's writing and argumentation. The black person (Fanon uses the term 'Negro') becomes a phobogenic object, in other words a stimulus that causes anxiety. As with all psychoanalytic interpretations of phobias, Fanon notes that there is a secret attraction to the object that arouses dread in the individual. Hatreds and racism are a means by which the individual hides from and detracts from their own sexual perversity. Drawing heavily on Sartre's existential writings, Fanon likens this phobic response to that of anti-Semitism:

> The Jew is feared because of his potential for acquisitiveness. 'They' are everywhere. The banks, the stock exchanges, the government are infested with 'them'. 'They' control everything.
>
> (Fanon, 1968: 157)

If the Jew is feared for his acquisitiveness, then for Fanon, the black person is revered for his sexual powers. After Fanon, McCulloch (1983) describes the imago (an imago being 'an unconscious prototypical figure'; Laplanche and Pontalis, 1973: 211) of the black man, and presumably woman, in European consciousness as a common phantasy of massive sexual powers. Fanon elucidates:

> As for the Negroes, they have tremendous sexual powers. What do you expect, with all the freedom they have in the jungles! They copulate at all times and in all places. They are really genital. They have so many children they cannot even count them. Be careful or they will flood us.
>
> (1968: 157)

Fanon argues that it matters little whether this image of the black man is real, the point is, it is cognate. In the same way that the Jew was perceived as a danger through the projection of a stereotype, the black person has suffered the same form of projection with an emphasis placed on sexual phenomena. As Elisabeth Young-Bruehl (1996) has noted, Fanon found much to admire in Sartre's (1976) *Anti-Semite and Jew,* and thus to understand Fanon's concept of a phobogenic object, or more specifically what he terms 'Negro-phobia', it is useful to examine the work of Sartre as an influential figure in the formation of Fanon's psychological and sociological theory.

In *Anti-Semite and Jew,* Jean-Paul Sartre (1976) argues that it is not the Jewish character that produces or induces anti-Semitism, it is the anti-Semite who creates this image of the Jew; indeed for Sartre, if the Jew did not exist, the anti-Semite would invent him. Again, as with the black person, the Jew becomes a phobogenic object – a stimulus that causes anxiety:

> If you so much as mention a Jew to an anti-Semite, he will show all the signs of lively irritation ... It is not unusual for people to elect to live a life of passion rather than one of reason. But ordinarily they love the objects of their passion: women, glory, power, money. Since the anti-Semite has chosen to hate, we are forced to conclude that it is the state of passion that he loves.
>
> (Sartre, 1976: 18)

This poses the question: Why invent the Jew, why choose to hate? The anti-Semite constructs this phobogenic object to project both the misfortunes of his country and himself onto some other, a ridding of unpalatable thoughts onto a bad object. Sartre argues that this reason based in passion is a form of reason in which the individual becomes impenetrable. Whereas the rational man forever lives in doubt of his reason and is tentative in his search for truth, the anti-Semite does not wish to change, he is not reflexive because he is in fear of both himself and the truth; reasoning plays a subordinate role in the life of the anti-Semite. For Sartre, the anti-Semite is impervious to reason, to experience, and therefore to change. The anti-Semite is terrifying because his actions are based in irrational convictions, in passion; he is nothing but the 'fear he inspires in others'. The anti-Semite is, for Sartre, a mediocre person, a 'man of the crowds', lacking in any form of authenticity or individuality. Indeed, deindividuation allows the individual to become immersed in the anti-Semitic following. The true purpose of this immersion is to hide from one's own self, while attributing value to mediocrity: to create an *elite* out of the *ordinary*. There is in some sense a strong parallel with Eric Fromm's (1942) notion of 'authoritarianism' as a means of escape from the self. Sartre describes the anti-Semite:

> He chooses the irremediable out of fear of being free; he chooses mediocrity out of fear of being alone, and out of pride he makes of this irremediable mediocrity a rigid aristocracy. To this end he finds the existence of the Jew absolutely necessary. Otherwise to whom would he be superior.
>
> (1976: 28)

Thus for Sartre, the anti-Semite demonstrates all the characteristics of Fromm's authoritarian character. He has a weak ego, he cannot cope with his own freedom, he escapes into the herd, the masses, surrendering himself to mediocrity. Hence, we can see what Sartre means when he talks of the anti-Semite inventing the Jew. The Jew is the phobogenic object that the anti-Semite has to invent – an object that both holds a secret attraction and arouses dread in the individual; it is a paradoxical construction that is both repulsive and attractive to its originator. Sartre is clear about this point, the anti-Semite holds a profound sexual attraction towards the Jew based in a 'curiosity fascinated by evil' and the pleasure of sadism. Sartre notes, 'the Jew only serves him as a pretext; elsewhere his counterpart will make use of the Negro or the man of yellow skin' (*ibid.*: 54).

Sander Gilman (1985) has also lucidly argued that the concept of colour is a quality of Otherness, not of reality, 'For not only are blacks black in this amorphous world of projection, so too are Jews' (1985: 30). Following in Sartre's philosophical footsteps, influenced by Freud and tinged with Lacan, Fanon argues in his description of Negrophobia that 'the cycle of the biological begins' (1968: 161). What Fanon means by this is that this phobia is found on the most basic of instinctual levels; in biological notions of physical difference and reinforced by the imago of the black person which has been constructed in phantasy. To understand racism from a psychoanalytic perspective, argues Fanon, we have to concentrate on sexual phenomena. Bulhan (1985) argues that there are strong reminders of Freud's (1930) *Civilization and Its Discontents* throughout *Black Skin White Masks*, and more generally Freud's notion of 'sublimated instinctual energies that must find socially acceptable means of expression' (1985: 70). Thus, revered for his or her sexual powers and potency in popular mythology, the black person becomes a phallus symbol:

> When a white man hates black men, is he not yielding to a feeling of impotence or of sexual inferiority? Since his ideal is an infinite virility, is there not a phenomenon of diminution in relation to the Negro, who is viewed as a penis symbol.
>
> (Fanon, 1968: 159)

Fanon argues that the white person has a secret desire to return to an era of 'unrestricted sexual licence' and orgiastic scenes of rape and unrepressed incest; everything he sees, creates and projects in the image of the black person. This is reminiscent of Max Horkheimer and Theodor Adorno's thesis in *Dialectic of Enlightenment* (1994). The Fascist longs to return to a presocial state of nature, seeing in the Jew what he really *feels* in his self. For Fanon, the white person projects desire on the black person, and the white person behaves as if the black person is the owner of these desires: 'what appears repellently alien, is in fact, all too familiar' (Horkheimer and Adorno, 1994: 182). The Jew is associated with wealth and power, the black person has been fixated at a bodily, biological, genital plane:

> Two realms: the intellectual and the sexual. An erection on Rodin's thinker is a shocking thought. One cannot decently 'have a hard on' everywhere. The Negro symbolises the biological danger, the Jew, the intellectual danger.
>
> (Fanon, 1968: 165)

Thus, if we were to clarify Fanon's position thus far, Negrophobia emanates from a basic biological and instinctual need; the phobogenic object arouses both dread and anxiety, in tandem with a secret sexual attraction for the object. The attraction is twofold. First, the racist perceives in the black person what he or she secretly desires, and, second, this is a constant reminder of a longing to return to an era of unrepressed sexual activity. It would seem that Fanon is suggesting that we attack the black Other because we cannot accept the nature of our own instinctual desires. It may also be the case that we attack and destroy because we cannot have what we want. It is in this sense, for Fanon, that the racist like the anti-Semite is in fear of both his or her own self and the truth, an irrational passion that is resistant to change. As with the anti-Semite, white would invent black if black did not exist.

David Macey (2000, 2001) provides an interesting and very readable portrait of Fanon's life, work and politics and draws our attention in particular to Fanon's relationship to psychoanalysis and Lacan. There are two important strands of thought in Macey's work which I think should be noted. First, for Macey there is often a tendency to overplay the psychoanalytic content of Fanon's work which often distracts from Fanon's philosophical and structural claims. Second, there is a gentle critique of psychoanalysis in a discussion of Fanon's analysis of Octave Mannoni's inferiority thesis.

Macey reminds us that although influenced by Lacan and Freud, Fanon's main philosophical framework is based in the existentialism of Sartre and Merleau-Ponty. Macey argues that many perceive Fanon as a psychoanalyst who was influenced by Lacan. Macey notes that Fanon quite clearly was not a psychoanalyst, 'and the influence of Lacan has been greatly overstated' (2001: 467). Reading Fanon it is hard to disagree with Macey's position. *Black Skin White Masks*, as I have argued earlier in this chapter, follows in Sartre's philosophical footsteps, is influenced by Freud and tinged with Lacan. I'm not sure whether the Lacanian influence is overstated, or it is merely the opposite in the sense that Fanon's writings provide a rich source of psychoanalytic interpretation from all fields of psychoanalytic thought. Macey is clear that,

> for Fanon, neuroses and psychoses do not arise from the sequence: desire, repression, symptom. And they are certainly not sexual in origin. They result from a brutal encounter with a hostile reality.
>
> (2001: 475)

Macey (2000) uses Fanon's critique of Mannoni's (1964) *Prospero and Caliban* to warn us about the problem of applying psychoanalysis to the 'black problem' which Fanon views as an honest but dangerous piece of work. As Macey notes, Mannoni's conclusion is that colonialisation is based in need and dependency – the colonised suffer an inferiority complex in relation to the colonisers. The inferiority is an inherent weakness which is revealed when the colonised are exposed to a superior society. No, says Fanon: 'Let us have the courage to say it outright: It is the racist who creates his inferior'

(1968: 93). Inferiority for Fanon is a result of both the physical and emotional oppression – the psychodynamic and political economy of imperial power.

I think what we can take from Fanon, and indeed I think this is what David Macey is hinting at, is that we should not consider the psychological without also considering the structural, material conditions of life – the two are inseparable. If we return to the psychoanalytic in Fanon's work, then what I find particularly intriguing is the reference to Lacan which appears in an extended footnote. Fanon suggests that it would be interesting to investigate how the image of the white person develops with the appearance of the 'Negro', with reference to Lacan's idea(l) of the mirror stage.

Jacques Lacan and the mirror stage

Jacques Lacan, like Fanon, trained in psychiatry before going on to become one of the most controversial and influential figures in contemporary psychoanalysis. Lacan undertook a medical degree at the Sorbonne before training in psychiatry under Gaëtan de Clérambault. As Lechte (1994) notes, Lacan was to change the whole orientation of psychoanalysis in France and elsewhere in his celebrated Seminar. Lacan is also well-known for the controversy that often surrounded him. He was expelled from the International Psychoanalytic Association in 1953 for the use of unorthodox methods in analytic practice. Lacan reinterprets the work of Freud through the lens of post-structuralism, emphasising the relationship between ego, the unconscious and language. Lacan achieved international notoriety with the publication of *Ecrits* in 1966, and *The Four Fundamental Concepts of Psychoanalysis* in 1977.

Lacan (1977a,b) argues in his seminal paper *The Mirror Stage* that the infant, at between six and eighteen months, becomes aware of its own body as a totality, by seeing in the mirror its own image. Thus for Lacan:

> We only have to understand the mirror stage *as an identification*, in the full sense that analysis gives to the term: namely the transformation that takes place in the subject when he assumes an image.
>
> (1977b: 2)

When the child sees its own image in a mirror, it will at first try and grasp this image as if it is real. There is then some recognition of similarity in this image proceeded by a realisation that the image is indeed the child's own. The child at this age is unable to fully coordinate its movements and has to be held in front of the mirror by some 'other'. The child is able to look in the mirror and say 'that is me', whilst turning to the parent and perceiving a sense of separation, a sense of identity. Sarup (1992) explains in detail:

> Why does the child turn around to look at the Other? The Other warrants the existence of the child, certifies the difference between self and other. This is the action in which all subjectivity is based, the moment in which the human individual is born.
>
> (1992: 64)

This process, argues Lacan, is a drama. The individual moves from a state of insufficiency to anticipation, that is, anticipation of the individual's image as an adult. A metamorphosis from a fragmented body image to a totality that Lacan describes as orthopaedic; orthopaedic in the sense that the mirror stage adds a 'prop' that enables the child to metaphorically stand up straight in the identity of a subject. This, however, for Lacan, is 'the armour of alienating identity, which will mark with its rigid structure the subject's entire mental apparatus' (1977b: 4). The subject is therefore alienated by the rigid structure of the mirror image, imprisoned by its own identity. There is no doubt the image we see in a mirror is never real, it is always a reversal of a projected image of the self. Malcolm Bowie (1991), reading Lacan, describes the mirror image as a *mirage* of 'I':

> The child, itself so recently born, gives birth to a monster: a statue, an automaton, a fabricated thing... From spare parts, an armoured mechanical creature is being produced within the human subject, and developing unwholesome habits and destructive appetites of its own.
>
> (1991: 26)

Lacan is arguing that what the child creates is an *identification* rather than an *identity*. What Lacan describes as a fiction, an imaginary projection, the *ideal-I*. As Sarup (1992) indicates, this *gestalt* is more stable than the child, giving an illusion of control. Crucially, self-identification represents a permanent tendency in the individual to seek and foster this 'imaginary wholeness of an ideal ego' (Sarup, 1992: 65). In other words, the ego has only an illusion (or delusion) of strength which has to be constantly reinforced throughout life.

It could be suggested that if this sense of self can only be validated in the realm of reality by the presence of some 'other' in the first instance, then this must continue throughout the subject's existence as the ego is constantly reinforced. It would seem that this was what Fanon was intimating in making reference to the formation of the image in the mirror stage:

> It would indeed be interesting, on the basis of Lacan's theory of the *mirror period*, to investigate the extent to which the image of his fellow built up in the young white at the usual age would undergo an imaginary aggression with the appearance of the Negro.
>
> (1968: 161)

Can it be that the 'other' for the racist will always be the black person, as Fanon suggests? If we return to Lacan's theory, the 'other' warrants the existence of the child, marking a separation and difference in which subjectivity is based. In other words, the self is defined in relation to some other, and other is not what 'I' am. The 'other' is idealised in the mirror on the level of a body image. The image of the black person as we have seen is threatening, based in myths of sexual prowess and potency. Aggression is directed at the other in two forms: first, aggression which separates and defines who I am, or perhaps more importantly, who I am not. Second, who I would like to be: powerful, sexual, potent. Desire for Lacan, is always desire for the other. Instinctually, I desire what the other is, but I cannot have it, so I will destroy it.

The mirror stage, for Fanon, has a double edge. The black person, he argues, perceives in terms of whiteness. The I is constructed with reference to white, black is both other and I. In this sense the black person is doubly disadvantaged. She or he is both persecuted as other, and in the same instance is oppressed by making his or her I a white mask – *Black is white is black*. In the final sections of this chapter I want to suggest how we may start thinking about Fanon's work psychoanalytically from a Kleinian perspective. This is because I feel that despite the insights that a Lacanian perspective can and does give to Fanon's writings, there are some basic theoretical and epistemological problems which need to be highlighted. First, though, I want to make an interesting diversion to look at the work of Slavoj Zizek. Zizek has been prolific in the field of psychoanalytic studies and has become well-known for his Lacanian philosophical commentaries on ethnic and intergroup hatred.

Do we fear the theft of our own enjoyment?

In *Tarrying with the Negative* Slavoj Zizek (1993) asks us why the West
was so fascinated by the disintegration of communism in Eastern
Europe. The answer, for Zizek, is obvious: 'what fascinated the
Western gaze was the re-invention of democracy' (1993: 200).
Democracy, for Zizek, whilst showing signs of decay and crisis, has
been rediscovered in Eastern Europe in a new and novel form. This
fascination has a function in that the West seeks in Eastern
European politics the lost original experience of democracy. Zizek
argues that Eastern Europe functions as the West's ego-ideal, the
point at which the West sees itself in a likeable, idealised form –
a good object. The object of fascination for the West, according to
Zizek, is the gaze. In other words, the way in which the East stares
West in fascination at democracy, and particularly the enthusiasm
for democracy that Zizek argues that the West has long lost the taste
of. The reality is, however, somewhat different:

> The reality emerging now in Eastern Europe is, however, a disturbing
> distortion of this idyllic picture of two mutually fascinated gazes: the
> gradual retreat of the liberal-democratic tendency in the face of the
> growth of corporate national populism which includes all its usual
> elements, from xenophobia to anti-Semitism. To explain this
> unexpected turn, we have to rethink the most elementary notions
> about national identification – and here, psychoanalysis can be of help.
> (*Ibid.*: 200)

Thus, Zizek introduces us to the idea of the 'Theft of Enjoyment'.
Zizek argues that the bond which holds a given community together
is a shared relationship to a Thing – 'to our enjoyment incarnate'.
The relationship we have to our Thing is structured by fantasy and
is what people talk of when they refer to a threat to 'our' way of life.
This nation Thing is not a clear set of values from which we can
refer, but a set of contradictory properties that appears as 'our'
Thing. This Thing is only accessible to us, but tirelessly sought after
by the Other. Zizek argues that others cannot grasp it, but it is constantly menaced by 'them'. So, this Thing is present, or is in some
way to do with what we refer to as our 'way of life'; the way we organise our rituals, ceremonies, feasts, 'in short, all the details by which
is made visible the unique way a community *organises its enjoyment*'
(1993: 201). Zizek cautions, however, that this Thing is more than

simply a set of features that comprise a way of life, there is something present in them, people *believe* in them, or more importantly 'I believe that other members of the community believe in this thing'. The Thing exists because people believe in it, it is an effect of belief itself:

> Nationalism thus presents a privileged domain of the eruption of enjoyment into the social field. The national cause is ultimately nothing but the way subjects of a given ethnic community organise their enjoyment through national myths. What is therefore at stake in ethnic tensions is always the possession of the national Thing. We always impute to the 'other' an excessive enjoyment: he wants to steal our enjoyment (by ruining our way of life) and/or he has access to some secret, perverse enjoyment. In short, what really bothers us about the 'other' is the peculiar way he organises his enjoyment, precisely the surplus, the 'excess' that pertains to this way: the smell of 'their' food, 'their' noisy songs and dances, 'their' strange manners, 'their' attitude to work.
>
> (*Ibid.*: 203)

Thus Zizek notes the paradoxical nature of this Thing; for the racist the Other is either a workaholic who steals our jobs and labour, or an idler, a lazy person relying on the state for benefits. Our Thing is therefore something which cannot be accessed by the Other but is constantly threatened by 'otherness'. What Zizek's work highlights is the role of myth and phantasy in the construction of national identity, and more importantly the way in which this identity is imagined rather than grounded in some reality. As Zizek notes, what we cover up by accusing the Other of the theft of our enjoyment is the 'traumatic fact' that we never possessed what we perceive has been stolen in the first place. It is a fear of the theft of enjoyment, a fear of the theft of imagination, of phantasy, of myth. Every nationality, argues Zizek, has its own mythology which describes how other nations deprive it of a part of its enjoyment, the part which allows it to live fully. Zizek likens this to an Escher drawing where in a visual illusion water pours from one basin to another until eventually you end up at the starting point.

The theft of enjoyment in Lacanian terms is about imaginary castration. As Zizek notes, we do not need many real Jews to imbibe the phantasised imago of the Jew with mysterious powers that threaten us; as Sartre remarked, if the Jew did not exist the anti-Semite would invent him. For Zizek, the real secret of the Jew is in our own antagonism – enjoyment in Lacanian terms is enjoyment of

---

Example 7.1   The former Yugoslavia and the 'theft of enjoyment'

We can use Zizek's example of the former Yugoslavia to describe the network of decantations and thefts of enjoyment:

> Slovenes are being deprived of their enjoyment by 'southerners' (Serbians, Bosnians ...) because of their proverbial laziness. Balkan corruption, dirty and noisy enjoyment, and because they demand bottomless economic support, stealing from Slovenes their precious accumulation of wealth by means of which Slovenia should otherwise have already caught up with Western Europe. The Slovenes themselves, on the other hand, allegedly rob the Serbs because of Slovenian unnatural diligence, stiffness, and self-ish calculation. Instead of yielding to life's simple pleasures, the Slovenes perversely enjoy constantly devising means of depriving Serbs of the results of their hard labour by commercial profiteering, by reselling what they bought cheaply in Serbia. The Slovenes are afraid the Serbs will 'inundate' them, and that they will thus lose their national identity.
>
> (Zizek, 1993: 204)

The basic premise of both Serb and Slovene, argues Zizek, is we don't want anything foreign and we want what rightfully belongs to us. This, as Zizek suggests, is a sure sign of racism. A clear line of demarcation is drawn and a psychological border erected, where in reality this clarity is mere fiction. If we return to the theme of this book: explaining racism psychoanalytically, then there are very clear Freudian and Lacanian ideas in Zizek's work. As Zizek points out, the theft of enjoyment is not about immediate social reality, it is not about different ethnic groups living together, as we know this is possible and exists all over the world. The theft of enjoyment is about inner tensions and conflicts within communities and the way these are projected out onto others in the form of hatred and loathing, this in turn is justified in terms of a something stolen, and/or the community being deprived by others.

---

the Other. The hatred of the Other's enjoyment is hatred of one's own enjoyment. A classic case of projection and introjection – back to Horkheimer and Adorno and ultimately Freud – what appears repellently alien is, in fact, all too familiar. Zizek elucidates:

> Does not the Other's enjoyment exert such a powerful fascination because in it we represent to ourselves our own innermost relationship to enjoyment? And, conversely, is the anti-Semitic capitalist's hatred of the Jew not the hatred of the success that pertains to capitalism itself, i.e., of the excess produced by its inherent antagonistic nature? Is capitalism's hatred of the Jew not the hatred of its own innermost,

essential feature? For this reason, it is not sufficient to point out how the racist's Other presents a threat to our identity. We should rather inverse this proposition: the fascinating image of the Other gives a body to our own innermost split, to what is 'in us more than ourselves' and thus prevents us from achieving full identity with ourselves.

(1993: 206)

Thus, the threat from the Other is not to our own particular identity, but a reminder of our own innermost tensions and feelings. So, for Zizek, post-communist Eastern Europe, far from developing a form of democratic pluralism, has moved towards authoritarian nationalism, a nationalism which is obsessed by the theft of enjoyment. The question is: why does this attachment to ethnic identity, or more specifically ethnic cause, persist even after the power structures that have fostered it have collapsed. Zizek, again, turns to Lacanian psychoanalysis for an answer.

It is interesting to note that Zizek, like Fanon, also uses classical sociology and political economy to support his psychoanalytic explanations. Capitalism, argues Zizek after Marx, is inherently imbalanced; it has no normal state, it is in constant flux, ever producing an excess, ever expanding in order to survive. It is a paradoxical loop: the more that is produced, the more we have dissatisfaction, 'the greater the wealth, the greater need to produce more wealth' (*ibid.*: 209). For Zizek, after Lacan, capitalism represents the reign of the discourse of the hysteric, where the vicious circle of desire's apparent satisfaction only widens the gap of dissatisfaction. Zizek likens this to the Freudian superego, the more we obey its command the more we feel guilt, which in turn calls for repentance and thus more guilt: 'as in capitalism, where an increase in production to fill out the lack only widens the lack' (*ibid.*: 210).

Zizek asks us to consider against this background the role of the master. The role being to regulate excess and to restore some semblance of balance. We have seen in Adorno's work the emergence of the authoritarian personality and the authoritarian leader figure. This is a mark of Fascism. Capitalism without excess – the leader restores the structural imbalances in the social fabric while attributing the cause of imbalance to an outsider, to the Other, to the Jew. Thus the elimination of the Other will restore the balance of the social fabric of the nation:

The function of the master is to dominate the excess by locating its cause in a clearly delimited social agency: 'It is *they* who steal our enjoyment, who, by means of their excessive attitude, introduce imbalance and antagonism'. With the figure of the Master, the antagonism *inherent* in the social structure is transformed into a relationship of *power*, a struggle for *domination* between *us* and *them*, those who cause antagonistic imbalance.

(Ibid.: 210)

Zizek argues that the reemergence of national chauvinism in Eastern Europe may be a form of shock absorber against the excesses of unregulated capitalism. The systematic replacement of communism with capitalism without excess, without formal external relations with individuals, and without an alienated civil society has brought about fantasies of the theft of enjoyment, rekindled anti-Semitic feeling, and has borne witness to some of the worst and most horrific scenes of ethnic hatred of the twentieth century. This, for Zizek, is the price to be paid for this impossible desire.

Zizek's work is interesting in that it draws on both psychoanalytic references and the political economy of hatred. It specifically addresses the relationship between self and Other in a way which reveals Other as a manifestation of our own inherent and innermost tensions. I have deliberately provided a very un-Lacanian reading of a text which is fuelled by Lacanian theory. This is because there is a certain quality in Zizek's work which appeals to a wider audience. The clarity of his ideas introduce and use many of the basic concepts in all schools of psychoanalysis to address very real social problems. You can read Zizek psychoanalytically without reference to Lacan and still benefit from this reading. Zizek's work in some sense bridges the gap between psychoanalytic schools of thought. Next I want to turn to contemporary Lacanian ideas about race, and particularly the work of Kalpana Seshadri-Crooks.

Desiring whiteness

Kalpana Seshadri-Crooks describes her work, *Desiring Whiteness* (2000), as a tentative foray into a territory that has been left uncharted; that is, 'race' as a system of organising difference around a privileged term – 'whiteness'. What Seshadri-Crooks actually delivers is an intriguing thesis which examines in detail, and far from tentatively, how a chain of symbolic structuation which operates through a process of inclusions and exclusions constitutes a pattern for organising human difference. As Seshadri-Crooks notes, although it is commonplace to hear phrases such as 'race is a construct' or 'race does not exist', 'race' shows no actual signs of disappearing and is still in common usage in everyday language. So, why do we hold on to the concept, and why is it so difficult to give up?

Seshadri-Crooks asks how we might begin to understand the concept of race and, more specifically, how can we decipher whiteness? She argues that race appears like sex, a fundamental fact of human embodiment, something we are inherently born with. This may seem obvious, in that the notion of race is dependent on the cosmetic characteristics of individuals, yet we have already argued that race is a construct. The point that Seshadri-Crooks seems to be making is that despite what we know about the construction of racial typologies, the pseudo-sciences of the nineteenth and twentieth centuries, the rise and fall of Social Dawinism, race itself as a concept, or container, has been successfully grafted to nature. In other words, the racial category appears natural. This leads Seshadri-Crooks to her central argument:

> Race is a regime of visibility that secures our investment in racial identity. We make such an investment because the unconscious signifier Whiteness, which founds the logic of racial difference, promises wholeness...what guarantees Whiteness its place as master signifier is visual difference.
>
> (2000: 21)

Whiteness therefore makes possible difference, it orders and classifies and separates people on the basis of what is considered a natural epistemology. Seshadri-Crooks quotes Foucault (1990), to illustrate this point, but this is also reminiscent of Bauman's (1991) *Modernity and Ambivalence*. The structure of race forever asserts difference, for the sake of sameness, to reproduce the desire for whiteness, or in Foucault and Bauman's case the rational modern subject and the 'gardening state'. The difference for Seshadri-Crooks, however, is that the visible bodily marks of race 'serve to guarantee Whiteness as more than a discursive construction' (Seshadri-Crooks, 2000: 59). Using the example of Joseph Conrad's (1966) short story *The Secret Sharer*, the author attempts to show how Lacan's notion of the *gaze* relates to the structure of Whiteness. This is important because it demonstrates the application of Lacanian thinking in the analysis of 'race'. This quote gives a taste:

> The secret sharer can be interpreted as a story about the successful reaching of the goal of whiteness – the *jouissance* of absolute mastery and

Example 7.2   The racist joke

If for Seshadri-Crooks, Conrad's *Secret Sharer* is about the successful accomplishment of Whiteness, then her analysis of colonial discourse and jokes portrays the failure of such an accomplishment. Using George Orwell's writings of India, Burma and Morocco, Seshadri-Crooks argues that the repression of the historicity of race often appears in jokes as an uncanny encounter. A Lacanian reading of Freud's (1919) notion of the Uncanny (*Das Unheimlich*, see Chapter 5) in relation to jokes, offers the uncanny object placed in a joke, as lack of lack. In other words, in a place that should have been empty, thus causing anxiety. Jokes, argues Seshadri-Crooks, after Freud, can be of two types. First we have the innocent verbal joke that plays on words. Second, we have the more sinister tendentious joke which engages with a thought or concept. This category can be subdivided into obscene, aggressive, cynical and sceptical jokes. Whilst tendentious jokes are the most appropriate or pertinent for understanding the anxiety entailed by whiteness, the author argues that we must first look at the persistence of the comic in colonial humour. This enables us to discern the uncanny joke implied by whiteness. Most racial humour is of a comic kind, that is caricature and infantalisation which sustains the logic of colonialisation and portrays a scenario of domination. The comic is anything but subtle and is direct in achieving its purpose. Mimicry, exaggeration, slapstick and parody denigrate the racial 'other'. Seshadri-Crooks argues that the racist joke is an aggressive joke which substitutes for the violence that is forbidden in society. It is a recycler of violence and used by the weak in society.

fullness. While the inevitable failure of such a goal could produce anxiety, and the captain is often on the brink of such affect, it is here presented as triumphant.

(Seshadri-Crooks, 2000: 78)

The lethal fantasy at the core of race for Seshadri-Crooks is the possibility of transcending the visible phenotype; that is, reaching beyond the bodily to a place of being itself where difference and lack are wholly extinguished. The fantasy of encountering Whiteness would be to recover the missing substance of one's being, coinciding not with some model of bodily perfection, but with the 'gaze', the void in the Other which could annihilate difference.

How does race as a symbolic system sustained by a regime of visibility translate into social policy? Identity politics work, but ultimately reinforce the very system that such politics are trying to redress. Seshadri-Crooks argues that her theory is anti-policy, it is race itself which should be dismantled. We should develop new adversarial aesthetics which will throw racial signification into disarray, use the visual against the visual. We should stress doubt in the concept of race to the extent that everyone mistrusts their knowledge of racial belonging in the practice of *discoloration*. Seshadri-Crooks explores theory, the visual and written text in tandem in attempt to reveal the complexities of race and of identity in a psychoanalytic account of a social problem.

In the final section of this chapter I want to return to Lacan and consider some of the criticisms of Lacanianism. I do not want to dwell on them, however, rather I want to use them as a bridge, as an introduction to the final two chapters of this book which address the work of Melanie Klein.

Lacanian and Kleinian interconnections: moving on...

Fanon's treatment of Lacan is interesting, as is Zizek's, but they are still subject to some of the theoretical and conceptual problems present in Lacan's ideas. I do not want to dwell on these problems in depth (although we should be aware of them), but move on, as both Winnicott (1971) and Leader (2000) have done, to build on Lacanian ideas in a positive way, as these criticisms have been well-documented and rehearsed by other writers. The reasoning for this is that these theoretical problems do not add to our understanding of racism and ethnic hatred, rather they distract and prevent us from developing a critical sociological theory of racism.

If we return to Lacan's concept of the mirror stage, Anthony Elliott (1994) draws our attention to Lacan's failure to specify the processes which enable the individual to misrecognise his or her self in the mirror stage. Surely the individual must have some sense of self and some capacity for emotional response to be able to respond in this way to the mirror. Similarly, Ferrell (1996) argues that the mind must be active in its interpretations of the mirror image. Again, there must therefore already be some sense of self for the child to be able to interact with the mirror image in this way. A second criticism of Lacan's thinking stems from the often dense and difficult nature of Lacan's linguistic style. Bowie (1991) has noted that Lacan's use of language and frequent puns leave the reader in a state where much has to be speculated about, or inferred, as the language becomes more impenetrable. Francois Roustang (1990) is particularly scathing of Lacan's work, suggesting that Lacan is prone to splitting and setting up unreconcilable dichotomies. Indeed for Roustang:

> He constantly isolates one side of an opposition, and hurls the other side into oblivion ... Like the psychotic, the Lacanian system is cut off from life, from affects, from subjectivity and from all appropriation.
>
> (1990: 118)

The final, and perhaps most difficult aspect of Lacan's work is articulated by Elliott (1994). Elliott focuses on an epistemological dilemma with specific implications for freedom and anti-racism. If the self is illusory, a trick, something imaginary and alienating, then any political project aimed at emancipation and freedom would be caught in the same illusory trap. I feel, however, that a careful reading of Zizek's work can help us move past some of these criticisms. Zizek has specifically addressed the relationship between self and other in a way that reveals some of the paradoxes and innermost tensions within our self in relation to others, the nature and fragility of the human condition – of human frailty. Fanon has also shown us how we relate to others, and specifically he addresses the construction of the racist's self in relation to an imaginary other. Both writers demonstrate a synthesis of psychoanalytic and sociological theory examining both the psychodynamic processes of racism and the political economy of hatred. There are clear links between the use of psychological mechanisms and socioeconomic processes. In this way Fanon and Zizek provide us with the big picture (without resorting to metanarrative), the way in which the social fabric, the political climate and the individual interact in society walking a tightrope between love and hate.

Darian Leader (2000) discusses the similarities in the work of Lacan and Klein. Leader's work is particularly helpful in providing a bridge between Lacanian and Kleinian psychoanalytic concepts. He provides an introduction from which we can go on to examine Klein's contribution to psychoanalysis in the following chapters of this book and start to think about how we may explore racism and exclusion through a Kleinian lens. Leader argues that because of the similarities (as well as contradictions) between the two positions, a 'dialogue between Kleinians and Lacanians makes more sense than divorce' (2000: 236). Leader highlights the interconnections

---

Example 7.3 Developing the mirror: Donald Winnicott –
Playing and Reality

There have been some interesting and positive developments of Lacan's work in the clinical environment, and such a development was proffered by Donald Winnicott (1971) in *Playing and Reality*. The mirror for Winnicott is not an actual mirror, it is a metaphor for the mother's face. Rather than a delusion, a trick, it is a transitional illusion which enables the infant to separate 'me' from 'not-me':

> What does the infant see when he or she looks at the mother's face? I am suggesting that ordinarily, what the baby sees is himself or herself.
>
> (Winnicott, 1971: 112)

Winnicott argues that this marks the beginning of self-consciousness: '*When I look I am seen, So I exist. I can now afford to look and see*' (ibid.: 114; my emphasis). The infant therefore forms a self, albeit illusory, in the mirror of the mother's face. A mirror because the mother returns the self to the child, by being seen and therefore being able to see. The self is therefore a transitional illusory self that enables the infant to identify me from not-me, to grow and to develop. The concept of the mirror stage in Winnicott's writings synthesises Lacan's ideas into an object-relations scheme of interpretation, offering a positive form of illusion in which the self is not alienated. The self does not develop at the expense of some Other, but matures in relation to the mirror role of the child's parents or primary carers. There is in some sense built into Winnicott's model the idea of positive self-reflection.

---

of interest between the two analysts, as well as drawing a parallel between the mirror stage and the depressive position (see Chapter 8). Leader notes that both Klein and Lacan were responding to Freudian problems, but proposing different solutions:

> If we are trying to link the mirror phase theory and the depressive position, there is the problem of reconciling this apparent joy of the Lacanian child with the sad, concerned mood of the Kleinian one.
>
> (*Ibid.*: 201)

For Leader, Klein herself provides the solution. In the depressive position there is a division of feelings between the destruction of the ego, and pining; the wish to make reparation. Leader offers a similarly analogous split in the mirror stage between the 'fragmented body and the wholeness promised by the mirror' (*ibid.*). It is with this in mind that I wish to devote the rest of this book to exploring the ideas and concepts of the object-relations school and particularly the work of Melanie Klein.

Conclusion

Thus far, I have examined the psychoanalytic contributions that Frantz Fanon and Slavoj Zizek have made to our understanding of racism and the construction of black identity. Fanon's and Zizek's work in this area is important as it provides a platform from which to explore these issues from a Kleinian perspective which both complements and completes Fanon's original work. Thus far we have investigated the relationship between the work of Jean-Paul Sartre and Frantz Fanon, taking up Fanon's suggestion that it might be interesting to investigate the construction of white and black identity with reference to Lacan's mirror stage. Two strong themes arise from this investigation. First, the production of black identity by the white person is inextricably linked with the way in which we perceive, react to and ultimately treat our constructed Other. In other words, there is a strong link between identity construction and racism. Second, and following from the first point, many of the ideas of Lacan in relation to identity construction are complementary rather than contradictory to Kleinian ideas.

Fanon's psychoanalytic treatment of Sartre's work provides us with an explanation which is firmly rooted in our biological instincts. Negrophobia emanates in biological notions of physical difference which are re-enforced by an unconscious prototypical figure, an imago of the black person. Hatreds and racism are a means by which the individual hides from their own sexual perversity. In Sartre we see a construction of the phobogenic Jew, the object in some sense becomes a container in which to place the individual's misfortunes. The Jew, for Fanon, has been fixated at an intellectual level, the black person on a bodily, biological, genital plane. The idea that we see in the imago of the black Other what we feel in our self, I have argued, is nothing new; Horkheimer and Adorno have already suggested this in *Dialectic of Enlightenment* – we attack the Other because we cannot accept our own sexual desires; we attack and destroy what we cannot have.

Zizek's work also give us an example of the practical application of psychoanalytic ideas in tandem with sociological theory in the explanation of social, political and psychological phenomena. There are clear Freudian and Lacanian ideas in Zizek's work, and through the concept of the theft of enjoyment Zizek illustrates the inner tensions and conflicts within communities and the ways in which these tensions affect our relationship to others. Again, Zizek's use of the concept of 'master' is reminiscent of Adorno's and Fromm's formulations of the authoritarian leader. In Chapter 5 we examined Freud's work and looked at his concept of the Uncanny, in this chapter I have examined a contemporary reworking of this thesis through the work of Seshadri-Crooks, whose work is helpful again because it demonstrates a multidisciplinary approach to the analysis of postcolonial discourse.

A Lacanian reading of Fanon's work provides a bridge between Freudian and relational ideas of the formation of black identity. In Lacan's theory the 'other' warrants the existence of the child, marking a separation and difference in which subjectivity is based; the self is defined in relation to some other, and 'other' is not what 'I' am. Aggression, I have argued, is directed in two forms, first aggression which separates and defines who I am, and second who I would like to be. The mirror stage has a double edge: the black person perceives in terms of 'whiteness', the I is constructed with reference to white, and therefore black is both other and I. This leads to a double disadvantage, the black person is persecuted as other and oppressed as I.

As Christopher Lane (1998) notes, 'Every citizen of Europe and North America is haunted by the specter of racism'. Although I have provided a critique of Lacan's notion of the mirror stage, I would rather not dwell on the negative aspects of Lacan's thesis. Lacanian ideas and authors writing after Lacan have provided some rich and insightful interpretations of race and racism. I have touched on a few of them, from Lacan himself, from Zizek and Seshadri-Crooks, but I think it is also worth highlighting Lane's (1998) edited collection *The Psychoanalysis of Race,* which has as its focus the irrational nature of racism in many forms and emphasises the need for a psychoanalytic approach to fantasy and identification. I feel that these ideas provide us both with an insight and a platform, indeed a positive critique, from which to develop a Kleinian perspective of the construction of black identity and to develop further our understanding of racism.

In the following chapters I will outline Melanie Klein's concepts of phantasy position, and in particular projective identification, and argue that these ideas are crucial to our understanding of the construction of 'otherness', to our understanding of the construction of identity, and central to understanding racism and ethnic hatred. I will outline for the reader both the complexity and numerous interpretations of Klein's concepts before going on to reexamine Freud's, Fanon's and Zizek's work through a Kleinian lens. I place particular emphasis on the different interpretations of projective identification, which range from the prototype of all aggressive object relations to empathy. In words, from a violent attack to what Betty Joseph (1989) would describe as a 'subtle nudge'.

Summary of key terms

Fanon's phobogenic object describes an object that both holds a secret attraction and arouses dread in the individual; it is a paradoxical construction that is both repulsive and attractive to its originator.

Fanon's negrophobia is found on the most basic of instinctual levels; in biological notions of physical difference and reinforced by the imago of the black person which has been constructed in phantasy.

Lacan's mirror stage describes a metamorphosis from a fragmented body image to a totality that Lacan describes as orthopaedic; orthopaedic in the sense that the mirror stage adds a 'prop' that enables the child to metaphorically stand up straight in the identity of a subject.

Zizek's theft of enjoyment is about inner tensions and conflicts within communities and the way these are projected out onto others in the form of hatred and loathing; this in turn is justified in terms of something stolen, and/or the community being deprived by others.

Klein's depressive position (see in particular Chapter 8) is the concept developed by Melanie Klein to describe a certain cluster of attitudes and defences in which we learn to deal with anxiety, terror, love and hate. It is marked by a recognition of good and bad within the self and others and an urge to make reparation the paranoid schizoid position).

Melanie Klein, Racism and Psychoanalysis

Introduction

Kleinian psychoanalytic theory provides a powerful basis for our understanding of the ubiquitous and visceral elements of racial hatred and discrimination. In this chapter I will outline some of the basic concepts in Kleinian thought and argue that a Kleinian psychodynamic interpretation of racism can complete and build on Freudian theory, providing us with a critical analysis of the social and psychological dynamics in a racist society. It is the communicative aspect of Kleinian psychoanalytic theory which can help explain the ways in which we *think* of others, *feel* about others and, crucially, *how we make others feel*. I begin this chapter with several sections on the major theoretical underpinnings of Klein's work before going on to start thinking about how we can apply these concepts to racism and ethnic hatred.

There are several interrelated concepts in Klein's work which are crucial to our understanding of racism and hatred. The first of these is phantasy. Phantasy for Klein is a psychic representation of the instincts. Phantasy draws upon material from both internal and external worlds, modified by feelings and emotions and then projected at objects both real and imagined. Bound up with the concept of phantasy is the notion of splitting. An infant's fear takes the form of phantasies of persecution, and in defence the world is split into good and bad objects. The good is introjected and idealised, the bad projected out into someone or something. Splitting is essentially an attempt to create order out of chaos; the product of splitting is the formation of boundaries and a strong sense of 'us' and 'them', 'good' and 'bad'. In the following sections I also discuss the Kleinian idea of positions which are of a dynamic rather than linear nature. It situates psychical development firmly within a social relational context and can be best described as a group of attitudes and mechanisms which work together to protect the individual throughout life.

These contributions made by Melanie Klein to psychoanalytic thinking, and particularly child psychoanalysis and technique, are immeasurable. Grosskurth (1986) describes her as the parent of object relations, and Schwartz (1999) describes Kleinian thought as the paradigm shift in psychoanalysis – a significant reorientation in frameworks of understanding. Hanna Segal (1989) is in little doubt about the significance of Klein's work: 'her work not only had a profound influence on technique, but that it contributed to a change in the psychoanalytic approach to the understanding of mind – in the psychoanalytic *Weltanschauung*' (1989: 161).

Melanie Klein moved to and established herself in Britain in 1926 at the invitation of Ernest Jones, where she was to remain for the rest of her life. Klein was elected a member of the British Psycho-Analytic Society in October 1927, and went on to be a leading figure in the development of psychoanalytic theory and technique. Her major works include: *The Psycho-Analysis of Children* (1932, 1997), *Love, Guilt and Reparation* (1937, 1975), *Envy and Gratitude* (1957, 1997) and posthumously *Narrative of a Child Analysis* (1961). Klein died in 1960. The Kleinian tradition has continued and spread far beyond the bounds of clinical psychoanalysis; her concept of *positions* has made a huge impact on the philosophy of mind and theories of thinking. Her work has been refined by Kleinians, and particularly concepts such as projective identification have been further developed by the object-relations school. Klein, after Freud, is probably the most influential figure in psychoanalysis.

Phantasy

Infantile feelings and phantasies leave, as it were, their imprints on the mind, imprints which do not fade away but get stored up, remain active, and exert a continuous and powerful influence on the emotional and intellectual life of the individual.

(Klein, 1936: 290)

The word fantasy is used in everyday language and usually denotes something imagined or unreal. So, for example, we may daydream of a far-fetched and unattainable idea. Thus, if we fantasise we imagine pleasant but unlikely events or outcomes. If something or someone is fantastic, then excellence springs to mind. Fantasy is therefore about something *imagined, unreal* and *pleasant.* Phantasy (the ph denotes the fantasy is unconscious) for Klein, however, is a concrete representation of the mechanisms of defence (Segal, 1992: 30). Phantasy is a 'hard fact' (Guntrip, 1961: 223). Phantasy is about things good and bad, real and imagined and the influence of phantasy on everyday life, interaction, art and science 'cannot be overrated' (Klein, 1959: 251). As Guntrip notes:

> In the scientific age men continue as much as ever to produce their phantasies, often, it is true, disguised as political ideologies and even as scientific theories, but also as religious, artistic and literary symbolism, and tale telling – that immemorial, perennial interest of human beings.
> (1961: 223)

Klein's picture of the 'inner' world is of a world constructed in phantasy, that is, unconscious phantasy. As Ogden (1986: 11) notes, phantasy for Klein is a psychic representation of the instincts, the 'infant's attempt to transform somatic events in to a mental form'. Unconscious phantasies are not the same as daydreams, but an 'activity of the mind that occurs on deep unconscious levels and accompanies every impulse experienced by the infant' (Klein, 1959: 251). So, for example, a baby may deal with hunger by imagining the gratification of the breast on the one hand, but on another may feel deprived and persecuted by the breast that denies this satisfaction. These are phantasies – the mental expression of the life and death instincts. As Robert Young (1997) notes, 'Klein is operating well and truly in the most primitive parts of the inner world, where dream symbolism meets up with primitive bodily functions and body parts' (1997: 73).

Thus, for Klein, instincts are always attached to an object or are object-seeking, and therefore the experience of instinct in phantasy relates to an appropriate object: 'To the desire to eat, there is a corresponding phantasy of something which would be edible and satisfying to this desire – the breast' (Segal, 1964: 2). The infant from birth has to both cope with and interpret reality, to try and make some sense out of its environment and psychic reality. Reality influences, and is influenced by, unconscious phantasy. In this sense the instincts are set within a relational context, phantasy is not an escape from reality but can produce reality in that 'phantasies can determine what kind of causal sequence is attributed to events' (*ibid.*: 3).

Phantasy is therefore constructed from the material of the internal world of the infant, and external reality of the environment. Phantasy can be modified by feelings, emotions and affect, and then projected at objects both real, the breast for example, or imaginary, in other words phantasy is an integral part of perception enabling us to interpret and understand the world. Julia Segal illustrates:

> In these phantasies, people and parts of people live and die inside and outside the self; move around; give rise to enormous gratification and equally enormous fear, jealousy, or envy... In this way phantasies strongly influence expectations and interpretations of real events in the world.
>
> (1992: 31)

Phantasy is a crucial part of the Kleinian philosophy of mind. Phantasy, for Klein, enables the ego to perform one of its basic and important functions; the establishment of *object relations*. A world of good and bad objects is constructed through a process of projection and introjection (that is, taking in and internalising experience and part objects). These objects are both a source of internal persecution and anxiety on the one hand, and of stability on another. Internal objects are perceived by the child as having a life of their own. In *Envy and Gratitude* Klein (1957) describes both the harmonisation and conflict that the child experiences as a result of the interplay between ego, object, emotion and experience:

> When the infant feels that he contains good objects, he experiences trust, confidence and security. When he feels he contains bad objects he experiences persecution and suspicion. The infant's good and bad relation to internal objects develops concurrently with that to external objects and perpetually influences its course.
>
> (1957: 59)

Thus there is a constant interaction through the processes of introjection and projection between the internal (object) world and external reality, and the introjection of a good loving object is crucial for the stability and growth of the child. Hinshelwood (1994) notes that internal objects are closely related and deeply involved in the process of identity formation. Introjection operates through unconscious phantasy, and parts of the self are constructed in relation to internalised objects both good and bad. These objects are projected in the form of perception onto the external world giving 'meaning and emotional charge to the coolly perceived objects of external reality' (Hinshelwood, 1994: 67). The implication of this is that phantasy not only provides a vehicle for the construction of our own identity, but also, through projection, the construction of others. In other words, our perception of others is effected by our own emotional state, bad objects are expelled in a process of projective identification in which we not only attribute our own affective state to that of others, but make others *feel* the way we do. This, in some sense, appears to be what Segal (1964) is talking about when she refers to phantasy as a defence against internal reality: 'phantasies, moreover, may be used as defences against other phantasies' (1964: 5). Put simply, in phantasy the individual internalises a bad object and in defence projects that object into others. Julia Segal illustrates:

> The defence of identification with an aggressor might involve a phantasy of actually taking the aggressor inside the self in an attempt to control them, then feeling controlled by them and needing to get rid of other, threatened and vulnerable parts of the self into someone else (the new victim).
>
> (1992: 31)

This is why Klein thought object relations were so critical in that phantasy involves doing something to some other, an object which has become split off or separated from the self in a way that phantasy is no longer mere imagination but a concrete influence on reality. In Chapter 7 I explored the way in which the anti-Semite attempts to put bad or unpalatable parts of the self into some other. Klein's notion of phantasy gives us a clearer picture of the psychic mechanisms which facilitate this process. The Jew becomes the container for the object that has been split of and separated from the dis-owner, the anti-Semite.

The Kleinian notion of phantasy is not without controversy in the psychoanalytic community. Bateman and Holmes (1995) note that the subject of this controversy largely revolves around a debate about the degree of innate knowledge that the infant possesses, and the extent to which this knowledge is formed through interaction. Hinshelwood (1994) argues that if we grant experience from birth then we must accept that biological activity is accompanied by some form of 'pre-formed psychological meaning' (1994: 32). In other words, we are born with some form of innate psychology. This is a view that Klein would almost certainly agree with – the unconscious has a set of contents from birth and before, we are not born with a clean slate so to speak. Ogden (1986) is puzzled by the proposition: 'Does this mean that infant inherits thoughts, and thinks those thoughts from the beginning?' (1986: 11). Paraphrasing Isaacs (1952), Ogden suggests that if we define and think of phantasy as a 'corollary of the instincts', then instinct is characterised by a specific type of object relation that includes 'affective and ideational qualities not dependent on actual experience with objects' (*ibid.*: 13). In other words, what Ogden suggests is that we view the Kleinian concept of inborn knowledge as a set of biological codes that are an integral part of instinct, rather than a collection of inherited thoughts. What Klein is clear about is that phantasy continues through childhood and into adult life, we constantly phantasise, phantasy never leaves us, phantasy is at the heart of our mental activity:

> Phantasies – becoming more elaborate and referring to a wider range of objects and situations – continue throughout development and accompany all activities; they never stop playing a great part in mental life.
> (Klein, 1959: 251)

This aspect of phantasy is crucial to our understanding of racism, hatred and exclusionary practices, helping us understand how we perceive others in the way we do, and the mechanisms we use to create this perception in which the other really is frightening and dangerous. Unconscious phantasy is, to reiterate, after Isaacs (1952) a psychological representation of the instincts, a representation that involves the imaginary relationship between objects. There is a relationship in which the subject wishes to do something to the object 'other' in which phantasy can become concrete reality. In other words, we can make the other embody our phantasies. Phantasy is constructed from external reality and modified by feelings and emotions, it is an integral part of perception enabling us to interpret and understand the world – a form of reality-testing. The implication of this is that our perception of others is both effected and constructed

---

Example 8.1   Susan Isaacs: phantasies and words

In the classic paper 'The Nature and Function of Phantasy' (1952), Susan Isaacs gives an example of how a particular phantasy can dominate the mind of a small child long before the content of the phantasy can be put into words. Isaacs describes how a child of 20 months was horrified and screamed in terror at the sight of her mother's shoe which had a loose and flapping sole. For a week afterwards the child would shrink in terror if she saw her mother wearing any shoes at all. For some time afterwards the mother could only wear a pair of brightly coloured slippers. As the months passed the child gradually forgot about the terror. Some time later, as Isaacs notes, the child was able to verbalise the phantasy:

> At two years and eleven months, however (fifteen months later), she suddenly said to her mother in a frightened voice, 'Where are Mummy's broken shoes?' Her mother hastily said, fearing another screaming attack, that she had sent them away, and then the child then commented, 'They might have eaten me right up'.
>
> (Isaacs, 1952: 91)

The point for Isaacs is that this demonstrates a preverbal reaction to a phantasy in which the child perceived the shoes as a dangerous and threatening mouth that might devour her and responded as such, despite the fact that the young child could not put the phantasy into words until much later. Indeed for Isaacs 'Here we have the clearest possible evidence that a phantasy can be felt, and felt as real, long before it can be expressed in words'.

---

by our emotional state. In the following section of this chapter I will examine the Kleinian concept of *splitting*, and then *position*, which should enable us to understand the psychological mechanisms which turn phantasy into reality, which in turn help explain the powerful affective forces which pervade a racist society.

Splitting the self

The projection of split off parts of the self into another person essentially influences object relations, emotional life and the personality as a whole.

(Klein, 1946: 13)

Splitting, for Klein, is a mechanism of defence, and the most primitive form of controlling danger in which good and bad are separated. Klein argues that the ego is developed enough at birth for the child to feel anxiety and therefore deploy mechanisms to protect the fledgling ego. The operation of the death instinct gives rise to internal phantasies of annihilation. Because the early ego is particularly weak it tends to fragment when faced with anxiety. The fear of disintegration emanates from the work of the death instinct and evokes paranoid schizoid defences. The splitting of good and bad is a defence of the primitive and fragile ego in which the infant's fear takes the form of phantasies of persecution. In defence, the world is split into good and bad part objects. The good is introjected and idealised, the bad denigrated, anxiety is projected out into something or someone else – the bad object. This distinction between endangered and endangering is a biological impulse which Ogden (1986) likens to a chick's 'unlearned response to a hawk wing pattern' to flee, to separate itself from danger and, as Gomez (1997) argues, is basic to the functioning of political systems. We therefore have the notion of a mechanism which originates in our primitive biology which has become synthesised within everyday interaction at a socio-political and group level.

We have seen how anxiety is generated from an internal source, from the death instinct, but for Klein the first form of anxiety from an external force can be found in the experience of birth in which the pain and suffering felt by the child are experienced as an attack. It is, however, for Klein, the child's experience of feeding which initiates the child's first object relation with the mother. Klein's view is that object relations exist from birth, and the mother's breast is split into good and bad objects; in other words, into gratification and frustration. This splitting leads to a clear demarcation between love and hate:

> The baby's first object of love and hate – his mother – is both desired and hated with all the intensity and strength that is characteristic of the early urges of the baby ... [in hunger] Hatred and aggressive feelings are aroused and he becomes dominated by the impulses to destroy the very person who is the object of all his desires and in his mind is linked up with everything he experiences – good and bad alike.
>
> (Klein, 1937: 307)

The mother is therefore split into two persons, a person who is a loving provider and a mother who is frustrating and hated. Splitting is therefore a means of dealing with anxiety. I have used the example of the frustration of bodily needs, but if we return to primary anxieties in relation to the ego anxiety arises from the death instinct and is felt as 'fear of annihilation taking the form of fear of persecution' (Klein, 1946: 4). The fear of the destructive impulse is experienced as an overpowering and uncontrollable object. This object is projected outward, a fundamental mechanism of defence in which bad or frightening parts of the self are attached to an external object: the mother's breast. Klein notes that this process never entirely fulfils its purpose: 'therefore the anxiety of being destroyed from within remains active' (*ibid*.: 5). Klein's theory is complex and we have to understand that the mechanism of splitting is bound up with the concept of phantasy. Phantasy, as I have described in the previous section of this chapter, is a psychic representation of the instincts, and the anxieties that stimulate splitting are produced in phantasy and attached to objects:

> It is in phantasy that the infant splits the object and the self, but the effect of this phantasy is a very real one, because it leads to feelings and relations (and later on, thought processes) being in fact cut off from one another.
>
> (*Ibid*.: 6)

Idealisation intensifies the split between good and bad, perception becomes distorted, the other is seen as either excessively good or persecuting and dangerous. Idealisation, as Segal (1992) notes, covers a conviction that the other is really frightening. This idealised other is split off as a mechanism in defence of the self, a protection against humiliation, destructiveness and diminishment. Idealisation in this sense is a defence not against reality but against the self, against destructive or persecutory phantasies, in other words the good is exaggerated to offset the fear of the bad. Klein views this splitting process as essential to the stability of a young child. The security of the ego is enhanced, good objects are split away from bad objects and therefore preserved. Ogden (1986) perceives splitting as a basic mode of organisation of experience:

> This form of mental operation is used in the beginning to create order out of the chaos of the infant's earliest experience...Splitting is a boundary-creating mode of thought and therefore a part of an order generating process.
>
> (1986: 48)

The implication of Ogden's interpretation of splitting is that it has consequences for our social environment. Splitting can lead to the formation of strong boundaries around the self, in which the other is denigrated and is perceived as larger than life, threatening and wholly destructive. This is for the sake of the creation of order from disorder. Stephen Frosh (1989) equates racism with this form of splitting:

> If the racist's deep fear is of disorder – disorder within as well as without ... racist violence under these circumstances can be seen as an out-pouring of the racist's own disorder, directed at the boundary of the other to prevent it being directed against the self.
>
> (1989: 237)

Benjamin (1994) reiterates this view by describing splitting as both a form of defence and organisation in which the formation of boundaries and the use of discrimination are used to protect the self from the very same thing (boundaries and discrimination) that are used in defence. Similarly, Rustin (1991) argues that splitting between positive and negative attitudes towards others, and processes of idealisation and denigration, are inherit in racist attributions:

> Dichotomous versions of racial difference are paranoid in their structure, since they function mainly not as cognitive mapping devices intended to identify facts, but as ways of channeling and condensing basic feelings of positive and negative identification.
>
> (1991: 66)

Elliott (1994) supports Rustin's view by arguing that destructive and negative feelings intertwine with 'socially valorised' racial attributions, and thus the racist splits the world into rigid categories. Hatred and destructiveness permeate the social and political world and are characterised by the splitting of good and bad. I introduced this section with Gomez's notion that splitting is a basic function of the political system. In Britain each political party, or 'side' is under pressure to find some fault with anything the other suggests. Another example can be found in the speeches made by Enoch Powell:

> The disruption of the homogenous *we*, which forms the basis of *our* parliamentary democracy and therefore *our* liberties, is now approaching

the point at which the political mechanisms of a 'divided community'
take charge.

                                            (Powell in Barker, 1981: 21; my emphasis)

There is a clear split between 'us' and 'them' within the context of
a political debate on immigration policy. Anxieties are fostered
which play on cultural difference which in turn are used to tap into

---

**Example 8.2   Splitting as a paranoid solution to extreme
anxiety: September 11th**

Fakhry Davids (2002) gives a very good example of splitting and the reduction of quite complex psychodynamics into black and white accounts in
reaction to the events of September 11th. Davies notes that those events
were brought home vividly to us by the wall-to-wall media coverage – the
shocking images of the planes crashing into the twin towers of the World
Trade Centre, and then their collapse. Psychically unbearable events, argues
Davids, call into play powerful defences whose aim is to protect us from
perceived danger.

For Davids, the extent to which the event has been reframed in stereo-
typed racist terms is apparent everywhere:

> The problem has now been reduced to a conflict between the enlight-
> ened, civilised, tolerant, freedom loving, clean living democrat versus the
> bearded, robed, Kalashnikov bearing bigoted, intolerant, glint in the eye
> fundamentalist fanatic, or viewed from the other side, the humble believer
> with God on his side versus the infidel armed with all the worldly might
> of the devil.
>
> (Davids, 2002: 362)

For Davids, it is difficult for us to find neutral ground – you are either with
us, or against us – which side are you on? This reduction of a complex situation into black and white, good and bad is a paranoid solution to intense
anxiety. As Davids notes, this makes us feel that we know who we are, and
may justify actions that make us feel better. The problem is that we don't
face the problem.

Psychoanalysts, argues Davids, who see the murderous suicide attack as
carried out within a perverse psychotic state of mind come dangerously
close to the rhetoric of politicians who maintain that Bin Laden is paranoid
and psychotic (which may in itself be a mechanism of defence). Davids'
point is that we must not avoid the complexity of the issues, and at the same
time we should be aware of the limitations of our own knowledge.

primitive anxieties which arise from psychic mechanisms, all to gain popular support.

I have framed splitting in the context of the organisation of experience; splitting is therefore a means by which order is created from chaos and boundaries are formed and maintained around the self. If we relate this to racism, the 'other' becomes a denigrated object which on the one hand is deeply threatening and dangerous, on the other, a site of the creation of order from disorder. Splitting is somewhat paradoxical in this sense as it is a mechanism in which discrimination and boundaries are used to protect the self against the very same thing. Splitting has been aligned with dichotomous racial stereotyping, idealisations and negative racial attributions. In this sense splitting can be seen as a way of channelling and condensing both positive and negative feelings of identification. Put simply, the racist splits the world into rigid categories which permeate the social and political world and are exemplified in political discourse.

In the following section I will go on to discuss the Kleinian concept of 'positions', integrating the discussion of phantasy and splitting and setting these concepts within a social-relational context. This forms the backdrop for the discussion of projective identification in Chapter 9.

Between good *or* bad: the paranoid schizoid position

> I choose the term 'position' in regard to the paranoid and depressive phases because these groupings of anxieties and defences, although arising first during the earliest stages, are not restricted to them but occur and recur during the first years of childhood and under certain circumstances in later life.
>
> (Klein, 1952b: 93)

Klein's notion of position is at the centre of her understanding of both the development of the child and of basic mental functioning. Positions are part of a developmental schema in which the child constructs its 'self' in relation to good and bad objects. Although Klein's focus is on the first year of life in which we learn to deal with anxiety, terror, love and hate, she does stress, however, as with many of her explanatory concepts, that mechanisms of defence and communication developed in the first year continue to be used in adult life and are evoked by certain psychological conditions.

Segal (1992) argues that Klein found Freud's idea of developmental stages too limiting. Rather than suggesting that a child passes through some ordered, sequential and well-defined stages of development, Klein argues that the child moves between positions 'with a specific set of attitudes through which events can be interpreted' (Gomez, 1997: 36). The difference between a stage and position is clear: whilst a stage is something that we reach, is grown through, and we move on, a position is a perspective that can be returned to. In other words, as Hanna Segal (1964) notes, a position is 'a specific configuration of object relations, anxieties and defences which persist throughout life' (1964: xiii). Positions are therefore groupings of anxieties and defences against those anxieties which enable the child to develop and the ego to strengthen; they are configurations of attitudes and mechanisms which work together. Bateman and Holmes (1995) explain: 'In essence the Kleinian "positions" are constellations of phantasies, anxieties and defences which are mobilised to protect the individual from internal destructiveness' (1995: 39).

The paranoid schizoid position is the earliest form of the organisation of the defences. Good and bad, as I have described, are split, the good is introjected, the bad denigrated, made larger than life, and projected out into someone or something else. Interestingly, Ogden (1986) argues that entry into the paranoid schizoid position marks the shift from the biological to the psychological:

> Klein's view of psychological development can be viewed as a biphasic progression from the biological to the interpersonal-psychological, and the interpersonal psychological to the subjective. The first of these developmental advances involves a transformation of the infant as a purely biological entity into the infant as a psychological entity.
>
> (1986: 41)

In others words the paranoid schizoid position presents the infant as a psychological rather than a biological entity. As Ogden notes, in this phase the self exists predominantly as an object: 'thoughts and feelings happen to the infant, rather than being thought or felt by the infant' (*ibid.*: 42).

Anxiety stems initially from the social relationship between mother and infant, and the internal anxiety associated with the death drive. As we have noted previously, for Klein (1952b) the first source of anxiety from an external force can be found in the experience of birth. The pain and discomfort that have been suffered are perceived as an attack; 'As persecution. Persecutory anxiety, therefore, enters from the beginning in his relation to objects' (1952b: 62). The child's experience of feeding initiates for Klein the infant's first object relation with the mother. The breast is split into good and bad, satisfying and frustrating. The infant does not perceive the mother as something whole, rather it reacts to the experience of something good or something bad, quite literally as an object, to the experience of having something done to it. As Gomez notes, this differentiation or split between good and bad enables the infant to experience goodness, or the good object 'as a base for his sense of self' (Gomez, 1997: 37). This is the basis in Kleinian psychoanalysis for the development of trusting and loving.

This is not without problems, as Craib (1989) argues; whilst the introjection of the good object may provide some stability, the expulsion, denigration and projection of the bad object onto the outside world leaves the child in paranoid fear of external attack – 'the fear is that bad objects will come back and destroy it from the outside' (1989: 146). Or, as Gomez puts it: 'The price of experiencing goodness uncontaminated by badness is that at other times the baby feels himself to be in the grip of pure evil ... This is the stuff of nightmare' (1997: 38).

Despite the frightening terminology of the paranoid schizoid position, Klein views the mechanisms employed as a defence against anxiety, particularly the splitting of internal and external objects, emotions and the ego as part of normal development in early childhood. Ogden (1986) provides a useful summary of the paranoid schizoid position:

> The Kleinian conception of the paranoid-schizoid position is a formulation of the infant's first foothold in the psychological sphere. This position involves a mode of generating and organizing experience in which experience is predominantly of an impersonal, non reflective nature ... Thoughts and feelings are not personal creations; they are events that happen. One does not interpret one's experience; one reacts to it with a high degree of automaticity ... Splitting allows the infant, child or adult, to love safely and to hate safely, by establishing discontinuity between loved and feared aspects of self and object. Without such discontinuity, the infant could not feed safely and would die. Basic to the state of being characterising the paranoid-schizoid position is the continual rewriting of history in the service of maintaining discontinuities of loving and

hating aspects of self and object. It is essential that only one emotional plane exists at a time. Otherwise object relations become contaminated and, as a result, unbearably complex for the primitive psyche.

(1986: 64–5)

Processes of splitting, idealisation, introjection and projection are a means of making some order out of chaos for the infant. The introjection of an idealised good object affords the child protection against persecutory anxiety out of which develops an integrated and stronger ego. The tendency to split good and bad lessens as the fear of bad objects diminishes; the child's world becomes less polarised, and both good and bad are seen in whole objects.

Between good *and* bad: the depressive position

If the paranoid schizoid position is characterised by a splitting of difference, between good *or* bad, then arguably the depressive position can be described as a reconciliation of difference, between good *and* bad:

> His relation to the external world, to people as well as things, grows more differentiated. The range of his gratifications and interests widens, and his power of expressing his emotions and communicating with people increases.
>
> (Klein, 1952b: 72)

Klein (1952b) identifies the depressive position as an integration of experience; the tendency to split good and bad part objects lessens and the perception of persons containing both good and bad develops: 'It involves not only a reduced need to split and project and an increased integration of good and bad objects, but also a move from perceiving a part object to a whole object' (Craib, 1989: 148). Conflicts in the internal world, from within the self are less likely to be split and pushed into others. There is a recognition of both good and bad within the self which allows a recognition of this in others. The depressive position marks for Kleinians, particularly the intersubjectivist thinkers, the birth of the historical subject (see Ogden, 1986). Klein notes that these processes of integration and synthesis of the inner world, self and ego, cause the 'conflict between love and hatred to come out in full force' (1952b: 72). Care for others develops, as does guilt. Guilt arises as the individual realises that the attacked 'other' contains good. The individual hates the hating self and tries to repair, to make reparation for the damage that has been done:

> At this stage, the drive to make reparation to the injured object comes into full play ... When the infant feels that his destructive impulses and phantasies are directed against the complete person of his loved object, guilt arises in full strength and, together with it, the over-riding urge to repair, preserve or revive the loved injured object.
>
> (Klein, 1952b: 74)

Klein cautions us in this interpretation. This is not wholly a case of altruism; it is another form of defence used by the ego against the onset of anxiety. Reparation in itself is an important defence mechanism, as Klein explains: 'My mother is disappearing, she may never return, she is suffering, she is dead. No, this can't be, for I can revive her' (1952b: 75). This is a form of mourning for the lost good object, and guilt which is induced from the way in which this object has been destroyed in phantasy by the aggression of the infant. The infant, faced with a multitude of depressive anxiety situations brought on by guilt, may deny that he loves the object at all, persecutory anxiety increases and there is a regression to the paranoid schizoid position. Thus in 'normal' development the infant in the depressive position will experience a decrease in persecutory anxiety associated with the paranoid schizoid position, and an increase in depressive anxiety accompanied by the desire to make reparation. A multitude of stresses and anxieties can cause the infant to move between the two positions.

Hinshelwood (1994) argues that the depressive position marks a transition from *fear* to *concern*. The success of this transition is based on the internalisation of a good loving object. Sadness, as Hinshelwood notes, is a feeling which is central to the depressive position; concern develops out of guilt and the sadness felt for the damage that has been done to the loved object. Hinshelwood notes that it is important to distinguish between sadness and clinical depression: 'Often Klein is criticised for confusing the two states by using the term "depressive position" for sadness and concern' (1994: 78). Sadness as we have seen, for Klein, is a feeling which relates to the damaged loved object. Depression is a complex and paranoid state, as Hinshelwood argues 'depression protects against the poignancy of sadness and concern' (*ibid.*: 80). Attention is drawn away from the object and focused on the self, depressive anxiety is ousted by a return to a paranoid state.

For Klein, the depressive position is the foundation for relating to both external and internal reality in a way which enables the infant to deal with his aggression in a more realistic and objective way:

> Gradually the process of splitting and synthesising are applied to aspects kept apart less widely from one another; perception of reality increases and objects appear in a more realistic light. All these developments lead to a growing adaptation to external and internal reality.
>
> (Klein, 1952b: 75)

Frosh (1987) notes that the depressive position, despite having a 'characteristically negative outline', has 'some crucial achievements under its sway' (1987: 126). There is this sense of concern that Hinshelwood talks of, and of reparation, making good and recognising both good and bad in a *whole* rather than *part* object. Alford (1989) argues that the depressive position may provide a foundation for morality based in love rather than aggression. On the one hand, for Alford, we have the 'talion' morality of the paranoid schizoid position, a morality based in 'revenge rather than reparation', a primitive morality emerging from the unconscious. On the other hand we have reparative morality:

> It is a morality based not merely on the desire to make sacrifices, in order to make reparation for phantasised acts of aggression; it is also based on an ability to deeply identify with others, to feel connected with their fates. Their pain becomes our pain.
>
> (Alford, 1989: 41)

Alford highlights in his discussion of morality the ability of Melanie Klein to analyse human nature within the features of relationships rather than biology. Indeed he is convinced that she discovers morality within the relational world of the depressive position. Similarly Elliott (1994), using the work of Rustin (1991), argues that Klein's explanation of unconscious pain, guilt and anxiety provides us with both 'a root of our moral concern for people' and an 'ethical norm for the assessment of political life and cultural organisation' (Elliott, 1994: 82). Frosh (1987) describes the move between paranoid schizoid and depressive positions in a graphic and very useful way, arguing that we have traveled through a world that emphasises the horrific side of human destructiveness to a world imbued with love, morals and understanding:

> Intriguingly, what has begun as a theory emphasising the negativity of human experience, its fundamental destructiveness and the damage caused to self and others through envy and hatred, resolves into a precise and luminous celebration of making good, of forming personal relationships of the deepest kind on an image of concern and loving consideration.
>
> (1987: 127)

Frosh's point is that Kleinian theory, although appearing pessimistic, is in fact realistic in that progress is based on a gradual strengthening of the ego leading to the possibility of enriched social relations; 'the trajectory of theory is towards construction rather than withdrawal' (Frosh, 1987: 128). As Ogden (1986) notes:

> What one gains is subjective humanness and the potential to be free to make choices. This is not a dilemma that one resolves: one is stuck with it, with all its advantages ad disadvantages, unless one regressively flees from it into the refuge and imprisonment of the paranoid-schizoid position or through the use of manic defences.
>
> (1986: 99)

Ogden's view is that of what we might call the intersubjectivist approach to object relations. As I noted earlier in the text, for Ogden the depressive position marks the birth of the historical subject. Ogden himself claims that his analysis of the depressive position goes significantly beyond the ideas which are explicit in Klein's original writings. Ogden builds on Klein's ideas to talk about fundamental background states of being, which I feel is particularly important for sociological theory as it tells us something of the construction of the subject from a psychoanalytic perspective.

We have seen in the previous section that Ogden describes the paranoid schizoid position as a means of rendering experience discontinuous, and ejecting dangerous or frightening bits of this experience into others in a process of projective identification. Ogden describes the paranoid schizoid position as a nonreflective state of being, thoughts and feelings just happen. In the depressive position, however, the infant is an interpreting subject:

> At the moment that the infant becomes capable of experiencing himself as the interpreter of his perceptions, the infant as subject is born. All

experience from that point on is a personal creation (unless there is sub-sequent regression). In the paranoid schizoid position, everything is what it is (i.e. events speak for themselves), whereas in the depressive position, nothing is simply what it appears to be.

(1986: 73)

Ogden is critical of Klein, arguing that her mapping of the depressive position is a mechanical one which does not allow for the transformations that the infant experiences in the actual quality of experience. Klein's emphasis is on the inner world with very little reference to the intrapersonal and intersubjective. This is an argument which we will return to in the next chapter where we will see that theorists are divided as to whether the mechanism of projective identification is intersubjective or remains a phenomenon which exists entirely in the inner world of the infant.

Depressive anxiety, envy and hatred

Envy... to look askance at, to look maliciously or spitefully into, to cast and evil eye upon, to envy or grudge anything.

(Klein, 1957: 181n)

Envy which seeks to destroy is characteristic of the paranoid schizoid position, but envy also stands as a barrier to the reconciliation of good and bad in the depressive position. Envy, for Klein (1957), as Craib (1989) notes is entirely destructive. Klein makes a clear distinction between envy, jealousy and greed. Jealousy excludes another from good; destructiveness is a byproduct of exclusion and usually involves a second party. Greed operates similarly by taking the whole of the good, regardless of the consequences that others may suffer; again destructiveness is a byproduct of the process. Envy, however, 'seeks to destroy the good itself' (Alford, 1989: 37). In other words, what makes envy so destructive or dangerous is that it attempts to destroy good rather than bad.

The sharpest distinction between envy and greed is that the former is bound up in projection, the latter in introjection. Klein (1957) notes:

Greed is an impetuous and insatiable craving, exceeding what the subject needs and what the object is able and willing to give. At the unconscious level, greed aims primarily at completely scooping out, sucking dry, and devouring the breast: that is to say, its aim is destructive introjection.

(1957: 181)

Envy on the other hand seeks to expel, to put bad objects into some other in order to destroy their peace and happiness. Envy is a destructive form of projective identification; to look maliciously or spitefully *into*, 'to produce misfortune by his evil eye' (*ibid.*: 181n). Envy is associated with anxiety, in that envy and anxiety stand as a barrier to the reconciliation of good and bad in the depressive position. Arguably, envy compounds the anxiety associated with reparation in the depressive position. We perceive others as possessing something good that has been stolen from us; jobs, cultures, ways of life. We try to take it back, but we cannot have it all (greed), so we destroy it (envy). In seeking to ethnically cleanse 'others', we are in fact cleansing ourselves, ridding ourselves of the discomfort of envy. The racist in envy seeks to destroy the good that he cannot have. The racist, unable to enjoy cultural difference is a manifestation of envy; making bad what is good and destroying what he cannot have because he is unable to accept and share.

In order to understand the role that depressive anxiety plays in the explanation of racism it is necessary to return briefly to Klein's notion of positions. As I have argued, the paranoid schizoid position is characterised by a splitting of difference. Good and bad objects are split, the good introjected, the bad projected outward into someone or something else. Persecutory anxiety stems from the fear of internal and external attack. Gradually the tendency to split good and bad lessens as the fear of bad objects diminishes, the child's world becomes less polarised and both good and bad are seen in whole objects. Thus we have the transition to the depressive position. The depressive position can be viewed as a recognition of the plurality of difference in which the individual hates the hating self and tries to repair, to make reparation for the damage that has been done. Care for others develops, as does guilt in realisation that the attacked 'other' contains both good and bad. Thus, depressive anxiety fuels the need to make reparation. The depressive position involves fear, anxiety and despair about the ability to both make reparation for those destroyed in phantasy and to overcome one's own destructiveness. The anxiety generated may be so great that it leads to the employment of paranoid schizoid defences. In the explanation of racism, anxiety is not created by acceptance and celebration of difference; rather, it is the doubt on the part of the individual of his ability to do so which leads to the employment of paranoid schizoid defences. If we take a hypothetical example: 'I am sorry that I have hurt you, I want to be your friend, accept you and love you, but I doubt my ability to do so, to make the situation good again. If you are bad, if I form a border, a boundary to stop you coming in, I need not confront my own guilt or anxiety.' Thus the urge to make reparation, in itself, perpetuates and justifies racism for the racist. This is exemplified by the double bind of the 'new racism': 'we' the British nation are tolerant, 'we' open our arms to you, but in doing so the 'we' marginalises 'you'. 'You' cannot be like 'us' because you are not like 'us'. We make reparation to you, but in doing so we are unable to cope with the anxiety that we feel, the guilt of treating you the way we have. Intolerance, as Bauman (1991) so lucidly comments, hides under a mask of toleration.

Envy is therefore a projective and destructive attack which stands as a barrier to reconciliation in the depressive position. The racist seeks to destroy the good that he cannot have. Excluding and persecuting others not only alleviates the discomfort of envy but also of guilt and depressive anxiety. The urge to make reparation, as I have argued, in itself perpetuates and justifies racism for the racist. Depressive anxiety can often invoke schizoid defences which produces a vicious spiral of racism.

Summary

The Kleinian 'position' represents a perspective, a configuration of object relations, in other words: attitudes and mechanisms which work together and persist throughout life. In the paranoid schizoid position good and bad are split as a form of defence against both the internal and external world. Persecutory anxiety stems initially from the social relationship with the mother and internal anxiety associated with the death drive. Splitting occurs in the paranoid schizoid position within the context of phantasies of annihilation and destruction. The infant does not perceive the mother as a whole object, but reacts to the experience of something good or bad. The good is introjected, the bad idealised and projected out onto someone or something else. The introjection of the good enables the infant to experience goodness as a base for his sense of self. The projection or expulsion of the bad is problematic as it leaves the infant in constant fear of attack; the bad object will return and destroy him from outside. The infant lives in a schizoid state; on the one hand he experiences uncontaminated pure goodness, but at other times he is in the grip of frightening phantasies of annihilation. It must be noted, however, that despite the frightening terminology of the paranoid schizoid position, Klein views it as a normal defence against anxiety in early childhood. Processes of splitting, idealisation, projection and introjection are essentially about making order out of chaos. Out of the paranoid schizoid position there develops a base for the development of love, empathy and psychic integration in the depressive position. Splitting fends off persecutory anxiety allowing the ego to develop.

The depressive position, as I have argued, can be seen as an integration of experience. As the fear of bad objects diminishes so does the tendency to split, the child's experience becomes less polarised and both good and bad can be seen in whole rather than part objects. It is in the depressive position that the conflict between love and hate appears in full force. Guilt develops in realisation that the attacked other contains good as well as bad. The individual hates the hating self and attempts to make reparation for the damage that has been done. Persecutory anxiety is replaced by depressive anxiety, a move from fear to concern. I have noted that an excess of depressive anxiety may lead the individual to employ schizoid defences, in other words to return to the paranoid schizoid position.

Projection and *Identification* are an intrinsic part of psychical life. How do we relate these concepts to racism and other hatreds? In the following chapter I will explore the mechanism of projective identification which I feel is at the heart of these processes and crucial to our understanding of the psycho-social dynamics of exclusion.

Summary of key terms

Phantasy is an activity of the mind that occurs at deeply unconscious levels – the mental expression of the life and death instincts. The experience of instinct in phantasy always relates to an object, for example the breast; it enables the ego to perform one of its basic and most important functions – the establishment of Object Relations. Phantasy continues through childhood and into adult life; we constantly phantasise, phantasy never leaves us, it is at the heart of our mental activity.

Splitting is a mechanism of defence and the most primitive form of controlling danger in which the world is split into good and bad part objects to protect the fledgling ego. The good is idealised and introjected, the bad denigrated and projected out. It is particularly associated with paranoid schizoid functioning.

The paranoid schizoid position describes a specific configuration of object relations, anxieties and defences which persist throughout life. The paranoid schizoid position is the earliest form of the organisation of the defences characterised by the splitting of good and bad part objects, splitting of the ego, persecutory anxiety, idealisation of the good and denigration of the bad, and projective identification. It enables the infant to experience good while keeping the bad at a safe distance.

The depressive position. Here the small child's world becomes less polarised in a move towards an integration of experience. Splitting lessens and people are percieved as whole objects containing both good and bad. Conflicts within the internal world are less likely to be split and pushed into others. It is marked by depressive anxiety and the need to make reparation for the damage done by paranoid schiziod functioning. For Kleinians, and in particular intersubjectivist thinkers, the depressive position marks the birth of the historical subject. For Klein, this process of integration and synthesis of the inner world, self and ego allows the conflict between love and hate to come out in full force.

CHAPTER 9

Projection, Projective Identification and Racism

The drive to project (expel) badness is increased by the fear of internal persecutors. When projection is dominated by persecutory fear, the object into whom badness (the bad self) has been projected becomes the persecutor par excellence. The re-introjection of this object reinforces acutely the fear of internal and external perse- cutors... an interaction in which the processes involved in projective identification play a vital part.

(Klein, 1952b: 69)

Projection and projective identification

Projective identification is for Klein (1946) a crucial mechanism of defence. As we have seen in Chapters 5 and 6, projection *per se* is a relatively straightforward mechanism in which unpalatable impulses, feelings and parts of the self are projected out and onto others. In other words, we project onto the world experiences and qualities that are part of ourselves as if they are part of someone else. Hence we have Freud's notion of the uncanny: 'what appears repellently alien is in fact all too familiar'. Klein's notion of projective identification, however, differs significantly and it is important to differentiate between the terminology at the onset. As I have argued, Horkheimer and Adorno's use of projection in explanation of anti-Semitism provides us with a useful insight into the psychodynamic processes that underpin racism and ethnic hatred. What Horkheimer and Adorno fail to explain is the way in which the recipient of the projection is made to feel, for example, inferior. This is a useful way of differentiating between projection and projective identification. Whereas projection is a relatively straightforward process in which we attribute our own affective state to others, for example we may feel depressed and view our colleagues in the workplace as being miserable, or blame others for our mistakes. Projective identification involves a deep split, a ridding of unpalatable parts of the self *into* rather than *onto*, someone else. Projection *per se* may not be damaging, as the recipient of the paranoid thoughts may be blissfully unaware as such. Projective identification, however, involves a forcing of such feelings into the recipient and is therefore interactional and communicative. Klein (1952b) argues that the processes that underlie projective identification operate in the earliest relation to the breast: 'The "vampire like" sucking, the scooping out of the breast' (1952b: 69), as the infant in phantasy attempts to make his way into the mother's body. This corresponds to 'oral-sadistic' attacks on the breast which are bound up with greed, to introject and empty the mother's body of all that is good and desirable. At the same time, driven by persecutory anxiety, the bad self is projected into the object, the breast:

> split off parts of the ego are also projected on to the mother or, as I would rather call it, *into* the mother ... Much of the hatred against parts of the self is now directed towards the mother. This leads to a particular form of identification which establishes the prototype of an aggressive object-relation. I suggest for these processes the term projective identification.
>
> (Klein, 1946: 8)

Is important to bear in mind that it is not just bad parts of the self which are split off and projected into others, but also the loving part of the self. The point, for Klein, is that a balance can be struck between expulsion of good and bad which is essential for the development of healthy object-relations. The notion of projective identification is complex, and it becomes more so as we study the concept. Forcibly entering an object in phantasy stimulates anxieties which threaten the subject:

> For instance, the impulses to control an object from within it stir up the fear of being controlled and persecuted inside it. By introjecting and re-introjecting the forcibly entered object, the subject's feelings of inner persecution are strongly reinforced.
>
> (*Ibid*.: 11)

This situation of introjection and reintrojection of the bad object is at the very heart, for Klein, of paranoia. The fear of being imprisoned in another body (or culture) or the fear of another object (or culture) forcing itself inside our self. The implication of this is that by using projective identification to expel our bad bits into others, we live in fear of being invaded by others and thus perpetuate the cycle of persecution.

Robert Young (1994) suggests that projective identification is 'the most fruitful psychoanalytic concept since the discovery of the unconscious' (1994: 120). Young points both to the complexity of the nature of projective identification and the numerous interpretations of Klein's material. Young notes that psychoanalysts are divided on this score; 'whether or not a real, external Other, who has been affected by projection, is essential to the concept' (1994: 124). Bott-Spillius (1988) takes a wide approach arguing that projective identification is used and directed at both internal and external objects. Segal (1964) defines projective identification in terms of projection into an external object: 'parts of the self and internal objects are split off and projected into the external object' (1964: 14). Bion (1992) in Young (1994) talks also of projection into an external object. Klein herself used the term projective identification in several ways as her work evolved over a number of years, but in *The Emotional Life of the Infant* (1952b) she is clear that projective identification plays a vital role in the interaction between internal and external worlds. In the following two sections I will outline intrapsychic and intersubjective interpretations of this phenomena, but the reader has to bear in mind that there is often a crossover and very fine line between the use of psychological mechanisms in the internal and external worlds of the subject.

Intrapsychic projective identification

It should also be noted that the process of projection identification is closely bound up in phantasy. Projective identification is the vehicle or tool which enables phantasy to become reality by projecting our perception and emotion into others. Projective identification can be viewed as both directed at external and internal objects, but as Young (1994) cautions:

> It is important to emphasize that projective identification can occur wholly inside the unconscious of the projecting person and need not be involved at all with behaviour which is unconsciously designed to elicit a response from another person. The Other can dwell exclusively in the

inner world of the person who creates the projective identification and supplies the response for his or her phantasy.

(1994: 125)

Joseph Sandler (1987) also offers a critical reading of the usage of the concept of projective identification in *Projection, Identification and Projective Identification*. He traces the historical and progressive development of the concept highlighting three stages of its use. Sandler argues that for convenience the stages have been delineated, but in practice there is considerable overlap between the conceptualisations of projective identification. Sandler's first stage is concurrent with Klein's early writings:

> I speak here of *first stage projective identification* to emphasize the point that for Mrs. Klein projective identification was a process that occurs in *fantasy*. Let me put it another way. The real object employed in the process of projective identification is not regarded as being affected – the parts of the self put into the object are put into the phantasy object, the 'internal' object, not the external object.
>
> (Sandler, 1987: 17)

Projective identification, therefore, is a mechanism that operates within the psychic and internal world of the individual, a process which occurs in phantasy and has little impact on the external object world, a view supported by Robert Young's (1994) writings. Second-stage projective identification, for Sandler, represents an extension of Melanie Klein's original concept:

> whereas projective identification occurring within the person's phantasy life (reflected in the phantasy distortion of the analyst), can be called first stage projective identification. If either the self or the object represented in such unconscious fantasies is identified with by the analyst to a degree sufficient to contribute to the analyst's countertransference, we have an instance of second stage projective identification.
>
> (*Ibid.*: 18)

In other words, the analyst identifies with the projector's transference phantasy and this is shown in the countertransference of the analyst. Projective identification has simply added another layer to what we regard as transference and countertransference. The transference is not simply a repetition of the past, but a result, through projective identification of the present, of the unconscious relationship between analyst and analysand. Third-stage projective identification, for Sandler, involves a psychodynamic with the external word, with external reality and external objects, and is exemplified in Bion's (1962) and Ogden's (1986) writings:

> The analyst as 'container' is, as I see it, the analyst who can tolerate the patient's distress, hostility, and love – indeed, all his phantasies and feelings – and who as a consequence of his reverie can return them to the patient in the form of interpretations which will allow the patient to accept as aspects of himself those parts that he had previously considered dangerous and threatening.
>
> (Sandler, 1987: 23)

Projective identification in this form is intersubjective, communicative and exists in both internal and external worlds. Sandler makes a series of critical points which can only add to our understanding of projective identification. First, Sandler argues that projective identification need not always be accompanied by phantasies of invading and entering. The notion of 'into' the object is still commensurable with the idea of projective identification as a self and object representation. Second, projective identification is more than a psychotic mechanism, it is ubiquitous. Third, when examining second-stage projective identification, Sandler argues that it is insufficient to say that the internal phantasy object is put into the analyst. Rather, the patient attempts to actualise the phantasy in a process of transference and countertransference which is based in identification with the patient's phantasy object. There is then a second, a further projective identification into the phantasy analyst object. Fourth, and this is the area in which Sandler is most critical, is the idea of projective identification as communication as exemplified by Bion's (1962) work. Indeed, Sandler argues:

> What I find unacceptable is the notion that this process is one of projective identification, unless the concept is stretched to extreme limits. We would have to say, for example, that the child's cry of distress is 'put into' the mother by projective identification, and it seems to me that this represents a caricature of the original concept.
>
> (1987: 23)

For Sandler, Bion's container model can be separated from the developmental theory in which it is based, as can the concept of projective identification. In other words, for Sandler, in Bion's notion of container and contained there is a lot more going on than simply projective identification.

Although critical of the concept of projective identification Joseph Sandler's work is important as it reminds us of several problems with this type of concept. First, there are so many different interpretations of projective identification that we have to be careful not to take the interpretation out of context. Second, projective identification is used as both an explanatory concept and a description. If we take the many different meanings of the concept, together with its use as a description, then we are open to 'pseudo-explanation' (Sandler, 1987: 23). In other words, if we are not careful we tend to see projective identification everywhere in a descriptive form. In order that we may retain the explanatory power of the concept we must lose sight of its specific meaning in the relevant context.

The problem with projective identification is that if we take it to be a wholly intrapsychic phenomena, then it is not really of any specific use in sociological analysis. We cannot study the complex psychodynamic interactions between individuals, groups and society and the concept remains a tool for use only in the consulting room. This position does not do justice to the rich insights that projective identification can bring to the sociological perspective. In the remaining sections of this chapter I want to explore projective identification as a communicative form through the work of Bion (1962) and Ogden (1986).

Projective communication: intersubjective projective identification

Julia Segal (1992) uses the term projective identification to describe a mechanism which is designed to evoke a response in others, 'It is a very powerful means of communication of feelings, used by babies or small children before they can talk' (1992: 36). Joseph (1989, cited in Young, 1994) talks of a 'subtle nudge' to elicit a response from others. In the clinical setting, the patient may consciously or unconsciously try to induce feelings and thoughts in the analyst to 'nudge' the analyst into a way of acting which is consistent with the patient's projections. This is often very subtle, consciously unintended, and the recipient is not always immediately induced to act or behave in a certain way, but importantly made to feel the projections of the projector. Joseph (1989) identifies three types of projective identification within the clinical environment. First, the attack on the analyst's mind: 'a kind of total invading' (1989: 174). Gianna Williams (1997) likens this form of projective identification to a feeling of being temporarily blinded, as if acid had been thrown in her face (1997: 928). Second, a partial invasion, a taking over of the analyst's capacities. And finally putting parts of the self, particularly inferior parts, into the recipient. This we can parallel with Bion's (1962) notion of containment. In the former it is the patient who becomes identified with analyst's capacities, whilst in the latter it is the analyst who is identified with the projected bad or inferior parts of the self. Ogden (1986) supports Bion (1962) in a more communicative than internal account of projective identification. Communicative in the sense that the projection is aimed at an external object and designed to illicit a response both consciously and unconsciously. Bott-Spillius (1995) notes that analysts have gradually come to widen their use of Klein's concept of projective identification, noting:

> This is, I believe, one of the few areas in which current Kleinian theory and practice is rather different from that of Klein herself, for we now accept without question the idea that projective identification often, although not always, affects the recipient.
>
> (1995: 1)

In other words, phantasy is accompanied with some form of communicative behaviour which has an affect on the external object, the recipient. Thus, Bott-Spillius argues, projective identification 'communicates something, even when communication is not the projecting individual's primary conscious or even unconscious aim' (*ibid.*: 1).

Herbert Rosenfeld (1988) distinguishes between two types of projective identification and points towards a third. The first, projective identification as a method of communication is an intensification or distortion of a normal infantile relationship, based in non-verbal communication between mother and infant. The child projects unbearable impulses and anxieties into the mother who is able to alleviate and contain the anxiety the infant feels by modifying or changing her behaviour. In an intensified form of this projection the patient:

> Projects impulses and parts of himself into the analyst in order that the analyst will feel and understand his experiences and will be able to contain them so they lose their frightening or unbearable quality and

become meaningful by the analyst being able to put them into words through interpretation.

(Rosenfeld, 1988: 117)

This situation, argues Rosenfeld, is of fundamental importance in that it enables the patient or person to learn to tolerate his or her own impulses and begin to think about experiences which were previously meaningless or frightening – to communicate with others.

A second form of projective identification identified by Rosenfeld involves the splitting off and projection of anxieties into the analyst with the sole purpose of evacuation. This emptying of frightening and disturbing mental content leads to a denial of psychic reality:

> As this type of patient primarily wants the analyst to condone the evacuation processes and denial of his problems, he often reacts to interpretations with violent resentment, as they are experienced as critical and frightening as the patient believes that unwanted unbearable and meaningless mental content is pushed back into him by the analyst.
>
> (*Ibid.*: 118)

A third form of projective identification aims to control the analyst or object's mind; the patient feels that he or she has forced their way into the analyst. Rosenfeld argues that the projection of 'mad' parts of the self often dominates and the projector lives in fear of recontamination, of counter projective identification in which the analyst will reinvade the patient with his or her own madness. All three of these projective processes may operate simultaneously and, for example, someone may use projective identification as *communication* and *control* to evoke in the analyst or recipient a 'concerned' object.

Hinshelwood (1989, 1992) positions all these interpretations on a continuum from a violent prototype of the aggressive relationship to empathy. 'If projective identification varies from expulsion to communication, then at the very furthest point on the benign end of the scale is a form of projective identification underlying empathy, or "putting oneself in another's shoes"' (1992: 133). Hinshelwood quite rightly highlights the parallel between this continuum and the movement between the paranoid schizoid and depressive positions. A number of forms of projective identification can be used or employed and these are closely related to the notion of positions.

Young (1994: 130) notes that there is 'no sharp line to be drawn between normal and pathological, between benign as compared to virulent or malignant projective identification'. In the study of racism we are interested in the form of projective identification that is meant to evoke a response in others, to make them feel in a certain way. An analogy we can draw on is the difference between prejudice and discrimination. If prejudice is about prejudging in the absence of evidence, and discrimination is acting on prejudice, then prejudice on its own is relatively harmless; it is action that hurts. Similarly, projections and projective identifications that are contained and lived out in the inner world have little impact on the external world. It is the violent expulsion, the attack, the impulse 'to suck dry, bite up, and rob', to make others feel in certain ways, which provides the explanatory power in projective identification; again, it is the action that hurts.

Projective identification and containment

Bion (1959, 1962) develops Klein's idea of projective identification, introducing the concept of 'container' and 'contained'; the recipient of the projection acts as a container of feelings, such as love, hate and anxiety. Bion (1962) explains this model in relation to Klein's work:

> I shall abstract for use as a model the idea of a container into which an object is projected and the object that can be projected into the container: the latter I shall designate by the term contained.
>
> (1962: 90)

The relationship between container and contained is, as Symington and Symington (1996) note, either integrating or destructive. Depending on the level or degree of violence used in the projective identification, the communicative aspect of the projection can range from an attack resulting in destructiveness at one end of the spectrum, to a form of communication that leads to empathy and understanding at the other. As Ogden (1986) notes, under optimal conditions the recipient of the projection can reprocess the feeling evoked and then return it to the projector in a more manageable form, a communicative form. Problems arise when the projection takes the form of a violent expulsion in which the 'state of the object is not considered' (Hinshelwood, 1994: 130). Bott-Spillius (1988) explains:

> If the object cannot or will not contain projections, the individual resorts to increasingly powerful projective identification. Reintrojection is effected

with similar force. Through such powerful reintrojection the individual
develops within himself an internal object that will not accept projections,
that is felt to strip the individual greedily of all the goodness he takes in.

(1988: 155)

Bion provides a theory of emotion which has an environmental or
social aspect. Bott-Spillius (1988) argues that the notion of containment has lessened the divide between cognition and emotion. As
Bleandonu (1994) notes the 'container is penetrated and the contained penetrates whenever one emotion replaces another' (1994:
186). Thus the external object is central in attributing meaning to projected affect, a part of the thinking process. The implication is thus far
for Bion that projective identification is a communicative activity, a way
of transmitting meaning at one level by evoking empathy, at another a
form of violent expulsion. It is, as Bott-Spillius (1988) notes, a way of
seeing 'thinking' in terms of an emotional experience. In other words,
there is learning about yourself and others through projective identification. Meltzer (1978) takes this one step further by arguing that
Bion's notion of container and contained represents the first 'cogent
theory of the emotions in the history of psychoanalysis' (1978: 52).

For Bion (1962), therefore, projective identification is part of the
thinking process. Originally a procedure for 'unburdening the psyche of accretions of stimuli' (1962: 31), phantasy is projected into
the container and in a reprocessed form introjected back into the
projector. The point is that bad or intolerable feelings are transformed by the recipient, they are made tolerable. Bion calls this
process of transformation the 'alpha function'. If, as Bott-Spillius
(1988: 155) notes, all goes well, then the projector, the infant, eventually introjects this function of transformation and thus develops
a means of thinking and tolerance of frustration.

Ogden (1986) reformulates Bion's ideas and describes a manipulative interpersonal form of projective identification:

Interpersonal pressure is exerted on the recipient of the projective identification, pressure that is unconsciously designed to coerce the recipient
into experiencing himself and behaving in a way that is congruent with
the unconscious projective phantasy.

(1986: 145)

In Ogden's schema unwanted feelings are dumped on others by
inducing in a manipulative way that experience in the recipient, this
alters the behaviour of both projector and recipient.

Thus far I have differentiated between projection and projective identification and then discussed several forms of this mechanism, both intrapsychic and intersubjective. These interpretations range from the prototype of a violent aggressive relationship (Klein) to empathy (Bion). I have argued that the most important aspect of projective identification is the nature of the projection, in that it involves projecting *into* rather than *onto* the recipient. The implication of this is that the projection has some effect on the object or recipient.

It would be unwise and unfruitful to view projective identification as any less than a combination of the notions that I have discussed. As Hinshelwood (1989) notes, these interpretations can be placed on a continuum, and I would suggest that different forms of projective identification are used in differing psychological situations and this is relational to the paranoid schizoid and depressive positions. In spite of this complexity, there are clearly different forms of projective identification which can be usefully catergorised as *intrapsychic* and *intersubjective*. Whilst the intrapsychic provides us with a useful insight into early childhood development and is a key component of the clinical encounter, it is intersubjective account of projective identification that provides a valuable tool for the examination of social psychodynamics. In other words, the ways in which individuals interact with others in their social environment, how they communicate on both a conscious and unconscious plane, and how we make others feel. Projective identification can be both good, communicative and constructive, as easily as it can be pathological and destructive. This I believe is implicit in Klein's work. Bion (1962) and Ogden (1986) add depth to Klein's work, expanding on both interpersonal and intrapsychic elements of object relations.

Battered down by tom-toms: projective identification and racial hatred

> The other, the white man, who had woven me out of a thousand details, anecdotes, stories.
>
> (Fanon, 1968: 111)

The most obvious way to view projective identification in terms of the explanation of racism and ethnic hatred is as a violent expulsion of affect which renders the recipient in a state of both terror and self-hatred. Self-hatred is a state which is often brought about by others, and perhaps the most obvious example is that of Jewish people in the Holocaust. I recently went to a presentation by a Jewish survivor of Auschwitz, Bergen-Belsen and Dora camps in which he talked of his experiences growing up in Nazi Germany. The presenter went on to become a successful engineer and businessman in later life. Despite this, he still feels inferior when he walks into a room full of people, such is the power of projective identification. This is, however, only one way of viewing racism through the lens of projective identification.

In Chapter 7 we saw how the work of Zizek (1992) is useful for demonstrating the eruptive nature of the psychological mechanisms of ethnic hatred, in Zizek's case the former Yugoslavia. Although we noted that the psychoanalytic component of Zizek's sociological theory is based in Lacanian thought, it nonetheless provides some powerful examples of unconscious projections which we can recast in Kleinian terms. Fanon's (1968) work illustrates the lengthy if no less violent construction of black and white identity through the psychology of oppression and colonialism. Again, Fanon's psychoanalytic position is that of a Freudian who is starting to think about Lacanian concepts (see Chapter 7), but Fanon also provides some clear examples of the effects of unconscious projections. Projective identification operates at different levels and in different forms, but all have the same effect: to induce feelings of inferiority, misplacement, low self-esteem and of exclusion, a sense of not belonging; a sense that racism is something that you feel but rarely see, on one end of the continuum, on the other as a violent expulsion of hatred. Craib (1998) provides the most useful interpretation:

> Projective identification is a more profound form of projection. Instead of just seeing the feared quality or emotion in another person, I behave in such a way as to lead the other person to experience that quality in themselves.
>
> (1998: 17)

As I have argued in the previous section of this chapter, the implication for Bion (1959, 1962) is that projective identification is a communicative activity which can be normal or pathological. The former involves a form of communication in which mental states are communicated to others; it is a mechanism that can evoke empathy.

The latter involves a form of violent expulsion in which unbearable parts of the self are evoked in others. Pathological projective identification involves an enormous degree of hatred and violent splitting, loss of ego, omnipotent control and a desire to destroy awareness (Hinshelwood, 1989: 186). The recipient of these projections acts as a container of feelings such as fear, hatred and anxiety. The object of the projection becomes something inferior, repellant, someone or thing to be excluded, a container with which to detoxify our own self. Rustin (1991) cites by example Seabrook's (1973) account of racism in Blackburn in the 1960s. As parts of the Asian community started to take on some of the characteristics of white working-class life, the white community simultaneously, in response to economic decline and social disintegration, experienced a loss of these qualities. The white community projected into the Asian community the demoralised and disintegrated state which they were experiencing in the form of hostility towards the lifestyle adopted by the Asian community. Tension is again mounting at the time of writing this book as local people in the north of Britain perceive Kosovan asylum seekers to be stealing their housing, and benefits that are not rightly theirs. Again, the anger experienced because of clear socio-structual factors, poor housing and unemployment is projected onto and into an outgroup.

For Klein and Bion, projective identification is part of the thinking process and is arguably at the heart of ethnic and racial hatred. Thinking, for Bion, is in origin a procedure for unburdening the psyche of accretions of stimuli. Projective identification is the mechanism used to evacuate these build-ups and, in consequence, a way in which phantasy is made reality. Bion uses the example of people who have the impulse to force others to feel that they are capable of an act, for example, of discrimination, violence or murder. In the extreme, discrimination, violence and murder take place as a method of giving effect in the world of reality to phantasy through action (Bion, 1962: 32).

As we have seen, Frantz Fanon (1968) in *Black Skin White Masks* gives some powerful examples of the lived experience of the victims of racism in an analysis of the psychic consequences of colonialism. Although Fanon uses a Freudian analytic framework, his descriptions of the effects of unconscious projections enable us to point to the mechanisms of projective identification. Fanon's work concentrates on the psychology of oppression and on strategies to resist oppression which do not involve compromise or flight. The main feature of Fanon's understanding of the psychology of oppression is that inferiority is the outcome of a double process, both socio-historic and psychological: 'If there is an inferiority complex, it is the outcome of a double process: primarily economic; subsequently, the internalisation, or better, the epidermalization of this inferiority' (Fanon, 1968: 13). There is therefore a link between the socio-genesis and psychogenesis of racism and, as Jean-Paul Sartre (1976) demonstrates in *Anti-Semite and Jew*, these processes are violent and exclusionary. When Sartre talks of anti-Semitism as a passion it is not the Jewish person who produces the experience; rather, it is the (projected) identification of the Jew which produces the experience. Experience is made reducible to the object. Sartre argues that Jews have become poisoned by the stereotype others have of them, they live in fear that their actions will correspond to this stereotype and conduct is 'perpetually overdetermined from inside' (Sartre, 1976: 95). Fanon illustrates this internalisation of projection:

> My body was given back to me sprawled out, distorted, recoloured, clad in mourning in that white winterday. The negro is an animal, the negro is bad, the negro is ugly.
>
> (1968: 113)

If we understand the reference to the breaking up bodies, to being sprawled out and distorted, in terms of more than mere metaphor, then these processes which have consequences on the sociogenic level are the outcome of processes of projective identification. The white person makes the black person in the image of their projections, as Fanon notes:

> the white man has woven me out of a thousand details ... I was battered down with tom-toms, cannibalism, intellectual deficiency, fetishism, racial defects, slave ships.
>
> (1968: 112)

The black person lives these projections, trapped in an imaginary world that white people have constructed; trapped by both economic processes and by powerful projective mechanisms which both create and control the Other. This, of course, highlights the paradoxical nature of projective identification. White people's phantasies about black sexuality, about bodies and biology in general, are fears that centre around otherness, otherness which they themselves

Example 9.1   Paul Hoggett: the projection of a demoralised state

Paul Hoggett's (1992a) study of white people's resentment of Bangladeshi people in Tower Hamlets, London, illustrates the interplay between structural and psychological factors that give rise to ethnic hatred and tension. Hoggett notes how rapid social change has a profound effect on local communities. Social change also corresponds to a sustained period of uncertainty for groups and individuals in which the basis of both group and collective identity is challenged and undermined. Lifelong jobs are lost, as are traditional patterns of communal loyalty. Indeed, for Hoggett: 'A struggle for survival ensues but, for the most, this is primarily a struggle for collective psychological survival rather than physical survival' (1992a: 353).

Tower Hamlets is a multiracial area which has experienced massive social dislocation, poor housing, and a declining industrial base. Dislocation and a series of tit-for-tat stabbings between ethnic groups created a profoundly nostalgic anxiety amongst the white working classes for a way of life that has been lost. This led to tension between the two communities. A small beetle – the cockroach – became a focus of paranoia and defensiveness. Evidence suggesting that a major cockroach infestation has physical and structural causes was completely ignored. The actual improvement of homes by introducing double-glazing and central heating encouraged the cockroach to thrive by providing a warm breeding environment and a veritable insect motorway of pipes and ducts. This 'cuts no ice' with the white tenants; the cockroach comes to represent a complex body of resentment, paranoid anxiety, fear and hatred. Indeed for Hoggett: 'For the white tenant this Other is resilient, small in stature, multiplying fast, and impure, hence, no doubt, the symbolism of the cockroach' (1992a: 354). In this sense, phantasised and visceral elements of the white working class community are projected into the Bangladeshi community.

As with Seabrook's (1973) study, the white working class project their demoralised state in the form of hostility towards the lifestyle adopted by the Asian community, while simultaneously experiencing a loss or theft of their way of life:

> The resentment the whites feel toward the Bangladeshi community is made poignant by the fact that the latter community has many characteristics – extended and extensive kinship networks, a respect for tradition and male superiority, a capacity for entrepreneurship and social advancement – which the white working class in the area have lost.
>
> (Hoggett, 1992a: 354)

have created and brought into being. This is what Fanon means when he says that I was 'battered down', 'woven out of a thousand details' – the stereotype of the black person is constructed in the mind of the white person, and then forced back into the black person as the black historical subject. But this indeed is a false consciousness.

Similarly in *Tarrying with the Negative*, we have seen how Zizek (1993) has described the fear of a lost shared communal phantasy. To reiterate, Zizek argues that we have developed through phantasy a 'thing', a national thing: a shared relationship, a way of life, 'enjoyment incarnated' (1993: 201), a phantasy. This thing is contradictory because it is only accessible to us but is constantly under threat from the 'other'. Although Zizek is very influenced by, and uses, a Lacanian theoretical psychoanalytic framework, a Kleinian analysis of his work reveals some very good descriptions of projective identification using material based in an analysis of the former Yugoslavia: 'We always impute to the "other" an excessive enjoyment: he wants to steal our enjoyment (by ruining our way of life) and/or he has access to some secret, perverse enjoyment' (*ibid.*: 203).

For Zizek, the former Yugoslavia is a case study in the paradoxical nature of the theft of enjoyment. Something stolen from us that we never possessed in the first place, a way of life that was never complete, something constructed in phantasy and projected into and onto others. If we look at a small section of the passage I used in Chapter 7 we can see that projective identifications abound in the construction of difference, otherness and psychological boundaries:

> Slovenes are being deprived of their enjoyment by 'southerners' (Serbians, Bosnians ...) because of their proverbial laziness, Balkan corruption, dirty and noisy enjoyment ... The Slovenes themselves, on the other hand, allegedly rob the Serbs because of Slovenian unnatural diligence, stiffness and selfish calculation.
>
> (Zizek, 1993: 204)

The circle continues in a series of 'decantations' of the theft of enjoyment (*ibid.*); the basic premise for both Serb and Slovene is, 'we want our thing, that which belongs to us and we don't want anything foreign'. If we think about this within a Kleinian theoretical framework, then the 'other' is a psychological manifestation within us, a phantasy, which we project onto others. Ethnic hatred is a manifestation of phantasy that is locked up in a circle of projective identification in which the object produces experience, rather than experience producing the object. Ethnic tensions arise from the possession of a 'thing' produced in phantasy that others may steal, and this thing is a manifestation of our own psychotic or schizoid anxieties. Slovene is trapped in an image created by Serb, Serb in an image created by Slovene. Fears of otherness are paradoxical as they are created and brought into being by the projector. Thus we have the paradox of the confusion of perception in the paranoid schizoid position; we imagine the other in phantasy, while imagining what we have imagined has stolen something from us. This resonates in the projective elements of situations where a country can open its arms to people in a postwar boom, to do all manner of jobs, yet the other is perceived as stealing our jobs, jobs nobody wanted to do in the first place; the theft of something we never possessed.

I have argued that projective identification is a valuable concept in understanding the ubiquity and often explosive characteristics of ethnic hatred. Projective identification can be viewed as a continuum of affective force which ranges from attack to empathic communication. The work of Zizek (1993) reinterpreted in a Kleinian analysis illustrates the eruptive and violent end of the spectrum where ethnic hatred is a manifestation of phantasy locked in a circle of projective identification. Fears of 'otherness' are paradoxical as they are created and brought into being by the projector. This eruption of violence emanates from psychotic anxiety; we hate the group who may steal our enjoyment; we fear the theft of phantasy. Projection is violent, the object produces experiences in a series of decantations of the theft of enjoyment.

Frantz Fanon's (1968) work exemplifies, again within a Kleinian reinterpretation, the internalisation of projection. The white person creates the black person in their image (or imagination). For the black person these projective identifications become a lived experience. Again, there is a parallel with Zizek's work; white people's phantasies about black sexuality, bodies and biology are fears that centre around otherness, otherness that they themselves have created and brought into being. Hatred is of the group that we have constructed in phantasy, fear is of our own phantasy, projection takes the form of a violent intrusion.

I have also discussed the work of Seabrook (1973) and Hoggett (1992a). These are both interesting because they demonstrate the fusion of psychodynamic and socio-structural factors which give rise to ethnic tension. There is in both cases a sense of some form of loss or even theft of a way of life. If we use Bion's (1962) notion of container and contained, we can see that the Asian community are used as a container to detoxify the self. The white community project into the Asian community the demoralised and disintegrated state which they are experiencing in the form of hostility towards the lifestyle adopted by the Asian community. Similarly in Hoggett's (1992a) study, tension between white and Bangladeshi communities is exacerbated by the loss of certain qualities in the white working class which the Bangladeshi community are believed to still retain. Again, there is a strong sense of loss or theft of a way of life. We therefore hate the group who has stolen something from us. We fear those who possess what we mourn for. Projection takes the form of the transference of our demoralisation from subject to object.

The Kleinean account of projective identification gives a far more useful account of the ubiquity of racism and ethnic hatred than sociology alone. It helps us understand the psychodynamics that operate between the perpetrator and recipient. Larger groups can perpetuate anxiety about the 'other', and in this sense some forms of solidarity and community can be destructive in that they reinforce paranoid schizoid anxiety by giving it an objective focus, and this we have seen by example in Seabrook's and Hoggett's studies. The case studies that I have used represent the violent end of the continuum; rather than a 'gentle nudge' or an underlying feeling, they represent direct discrimination and racial hatred. If this continuum also represents the movement between paranoid schizoid and depressive positions, then this type of projection is synonymous with paranoid schizoid anxiety. In the final section of this chapter I want to briefly and tentatively look at the other end of this continuum, at projective identification as a subtle but coercive form of communication.

Projective identification as a subtle nudge: racism in institutions

We clearly live in a racist society, and racism is embedded in the structure of society as inequalities in access to housing, employment and education bear testimony. Institutions reflecting this society maintain rules and practices which perpetuate racism, which in turn are aimed at the individual: attitude manifests itself in action which becomes discrimination. The enquiry into the racist killing of

Stephen Lawrence has brought the problem of institutional racism to the forefront of public concern. It seems that institutional racism is prolific and not always quite as blatant as we may first assume. As I argued at the start of this book, institutional racism is an attempt to move away from the idea that inequality arises as a result of the attitudes of a few, sad, prejudiced white people. Rather racism is endemic in the structures, rules and practices of institutions, and in this context racism becomes self-perpetuating. Institutional racism, for Miles (1989), may be the cause of disadvantage for certain groups but may no longer contain explicit racist content. In this section I want to introduce the idea of the 'institution in mind' or the 'internal establishment', and argue after Menzies-Lyth (1989) that employees of large institutions tend to internalise the characteristics and central tenets of the institution that they are part of and use subtle forms of projective identification to alienate and exclude those who do not appear to fit into the commonly held practices or rules of the institution (in mind).

In a recent study of institutional racism in higher education (see Clarke, 2000), I have argued that experience is dominated, after Bion (1962), Joseph (1989) and Ogden (1986), by a series of subtle and not so subtle projective identifications and communications in which the black or Asian student is made to feel quite simply unwelcome by both members of the establishment and the student's own peers. Discrimination now takes the form where people are made to feel uncomfortable, anxious and different (in a pathological sense). This in turn impacts on the student's course of study and psychic well-being.

It is interesting to return to Ogden's (1986) description and analysis of projective identification. For Ogden, 'mature' forms of projective identification involve a phantasy of expulsion – expelling unwanted, split off parts of the self and in the process taking control of another. In tandem with this phantasy is an actual interpersonal interaction where the recipient of the projection is coerced to behave and feel in a certain way. It is important to note that the feeling and behaviour induced is congruent with the projector's internal phantasy. I do not think, for example, that the notion of white students projecting their unwanted and anxious selves on black students is explanation enough in itself. Again, as Menzies-Lyth (1989) has intimated, members, or in this case students, become like the institution by introjecting and operating its characteristic defence mechanisms; by sharing common attitudes and by carrying on traditional relationships. If we think, again in tandem, we have this psychodynamic operating on one level, while on another we have a complex construction of 'black'. A phantasised imago, an internal object which represents black people which has been constructed through a long history of racism, stereotypy and racial hatred. This is embedded in the structure of the institution and students expectations of it. The university as an institution is steeped in this history, and in some sense is a last great bastion of whiteness. Several students have commented: 'Its in the system, its not personal now', but the system seems to reduce racism back to a personal level, because the system excludes.

If we look at the concept of institutional racism psychoanalytically, then we can identify two broad areas of concern. First, institutions that reflect and reproduce the inequalities of society maintain rules and practices that perpetuate racism. Racism has become naturalised into established attitudes, procedural norms and social patterns. In other words, practices that we take for granted, that are not explicitly racist, may have their origins in racist discourse and are part of the affective organisation. Second, institutional racism has been seen as a move away from the idea that racism emanates from a few individuals and is endemic in the structure of society. I argue that while an institution may carry racist discourse within its tenets, which are then assimilated by members, this is reinforced by the prejudice and phantasy of individuals. Prejudice in itself is arguably enough to create an 'atmosphere', a feeling, to make others feel out of place, a subtle nudge. Thus, we have both individual prejudice, and a general social attitude which interact with a complex institutional psychodynamic which together generate feelings and processes of exclusion within institutions and the workplace.

This sense, or feeling, is perhaps what Freud (1919) really meant to articulate when he talked of the 'uncanny' – 'a class of frightening which leads us back to what is old and long familiar' (*SE XVII*: 220). A sense of old direct racism disguised as something else. It would seem that if we are to think about the policy implications of institutional racism, then we need to address the organisation as an affective or emotional group.

Summary

It has been the intention in this chapter to develop a critical sociological theory of racism. I have argued throughout this book that in order to understand racism we need to address the ways in which it operates at both a macro social level and on an individual affective plane. In other words, we need to address the dynamic between social forces that operate on a structural level and the affective emotional mechanisms that emanate from within the individual. I have discussed Kleinian theory at length in this chapter together with other theorists who build on Klein's work. Klein provides an account of how affect, feelings and emotions are formed in the social environment giving a social psychodynamic interpretation of conflict.

There are several interrelated concepts in Klein's theory which are crucial to our understanding of racism, hatred and exclusionary practices. Although I have broken down these concepts into discrete sections in this and the previous chapter to try and clarify and instruct, it should be noted that splitting, for example, is bound up with the concept of phantasy, as is projective identification, and they differ according to position. If we apply the notion of projective identification in terms of the explanation of racism and ethnic hatred, then we can see different forms and processes of projection. I have argued that the most obvious way of viewing projective identification in terms of the explanation of racism and ethnic hatred is as a violent expulsion of affect that renders the recipient in a state of both terror and inferiority – projective identification as an evacuation. This, however, is only one of the processes at work. By reinterpreting the work of Zizek (1993), Fanon (1968), Seabrook (1973) and Hoggett (1992a) within a Kleinian theoretical framework I have tried to demonstrate both the complexity of projective identification and the different processes involved between projector and recipient. In all four of these examples there is a complex interrelationship with socio-structural factors: colonialism, the collapse of nation-states, massive dislocation, poor housing and unemployment.

I have argued that the projection described above is synonymous with the paranoid schizoid position and persecutory anxiety. Envy and depressive anxiety arguably contribute to the use of and return to these mechanisms of defence. Envy stands as a barrier to the reconciliation of good and bad in the depressive position. Envy compounds anxiety associated with reparation and is an entirely destructive form of projective identification. We perceive others as possessing something good that has been stolen from us; ways of life, jobs, even culture; we try to take it back, but we cannot have it all so we destroy it in envy. The racist in envy seeks to destroy the good that he cannot have. The racist, unable to enjoy cultural difference is an embodiment of envy; making bad what is good and destroying what he cannot have because he is unable to accept and share.

A psychoanalytic reading of institutional racism reveals the more subtle usage of projective communication and the idea of the affective organisation. I have argued that if we are to address this problem then we have to take into account the emotive basis of organisations as well as the clear structural inequalities. I have put some considerable emphasis on the notion of projective identification as it clearly illustrates how we are able to make others feel in a certain way, for example to feel inferior. Projective identification is at the heart of racism and ethnic hatred; it is a major communicative dynamic which is at the centre of the thinking process; it is complex in form and operates on many levels of a continuum which ranges from violent expulsion to empathy. If we couch this in terms of racism, then at one end of the continuum we have a sense that racism is something you feel but rarely see. On the other it is a violent attack, and expulsion of fear and hatred. I do not think that psychoanalysis in itself explains racism any more than sociological ideas do; what I think psychoanalysis offers is *understanding*, or as Max Weber would say *Verstehen*.

Summary of key terms

Projective identification. Joseph Sandler (1987) describes the progressive development of the concept of projective identification thus:

Stage	Psychic domain	Effect
First	The internal world (intrapsychic)	None on external objects
Second	The internal world (intrapsychic/intersubjective)	Appears in countertransference
Third	Internal and external (intersubjective)	Communication/containment

Herbert Rosenfeld (1988) distinguishes between three types of projective identification:

Type of PI	Function	Effect
As communication	Unbearable thoughts contained	Toleration/ communication, intoleration of others

Type of PI	Function	Effect
As an evacuation	Evacuation of unbearable thoughts	Denial of psychic reality/resentment
As control	Forcing into some other to control	Fear of re-invasion/contamination

All three of these projective processes may operate simultaneously, and for example someone may use projective identification as *communication* and *control* to evoke in the analyst or recipient a 'concerned' object.

CHAPTER 10

Conclusion

We penetrated deeper and deeper into the heart of darkness ... The steamer toiled along slowly on the edge of a black and incomprehensible frenzy. The prehistoric man was cursing us, praying to us, welcoming us – who could tell? We were cut off from the comprehension of our surroundings; we glided past like phantoms and secretly appalled, as sane men would be before an enthusiastic outbreak in a madhouse. We could not understand because we were too far and could not remember, because we were travelling in the night of first ages, of those ages that have gone, leaving hardly a sign – and no memories.

(Conrad, 1902: 68)

It is well-known that Conrad's (1902) *Heart of Darkness* has a deeply psychoanalytic alter-ego. Initially Conrad's work seems an adventure which unfurled into a critique of the cruelty, greed and senseless barbarity of colonialism in which 'white' is the root of all evil in darkness. A further reading reveals a very different journey – a journey into the unconscious, the unknown, the heart of darkness. Of imaginary fears and enemies, of phantasy. It is both a journey into our psychological prehistory and, as O'Prey (1983) argues, 'the darkness is a deeply suppressed inner anarchy which is impossible to comprehend, or explain and better not to imagine' (1983: 22). I would of course disagree that it is impossible to comprehend; an exploration of both inner and outer worlds has been central in this book and this disagreement has been fundamental in the writing of this work.

This text brings together some of the main critical and theoretical contributions to the psychoanalytic and sociological study of racism. The book in part is intended to be an introduction to psychoanalytic ideas, and the application of those ideas through the study of racism. I have also tried to engage the reader with my own passion for Kleinian thinking. The work of Melanie Klein has helped me understand racism and hatred within a social relational context that explores the interface between the inner and outer worlds in our life. As such, I feel that Klein's contribution to psychoanalytic understanding provides an array of theoretical tools for the student of social, political and cultural studies. I have also devoted much space in this book to Freudian, post-Freudian and Lacanian ideas, which all add differing levels of analysis and have been instrumental in the development of this field, in particular the work of Max Horkheimer, Theodor Adorno, Eric Fromm, Frantz Fanon, Homi Bhabha and Slavoj Zizek.

There has been a fairly long history of the use of psychoanalysis within sociological critique stemming back to the critical theory of the Frankfurt School. I have tried to chart sociological thinking about racism whilst simultaneously introducing a history of ideas around thinking about our inner world, that of psychoanalytic theory. My contention throughout this book is that sociology is lacking something in its ability to explain why we are racist, which all of us are to a lesser or greater degree. My conclusion is depressing – that we are all inherently racist, and that only sustained and critical self-reflection can move us on from this position. This stance will no doubt be challenged by many of my colleagues, some of who may scream biological reductionism. I have tried to counter this by critiquing reductionist accounts of racism and situating explanation in the way in which we relate to each other in the social world using a Kleinian psychoanalytic sociology.

When I talk of us all as being inherently racist, or at least prejudiced, as many of us do not act on our prejudices, I cannot detach this from the social, economic and political conditions that promote prejudices, anxieties and fears. As Elisabeth Young-Bruehl (1996) has recently noted, prevention of depression and anxiety, of the states of mind that facilitate prejudices and of obsessional anti-Semitism should be at the forefront of our agendas in terms of both politics and education. I feel that sociology and sociologists have done an excellent job in pointing to and identifying different forms of racism, and the way in which racisms have become embedded in the structures of society. Sociology has told us *how we are racist*, pointing to inequalities in housing, welfare provision, education and the labour market; but these are, however, the appalling symptoms of a racist society, of a condition, and that condition is about *why* we respond and act to our fellow human beings in certain ways.

One of the problems with psychoanalysis is that on the one hand it makes all this very complex, but on the other the *complexity* gives us insight. People, things, objects and events are no longer clear-cut and black and white, we no longer have the racist who hates on the one hand, and the clear thinking liberal individual on the other, rather we have a view of the world and human nature where life is hard, painful and sometimes crazy. As Robert Young (2000) has noted, we are as human subjects intense, often fraught and ruled over by our inner world of phantasy, which is full of both *fear* and *desire*. We constantly live near, if not over the edge, and life is a balance between *love* and *hate*. In other words, we are all capable of outbursts of ethnic hatred, of racism and of discrimination, and it is the degree to which we recognise and therefore reflect on this condition that gives us a sense of how we feel in relation to others.

It is this critical and self-reflective element of psychoanalysis that provides, if you like, that which is missing or lacking in the sociological analysis of racism and other hatreds. It is difficult to understand or explain the irrational eruption of anger and loathing that characterises ethnic hatred without addressing what we could simply call the crazy or mad parts of our self. There is no reference point or analytic framework to do this in sociology, we would not get past discussing what we mean by irrational. Psychoanalysis and psychoanalysts are not afraid to confront these issues, to address our undesirable tendencies, thoughts, feelings, imagination – conflicts within our internal world, and conflicts between inner and outer worlds.

I want to conclude, then, by arguing that there are certain key concepts that are crucial for our understanding of the psychodynamics of racism, and these are the notions of phantasy, splitting and projective identification. After Kovel (1970), who argues that we cannot attribute human behaviour to mono-causal explanations, I also want to stress that the psychological is inextricably intertwined with the structural – the cultural, the historical, the social and political. As Fanon (1968) has told us, there is a both a political economy and a psychodynamic of racism – only a critical psychoanalytic sociology can address both.

As Sander Gilman (1985) notes, our internal world and mental representations of the world, *become the world*. In other words, there is a tendency to treat creations of thought as a given reality. This is why I feel that the concept of *phantasy* is so important if we are to understand how we come to construct our world, often in an imaginative and creative way but also in a destructive and exclusionary manner. Indeed, Rosalind Minsky (1996) notes that for Klein 'phantasy is a precondition of any engagement we can have with reality' (1996: 81). While many acts of racism may appear to be ruthlessly calculated, others appear as irrational eruptions of anger and hatred for the other. Both forms are fuelled by our unconscious phantasies, by fear of difference, and more importantly by the fear of the destruction of our own self. Difference highlights the fragility of our own ego, of our sense of self and of the inherent selfishness of human beings. It seems that we need some other, whether it be aged, gendered or racialised to maintain our identity amongst our selves. Cornelius Castoriadis (1999) has noted the essential *incon-vertibility* of the Other based in physical and irreversible characteris-tics, the object of hate can never be confused with I – 'The colour of the skin and facial traits are the most appropriate support of this hate, for they supposedly would mark the irreducible strangeness of the object and eliminate all risk of it being confused with the racist' (Castoriadis, 1999: 413).

I have used the work of Zygmunt Bauman (1989, 1990, 1991) throughout this book because I believe that his sociological account of the Stranger illustrates well the social manifestation of phantasy. The stranger, to paraphrase Bauman, brings the outside inside and poisons the comfort of order with the suspicion of chaos. The stranger is a psychic entity, a construction in phantasy that symbol-ises our fears and anxieties. The stranger lives both in our commu-nity and our psyche – a product of socio-historical forces, phantasy and our imagination. We attribute strangeness to other groups and real individuals. We are repulsed by what we see, as we are confronted by our own fears and chaos, by the contents of our unconscious mind. The stranger in a Freudian sense represents the uncanny and has been persecuted as Jew, as gypsy, as Muslim, as asylum seeker and as indigenous other. They, the stranger represent all our fears of chaos, of displacement, and represent a threat to our psychic stability.

As Julia Kristeva (2001) notes, although internal and external *splitting* are phantasy-like, the young child still experiences the effects as real. Splitting, as I have noted, is a basic mode of defence for the fledgling ego, and Klein argues that splitting and other defences continue throughout life as we resort to paranoid schizoid defences. If phantasy helps us understand why we are racist, then splitting bridges the how and why as it is so closely related to phan-tasy. It seems that under many forms of anxiety we are prone to split the world into dichotomous polarities, between good and bad, black and white. We idealise and introject the good, whether this be ways of life, objects, individuals or political leaders, and denigrate the bad – projecting these qualities into someone or something else. Very real acts of violence, and as we have seen recently terrorism, force fear into us, manipulate our psyche, and invade our inner world. Again we start to see the world in dichotomous entities – 'you are either with us, or against us'. From a Kleinian perspective this is a classic reaction to the fear of being destroyed from both within and without. If we think in terms of racism, then splitting has the effect of creating or forming strong boundaries around the self, in which the other is denigrated, stripped of his or her basic human rights as an individual, and is perceived as larger than life, threatening and wholly destructive. As Gilman (1985) observes, splitting between good and bad is at 'the root of all stereotypical perceptions' (1985: 17). In some sense the racist becomes self-justifying, and I feel that the whole project of defining 'race' as a category is about splitting, and this has the effect of cleansing, filtering and containing difference; the ultimate goal of which is to *control* others.

The final concept, and the one which I feel is of the most importance in the understanding of racism and ethnic hatred, is that of *projective identification*. I have devoted a whole chapter of this volume to the subject and therefore will not reiterate, but simply add a few observations. As Ros Minsky (1996) argues, the psychoanalytic concept of projective identification allows us to begin to see evidence for feelings and phantasies which are unconscious. The concept of projective identification for me enables conceptualisation of the processes by which we make others feel either the way we do, or the way we want them to feel. It is a form of violent expulsion, a form of communication, and can be as coercive as it is constructive. As Kristeva (2001) notes, after Segal (1964), projective identification is the first step in bonding with the outside world (Kristeva, 2001: 71). I feel that projective identification as a concept is central to our understanding of racism because it gives us a very good idea about how we are able to make others feel inferior and in some sense create their identity through our projections, not just through violent expulsions of unconscious phantasies but through the subtle nuances, nudges if you like, that are common in institutions and workplaces. Projective identification is often employed as the mechanism by which silent racist discourses are transferred from subject to object in a world where overt discrimination is monitored, and is again, I feel, at the heart of institutional racism.

Finally, if we view all three concepts – phantasy, splitting and projective identification – within the context of Freud's uncanny, then we have a very good discription of the social psychodynamics of racism and in some sense why we feel the need to treat others in the way that we do. In *Das Unheimlich*, the accent is on the quality of feeling, on the aesthetic, and as Freud notes the uncanny, proceeds from actual experience. The uncanny belongs to a set of experiences that can be classed as frightening, and the frightening element emanates from something familiar that we see in others that has been repressed in the self. The uncanny, I feel, is deeply entrenched in phantasy.

Phantasy, not only provides a vehicle for the construction of our own identity, but also through projection or more specifically projective identification the construction of others. Not only do we attribute our own affective state, our sense of uncanny, to others, but we also make others feel the way we do. Feelings of uncanniness produce an uncanny object. Phantasy in a Kleinian sense is therefore a relational rather than biological source of *Das Unheimlich*. These feeling are not produced by the repression of instincts and drives, but by the way we construct ourselves in relation to others through phantasy. Thus, racism and ethnic hatred emanate from a complex interaction between self and other, in which phantasy becomes the reality of containing uncanniness in a racial category.

The racial or ethnic other is created by both our fear and ignorance of difference. What appears repellently alien is the manifestation, a reflection, of phantasy in some other. In this way, that which is familiar turns to frightening and produces feelings of hate. I feel that it is in the depressive rather than the paranoid schizoid position that this is more likely to happen. As this phantasy is recognised in some other, the racist hates the hating self and tries to make reparation. The depressive anxiety associated with this position becomes too much and love turns to hate. The reintrojection of this object phanatasy acutely reinforces the fear of internal and external persecution. In other words, an excess of anxiety in the depressive position marks a return to paranoid schizoid defences. It is in this way that I argue that ignorance, anxiety and fear lead to racism, hatred and suffering. The racial 'other' is constructed in phantasy through ignorance, projected into others through fear, recognised in others as familiar, and experienced by us as *uncanny*.

If we can understand racism and acts of destructive hatred, then we can start to think about policy and practice to counter it.

This requires critical and sustained self-reflection. Psychoanalysis can give us some purchase on the affective elements of racism and ethnic hatred; it is that crazy, some call it irrational side of life that it addresses. The combination of socio-structural analysis and psychoanalytic interpretative theory allows us to look in parallel at how changing structures in society evoke certain emotions and anxieties. These powerful affective forces in turn support structures of discrimination which produce exclusionary practices leading to the maltreatment of people because of their specific 'otherness'.

Background and Further Reading

Below is a list of various texts which should be useful in pursuing most of the areas in this book. The areas are set out in distinct categories, but in reality many of the texts overlap. In particular the section on race and racism cannot be exhaustive as the field is huge, and the texts listed are those that I have found useful over the years and would recommend as a starting point.

Psychoanalytic sociology

Craib, I. (1989) *Psychoanalysis and Social Theory*. London: Harvester Wheatsheaf.

Craib, I. (2001) *Psychoanalysis: A Critical Introduction*. London: Polity.

Elliott, A. (1994) *Psychoanalytic Theory: An Introduction*. Oxford: Blackwell.

Elliott, A. (1999) *Social Theory and Psychoanalysis in Transition: Self and Society From Freud to Kristeva*. London: Free Association Books.

Richards, B. (1989) *Crisis of the Self*. London: Free Association Books.

Rustin, M. (1991) *The Good Society and the Inner World*. London: Verso.

Sigmund Freud

Freud, S. (1969) *Civilisation and its Discontents*. London: Hogarth Press.

Freud, S. (1991) *Two Short Accounts of Psychoanalysis*. London: Penguin.

Freud, S. (1953–1974) *The Standard Edition of the Complete Psychological Works of Sigmund Freud*. Vol 1–24. London: Hogarth Press. Trans. James Strachey.

Gay, P. (1988) *Freud: A Life for Our Time. London*: Papermac.

Jones, E. (1957) *Sigmund Freud: Life and Work*. London: Penguin.

Laplanche, J. and Pontalis, J.-P. (1973) *The Language of Psychoanalysis*. London: Hogarth Press.

Ricouer, P. (1970) *Freud and Philosophy: An Essay on Interpretation*. New Haven: Yale University Press.

Storr, A. (1996) *Freud*. London: Oxford University Press.

Melanie Klein

Hinshelwood, R. (1989) *A Dictionary of Kleinian Thought.* London: Free Association Books.

Hinshelwood, R. (1992) *Clinical Klein.* London: Free Association Books.

Klein, M. (1992) *Love, Guilt and Reparation and Other Works 1921–1945.* London: Karnac Books.

Klein, M. (1993) *Envy and Gratitude and Other Works 1946–1963.* London: Karnac Books.

Klein, M. (1996) *Narrative of a Child Analysis.* London: Karnac Books.

Klein, M. (1998) *The Psycho-Analysis of Children.* London: Karnac Books.

Kristeva, J. (2002) *Melanie Klein.* New York: Columbia University Press.

Mitchell, J. (1986) *The Selected Melanie Klein.* London: Penguin.

Segal, H. (1964) *Introduction to the Work of Melanie Klein.* London: Heinemann.

Kleinian and post-Kleinian psychoanalysis

Alford, C.F. (1989) *Melanie Klein and Critical Social Theory.* Berkeley: Yale University Press.

Bion, W.R. (1961) *Experiences in Groups.* London: Tavistock.

Bion, W.R. (1962) *Learning From Experience.* London: Karnac Books.

Bott Spillius, E. (1988) *Melanie Klein Today: Developments in Theory and Practice.* Vols 1–2. London: Routledge.

Grosskurth, P. (1986) *Melanie Klein: Her World and Her Work.* London: Hodder & Stoughton.

Klein, M., Heimann, P., Isaacs, S., and Riviere, J. (1952) *Developments in Psychoanalysis.* London: Hogarth Press.

Joseph, B. (1989) 'Projective Identification: Some Clinical Aspects'. In M. Feldman and E. Bott Spillius (eds), *Psychic Equilibrium and Psychic Change.* London: Tavistock/Routledge, pp. 168–80.

Meltzer, D. (1978) *The Kleinian Development.* London: Karnac Books.

Ogden, T.H. (1989) *The Primitive Edge of Experience.* London: Karnac Books.

Ogden, T.H. (1990) *The Matrix of the Mind: Object Relations and the Psychoanalytic Dialogue.* London: Karnac Books.

Sandler, J. (1987) *Projection, Identification and Projective Identification.* London: Karnac Books.

Winnicott, D.W. (1975) *Through Paediatrics to Psychoanalysis: Collected Papers.* London: Karnac Books.

Winnicott, D.W. (1971, 1991) *Playing and Reality.* London: Routledge.

Young, R.M. (1994) *Mental Space.* London: Process Press.

Lacan and post-Lacanian psychoanalysis

Bowie, M. (1991) *Lacan.* London: Fontana.

Dor, J. (1998) *Introduction to the Reading of Lacan: The Unconscious Structured Like a Language.* New York: Other Press.

Lacan, J. (1977) *The Four Fundamental Concepts of Psycho-Analysis.* London: Tavistock.

Lacan, J. (1977b) *Ecrits: A Selection.* London: Tavistock.

Lacan, J. (1988) *The Seminar of Jacques Lacan: Freud's Papers on Technique. 1953–54* (Vol 1). London: Cambridge University Press.

Lacan, J. (1988) *The Seminar of Jacques Lacan: The Ego in Freud's Theory and in the Technique of Psychoanalysis. 1954–55* (Vol 2). London: Cambridge University Press.

Laplanche, J. (1987) *New Foundations for Psychoanalysis.* Oxford: Blackwell.

Macey, D. (1988) *Lacan in Contexts.* London: Verso.

Roustang, F. (1990) *The Lacanian Delusion.* Oxford: Oxford University Press.

Samuels, R. (1993) *Between Philosophy and Psychoanalysis: Lacan's Reconstruction of Freud.* London: Routledge.

Verhaeghe, P. (2001) *Beyond Gender: From Subject to Drive.* New York: Other Press.

Zizek, S. (1988) *The Sublime Object of Ideology.* London: Verso.

Zizek, S. (1991) *Looking Awry: An Introduction to Jacques Lacan through Popular Culture.* London: MIT Press.

Psychoanalysis, racism and postcolonialism

Bhabha, H. (1994) *The Location of Culture.* London: Routledge.

Bulhan, H. (1985) *Frantz Fanon and the Psychology of Oppression.* London: Plenum Press.

Fanon, F. (1968) *Black Skin White Masks.* London: MacGibbon & Kee.

Fanon, F. (1990) *The Wretched of the Earth.* London: Penguin.

Frosh, S. (1989) Psychoanalysis and Racism. In B. Richards (ed.), *Crisis of the Self.* London: Free Association Books, pp. 229–43.

Gillman, S. (1985) *Difference and Pathology: Stereotypes of Sexuality, Race and Madness.* London: Cornell University Press.

Gordon, L., Whiting, T. and White, R. (1996). *Fanon: A Critical Reader.* Oxford: Blackwell.

Kovel, J. (1970) *White Racism: A Psychohistory.* London: Penguin.

Lane, C. (ed.) (1998) *The Psychoanalysis of Race.* Columbia: Columbia University Press.

Macey, D. (2000) *Frantz Fanon: A Life.* London: Granta Books.

Mannoni, O. (1964) *Prospero and Caliban: The Psychology of Colonization.* New York: Praeger.

McCulloch, J. (1983) *Black Soul White Artefact: Fanon's Clinical Psychology and Social Theory*. London: Cambridge University Press.

Rustin, M. (1991) Psychoanalysis, Racism and Anti-Racism. In *The Good Society and the Inner World*. London: Verso, pp. 57–84.

Sekyi Otu, A. (1996) *Fanon's Dialectic of Experience*. Harvard: Harvard University Press.

Seshadri-Crooks, K. (2000) *Desiring Whiteness: A Lacanian Analysis of Race*. London: Routledge.

Wolfenstein, E.V. (1981) *The Victims of Democracy: Malcolm X and the Black Revolution*. California: University of California Press.

Young-Bruehl, E. (1996) *The Anatomy of Prejudices*. Harvard: Harvard University Press.

Zizek, S. (1993) *Tarrying with the Negative*. Durham: Duke University Press.

Critical theory

Adorno, T. (1991) 'Freudian Theory and the Pattern of Fascist Propaganda'. *The Culture Industry*. London: Routledge, pp. 114–35.

Arato, A. and Gebhardt, E. (eds) (1984) *The Essential Frankfurt School Reader*. New York: Continuum.

Bernstein, J. (ed.) (1994) *The Frankfurt School: Critical Assessments*. London: Routledge.

Fromm, E. (1942) *The Fear of Freedom*. London: Routledge.

Fromm, E. (1973) *The Anatomy of Human Destructiveness*. London: Pimlico.

Habermas, J. (1971) *Knowledge and Human Interests*. London: Heinemann.

Held, D. (1980) *Introduction to Critical Theory*. London: Polity Press.

Horkheimer, M. and Adorno, T. (1994) *Dialectic of Enlightenment*. London: Continuum.

Hoy, D. and McCarthy, T. (1994) *Critical Theory*. Oxford: Blackwell.

Marcuse, H. (1972) *Eros and Civilisation*. London: Abacus.

Whitebrook, J. (1995) *Perversion and Utopia: A Study in Psychoanalysis and Critical Theory*. London: MIT Press.

Wiggershaus, R. (1994) *The Frankfurt School*. London: Polity Press.

Sociology of race and ethnicity

Anthias, F. and Yuval-Davis, N. (1992) *Racialized Boundaries*. London: Routledge.

Back, L. (1996) *New Ethnicities and Urban Culture: Racisms and Multiculture in Young Lives*. London: UCL Press.

Back, L. and Solomos, J. (2000) *Theories of Race and Racism*. London: Routledge.

Balibar, E. and Wallerstein, I. (1991) *Race, Nation, Class: Ambiguous Identities.* London: Verso.

Banton, M. (1997) *Ethnic and Racial Consciousness* (2nd edn). London: Longman.

Barker, M. (1981) *The New Racism.* London: Junction Books.

Bauman, Z. (1989) *Modernity and the Holocaust.* Cambridge: Polity.

Cashmore Ellis, E. (1984) *Dictionary of Race and Ethnic Relations.* London: Routledge.

Cohen, P. (ed.) (1999) *New Ethnicities, Old Racisms.* London: Zed Books.

Fryer, P. (1984) *Staying Power: The History of Black People in Britain.* London: Pluto Press.

Gilroy, P. (1997) *There Ain't No Black in the Union Jack.* London: Routledge.

Gilroy, P. (1993) *The Black Atlantic.* London: Verso.

Goldberg, D. (1993) *Racist Culture.* London: Blackwell.

Hall, S. (1992) 'The New Ethnicities'. In J. Donald and A. Rattansi (eds), *Race, Culture and Difference.* London: Sage, pp. 256–8.

hooks, b. (1990) *Ain't I a Woman.* London: Pluto Press.

hooks, b. (1992) *Black Looks.* New York: Turnaround.

Hutchinson, J. and Smith, A.D. (eds) (1996) *Ethnicity.* Oxford: Oxford University Press.

Mason, D. (1995) *Race and Ethnicity in Modern Britain.* Oxford: Oxford University Press.

Miles, R. (1993) *Racism After Race Relations.* London: Routledge.

Miles, R. (1995) *Racism.* London: Routledge.

Mirza, H.S. (1992) *Young, Female and Black.* London: Routledge.

Rex, J. (1996) *Ethnic Minorities in the Modern State.* London: Macmillan.

Said, E. (1995) *Orientalism.* London: Penguin

Smith, A.M. (1992) *New Right Discourses on Race and Sexuality.* Cambridge: Cambridge University Press.

Solomos, J. and Back, L. (1996) *Racism and Society.* London: Macmillan.

Werbner, P. and Modood, T. (eds) (1997) *Debating Cultural Hybridity: Multi-Cultural Identities and the Politics of Anti-Racism.* London: Zed Books.

Useful academic journals

There are numerous academic scholarly journals which publish cutting edge commentaries and papers on many of the issues discussed in this book. Below is a list of some of the most useful.

American Imago
Free Associations
International Journal of Psycho-analysis
Journal of Human Rights
Journal for the Psychoanalysis of Culture and Society

Journal for the Theory of Social Behaviour
Lacanian Ink
Psychoanalytic Studies
Ethnic and Racial Studies
Theory, Culture and Society

Web resources

There are several psychoanalytic websites which have papers that can be downloaded, and in some cases entire books. Because of the nature of the web, addresses tend to change frequently and sites appear as quickly as they disappear. This is just a sample.

American Psychoanalytic Association: **www.apsa.org**
British Psychoanalytic Society and Institute of Psychoanalysis: **http://www.psychoanalysis.org.uk/**
The Freud Museum London: **www.freud.org.uk/**
Human Nature.Com: **www.human-nature.com/**
International Psychoanalytic Association: **www.ipa.org.uk/**
Kleinian Studies Ejournal: **www.human-nature.com/ksej/index.html**
Melaine Klein Trust: **www.melanie-klein-trust.org.uk/**
Psychematters: **www.psychematters.com/**
Centre for Psycho-Social Studies, UWE (for links) **www.uwe.ac.uk/research/pssrg/**

Bibliography

Abel, E., Christian, B. and Moglen, H. (eds) (1997) *Female Subjects in Black and White: Race, Psychoanalysis and Feminism.* Berkeley: University of California Press.

Adorno, T., Frenkel-Brunswick, E., Levinson, D.J. and Sanford, R.N. (1950) *The Authoritarian Personality.* New York: Harper & Row.

Adorno, T. (1991) 'Freudian Theory and the Pattern of Fascist Propaganda'. In *The Culture Industry.* London: Routledge, pp. 114–35.

Afshar, H. and Maynard, M. (eds) (1994) *The Dynamics of 'Race' and Gender: Some Feminist Interventions.* London: Taylor & Francis.

Alexander, C. (1996) *The Art of Being Black.* Oxford: Clarendon Press.

Alford, C.F. (1989) *Melanie Klein and Critical Social Theory.* Berkeley: Yale University Press.

Alford, C.F. (1997) 'Hitler's Willing Executioners: What does Willing Mean?', *Theory and Society,* **26**(5).

Allport, G. (1954) *The Nature of Prejudice.* New York: Anchor Books.

Alvesson, M. and Skoldberg, K. (2000) *Reflexive Methodology: New Vistas for Qualitative Research.* London: Sage.

Anderson, R. (ed.) (1995) *Clinical Lectures on Klein and Bion.* London: Routledge.

Anthias, F. and Yuval-Davis, N. (1992) *Racialized Boundaries.* London: Routledge.

Anthias, F. (1998) 'Evaluating "Diaspora": Beyond Ethnicity', *Sociology,* **32**(3), pp. 557–80.

Anwar, M. (1998) *Between Cultures: Continuity and Change in the Lives of Young Asians.* London: Routledge.

Arato, A. and Gebhardt, E. (eds) (1984) *The Essential Frankfurt School Reader.* New York: Continuum.

Arendt, H. (1964) *Eichman in Jerusalem: A Report on the Banality of Evil.* New York: Viking Press.

Auden, W. (1952) *Selected Poems.* London: Penguin.

Back, L. (1996) *New Ethnicities and Urban Culture: Racisms and Multiculture in Young Lives.* London: UCL Press.

Balibar, E. and Wallerstein, I. (1991) *Race, Nation, Class: Ambiguous Identities.* London: Verso.

Banton, M. (1970) 'The Concept of Racism'. In S. Zubaida (ed.), *Race and Racialism.* London: Tavistock, pp. 17–33.

Banton, M. (1997) *Ethnic and Racial Consciousness* (2nd edn). London: Longman.

Bahr, E. (1994) 'The Anti-Semitism Studies of the Frankfurt School: The Failure of Critical Theory'. In J. Bernstein (ed.), *The Frankfurt School Critical Assessments*. London Routledge, pp. 226–33.

Barker, M. (1981) *The New Racism*. London: Junction Books.

Barot, R. (ed.) (1996) *The Racism Problematic: Contemporary Sociological Debates on Race and Ethnicity*. London: Edwin Mellen Press.

Barth, F. (1969) *Ethnic Groups and Boundaries*. Boston: Little, Brown & Co.

Bateman, A. and Holmes, J. (1995) *Introduction to Psychoanalysis: Contemporary Theory and Practice*. London: Routledge.

Bauman, Z. (1989) *Modernity and the Holocaust*. Cambridge: Polity.

Bauman, Z. (1990) *Thinking Sociologically*. Oxford: Blackwell.

Bauman, Z. (1991) *Modernity and Ambivalence*. Cambridge: Polity Press.

Bauman, Z. (1993) *Postmodern Ethics*. Oxford: Blackwell.

Benedict, R. (1940) *Race and Racism*. London: Routledge.

Benjamin, J. (1994) 'The Shadow of the Other (Subject): Intersubjectivity and Feminist Theory', *Constellations: An International Journal of Critical and Democratic Theory*, **1**(2), pp. 231–54.

Bernstein, J. (ed.) (1994) *The Frankfurt School: Critical Assessments*. London: Routledge.

Bhabha, H. (1986) 'Remembering Fanon: Self, Psyche and the Colonial Condition', Foreword to F. Fanon, *Black Skin White Masks*. London: Pluto Press, pp. vii–xv.

Bhabha, H. (1994) *The Location of Culture*. London: Routledge.

Bick, E. (1986) 'Further Observations on the Function of the Skin in Early Object Relations', *British Journal of Psychotherapy*, **2**(4), pp. 292–9.

Billig, M. (1978) *Fascists: A Social Psychological View of the National Front*. London: Harcourt Brace Jovanovich.

Billig, M. (1991) *Ideology and Opinions*. London: Sage.

Bion, W.R. (1961) *Experiences in Groups*. London: Tavistock.

Bion, W.R. (1962) *Learning From Experience*. London: Karnac Books.

Bion, W.R. (1967) *Second Thoughts*. London: Karnac Books.

Bion, W.R. (1988) 'Attacks on Linking'. In E. Bott Spillius (ed.), *Melanie Klein Today: Developments in Theory and Practice*, Vol 1. London: Routledge, pp. 87–101.

Bion, W.R. (1992) *Cogitations*. London: Karnac Books.

Bleandonu, G. (1994) *Wilfred Bion: His Life and Works 1897–1979*. London: Free Association Books.

Bollas, C. (1992) *Being A Character: Psychoanalysis and Self Experience*. London: Routledge.

Bollas, C. (1995) *Cracking Up: The Work of Unconscious Experience*. London: Routledge.

Bott Spillius, E. (1988) *Melanie Klein Today: Developments in Theory and Practice. Volume 1: Mainly Theory*. London: Routledge.

Bowie, M. (1991) *Lacan*. London: Fontana.

Braham, P., Rattansi, A. and Skellington, R. (1992) *Racism and Antiracism: Inequalities, Opportunities and Policies*. London: Sage.

British Sociological Association (1992) *Statement of Ethical Practice*. Durham: BSA.

Bulhan, H. (1985) *Frantz Fanon and the Psychology of Oppression*. London: Plenum Press.

Casement, P. (1985) *On Learning From the Patient*. London: Routledge.

Casement, P. (1990) *Further Learning From the Patient: The Analytic Space and Process*. London: Tavistock/Routledge.

Cashmore Ellis, E. (1984) *Dictionary of Race and Ethnic Relations*. London: Routledge.

Cashmore Ellis, E. and Troyna, B. (1990) *Introduction to Race Relations*. London: Falmer Press.

Castoriadis, C. (1999) 'The Psychical and Social Roots of Hate', *Free Associations*, **43**, pp. 402–15.

Cheshire, N. (1975) *The Nature of Psychodynamic Interpretation*. London: Wiley.

Clarke, R. (1980) *Freud. The Man and the Cause*. London: Cape.

Clarke, S. (1999) 'Splitting Difference: Psychoanalysis, Hatred and Exclusion', *Journal for the Theory of Social Behaviour*, **29**(1), pp. 21–35.

Clarke, S. (2000) 'Experiencing Racism in Higher Education', *Journal of Socio-Analysis*, **2**(1), pp. 47–63.

Clarke, S. (2000) 'Psychoanalysis, Psychoexistentialism and Racism', *Psychoanalytic Studies*, **2**(4), pp. 343–55.

Clarke, S. (2001) 'The Kleinian Position: Phantasy, Splitting and the Language of Psychic Violence', *Journal for the Psychoanalysis of Culture and Society*, **6**(2), pp. 289–97.

Clarke, S. (2001) 'Projective Identification: From Attack to Empathy?' *Journal of Kleinian Studies*, **2**.

Clarke, S. (2001) 'From Aesthetics to Object Relations: Situating Klein in the Freudian Uncanny', *Free Associations*, **48**, pp. 547–61.

Clifford, J. (1994) 'Diasporas', *Cultural Anthropology*, **9**, pp. 302–38.

Cohen, A. (1995) *Delinquent Boys: The Culture of the Gang*. New York: Free press.

Cohen, P. (1989) 'Reason, Racism and the Popular Monster'. In B. Richards, *Crises of the Self*. London: Free Association Books.

Cohen, P. (1997) *Rethinking the Youth Question: Education, Labour and Cultural Studies*. London: Macmillan.

Cohen, P. (1999) 'Through a Glass Darkly'. In P. Cohen (ed.), *New Ethnicities, Old Racisms*. London: Zed Books, pp. 1–17.

Cohen, R. (1994) *Frontiers of Identity*. London: Longman.

Cohen, R. (1997) *Global Diasporas: An Introduction*. London: UCL Press.

Conrad, J. (1909, 1966) *The Secret Sharer. Great Short Works of Joseph Conrad*. New York: Harper.

Conrad, J. (1902, 1983) *Heart of Darkness*. London: Penguin.

Cornell, S. and Hartmann, D. (1998) *Ethnicity and Race: Making Identities in a Changing World*. London: Pine Forge Press.

Cox, O. (1948) *Caste, Class and Race*. New York: Monthly Review Press.

Craib, I. (1989) *Psychoanalysis and Social Theory*. London: Harvester-Wheatsheaf.

Craib, I. (1994) *The Importance of Disappointment*. London: Routledge.

Craib, I. (1998) *Experiencing Identity*. London: Sage.

Crews, F. (1993) 'The Unknown Freud'. *New York Review of Books*. 18th November.

Davids, T. (2002) 'Sept 11th: Some Thoughts on Racism and Religious Prejudice as an Obstacle', *British Journal of Psychotherapy*, **18**(3), pp. 361–6.

Donald, J. and Rattansi, A. (1992) *'Race', Culture and Difference*. London: Sage.

Douglas, M. (1966) *Purity and Danger*. London: Routledge.

Elias, N. (1978) *The Civilising Process 1: The History of Manners*. Oxford: Blackwell.

Elliott, A. (1994) *Psychoanalytic Theory: An Introduction*. Oxford: Blackwell.

Elliott, A. and Frosh, S. (eds) (1995) *Psychoanalysis in Contexts*. London: Routledge.

Elliott, A. (1999) *Social Theory and Psychoanalysis in Transition: Self and Society from Freud to Kristeva* (2nd edn). London: Free Association Books.

Essed, P. (1991) *Understanding Everyday Racism: An Interdisciplinary Theory*. London: Sage.

Evans-Pritchard, E. (1965) *Witchcraft, Oracles and Magic Among the Azande*. London: Clarendon Press.

Fanon, F. (1952, 1968) *Black Skin White Masks*. London: MacGibbon & Kee.

Fanon, F. (1961, 1990) *The Wretched of the Earth*. London: Penguin.

Feldman, M. (1997) 'Projective Identification: The Analyst's Involvement', *International Journal of Psycho-Analysis*, **78**(2), pp. 227–41.

Ferrell, R. (1996) *Passion in Theory: Conceptions of Freud and Lacan*. London: Routledge.

Fitzherbert, K. (1967) *West Indian Children in London: Occasional Papers on Social Administration*, **19**, London: Bell & Sons.

Fordham, M. (1995) *Freud, Jung, Klein: The Fenceless Field*. London: Routledge.

Foucault, M. (1977) *Discipline and Punish: The Birth of the Prison*. London: Penguin.

Foucault, M. (1978) *The History of Sexuality: An Introduction*. Vol 1. London: Pantheon Books.

Foucault, M. (1995) *Madness and Civilisation: A History of Insanity in the Age of Reason*. London: Routledge.

Freud, A. (1970) *Research at the Hampstead Child-Therapy Clinic and Other Papers*. London: Hogarth Press.

Freud, S. (1914, 1961) 'The Case History of Schreber, Papers on Technique and Other Works'. In *Standard Edition* Vol. 12. London: Hogarth Press, pp. 12–34.

Freud, S. (1919, 1961) 'The Uncanny'. In *Standard Edition* Vol. 17. London: Hogarth Press, pp. 219–52.

Freud, S. (1923a, 1961) 'Consciousness and what is Unconscious', *The Standard Edition* Vol. 19. London: Hogarth Press, pp. 13–18.

Freud, S. (1923b, 1961) 'The Ego and the Id'. *In Standard Edition* Vol. 19. London: Hogarth Press, pp. 19–27.

Freud, S. (1930, 1961) 'Civilization and its Discontents'. In *Standard Edition* Vol. 21. London: Hogarth Press, pp. 64–145.

Freud, S. (1933, 1964) 'The Dissection of the Psychical Personality'. In *Standard Edition* Vol. 22. London: Hogarth Press, pp. 57–80.

Freud, S. (1940, 1964) 'Outline of Psycho-Analysis'. In *Standard Edition* Vol. 23. London: Hogarth Press, pp. 144–7.

Freud, S. (1937, 1964) 'Analysis Terminable and Interminable'. In *Standard Edition* Vol. 23. London: Hogarth Press, pp. 216–53.

Freud, S (1930, 1969) *Civilization and its Discontents.* London: Hogarth Press.

Freud, S. (1991) *Two Short Accounts of Psychoanalysis.* London: Penguin.

Fromm, E. (1942) *The Fear of Freedom.* London: Routledge.

Fromm, E. (1973) *The Anatomy of Human Destructiveness.* London: Pimlico.

Frosh, S. (1991) *Identity Crisis: Modernity, Psychoanalysis and the Self.* London: Macmillan.

Frosh, S. (1989) 'Psychoanalysis and Racism'. In B. Richards (ed.), *Crisis of the Self.* London: Free Association Books, pp. 229–43.

Frosh, S. (1987) *The Politics of Psychoanalysis.* London: Macmillan.

Fryer, P. (1984) *Staying Power: The History of Black People in Britain.* London: Pluto Press.

Gardner, S. (1992) 'The Unconscious'. In J. Neu (ed.), *The Cambridge Companion to Freud.* Cambridge: Cambridge University Press.

Garfinkel, H. (1967) *Studies in Ethnomethodology.* London: Prentice-Hall.

Gay, P. (1985) *Freud: A Life for our Time.* London: PaperMac.

Gellner, E. (1993) *The Psychoanalytic Movement: The Cunning of Unreason.* London: Fontana.

Gillborn, D. (1990) *'Race', Ethnicity and Education: Teaching and Learning in Multi-Ethnic Schools.* London: Unwin Hyman.

Gillborn, D. (1995) *Racism and Antiracism in Real Schools.* Buckingham: Open University Press.

Gillborn, D. (1996) 'Exclusion From School', *Viewpoint,* **5**(4), London: Institute of Education.

Gillman, S. (1985) *Difference and Pathology: Stereotypes of Sexuality, Race and Madness.* London: Cornell University Press.

Gilman, S. (1999) 'Sigmund Freud and the Epistemology of Race'. In A. Elliott (ed.), *Contemporary Social Theory.* London: Blackwell, pp. 220–30.

Gilroy, P. (1997) *There Ain't No Black in the Union Jack.* London: Routledge.

Gilroy, P. (1993) *The Black Atlantic*. London: Verso.

Glaser, H. (1978) *The Cultural Roots of National Socialism*. London: Croom Helm.

Glymour, C. (1992) 'Freud's Androids'. In J. Neu (ed.), *The Cambridge Companion to Freud*. Cambridge: Cambridge University Press.

Goffman, E. (1978) *The Presentation of Self in Everyday Life*. London: Penguin.

Goldhagen, D.J. (1996) *Hitler's Willing Executioners: Ordinary Germans and the Holocaust*. London: Abacus.

Gomez, L. (1997) *An Introduction to Object Relations*. London: Free Association Books.

Gordon, L., Whiting, T. and White, R. (1996) *Fanon: A Critical Reader*. Oxford: Blackwell.

Gordon, S. (1984) *Hitler, Germans and the 'Jewish Question'*. Princetown: Princetown University Press.

Gotz, Pross and Chroust (1994) *Cleansing the Fatherland*. New York: Johns Hopkins University Press.

Griffin, R. (1991) *The Nature of Fascism*. London: Routledge.

Grosskurth, P. (1986) *Melanie Klein: Her World and Her Work*. London: Hodder & Stoughton.

Grunbaum, A. (1984) *The Foundations of Psychoanalysis: A Philosophical Critique*. Berkley: University of California Press.

Guntrip, H. (1968) *Personality Structure and Human Interaction*. London: Hogarth Press.

Habermas, J. (1971) *Knowledge and Human Interests*. London: Heinemann.

Hakluyt, R. (1972) *Voyages and Discoveries*. Harmondsworth: Penguin.

Hall, S. (1990) 'Cultural Identity and Diaspora'. In J. Rutherford (ed.), *Identity: Community, Culture, Difference*. London: Lawrence & Wishart.

Hall, S. (1992) 'The New Ethnicities'. In J. Donald and A. Rattansi (eds), *Race, Culture and Difference*. London: Sage, pp. 256–8.

Harré, R. (ed.) (1986) *The Social Construction of Emotions*. London: Blackwell.

Hayes, P. (1973) *Fascism*. London: Allen & Unwin

Heidegger, M. (1927, 1987) *Being and Time*. Oxford: Blackwell.

Held, D. (1980) *Introduction to Critical Theory*. London: Polity Press.

Heald, S. and Deluz, A. (1994) *Anthropology and Psychoanalysis: An Encounter Through Culture*. London: Routledge.

Hinshelwood, R.D. (1987) *What Happens in Groups: Psychoanalysis, the Individual and the Community*. London: Free Association Books.

Hinshelwood, R.D. (1989) *A Dictionary of Kleinean Thought*. London: Free Association Books.

Hinshelwood, R.D. (1994) *Clinical Klein*. London: Free Association Books.

Hoggett, P. (1992a) A Place for Experience: A Psychoanalytic Perspective on Boundary, Identity, and Culture. *Environment and Planning D: Society and Space*, **10**, pp. 345–56.

Hoggett, P. (1992b) *Partisans in an Uncertain World: The Psychoanalysis of Engagement*. London: Free Association Books.

Hoggett, P., Jeffers, S. and Harrison, L. (1994) 'Reflexivity and Uncertainty in the Research Process', *Policy and Politics*, **22**(1), pp. 59–70.

Horkheimer, M. and Flowerman, S. (1950) *Studies in Prejudice*. New York: Harper.

Horkheimer, M. and Adorno, T. (1994) *Dialectic of Enlightenment*. London: Continuum.

Hoy, D. and McCarthy, T. (1994) *Critical Theory*. Oxford: Blackwell.

Hutchinson, J. and Smith, A.D. (eds) (1996) *Ethnicity*. Oxford: Oxford University Press.

Innes, B. (1998) Experiences in Difference: An Exploration of the Usefulness and 'Relevance of Psychoanalytic Theory to Transcultural Mental Health Work', *Psychodynamic Counselling*, **4**(2), pp. 171–89.

Irigaray, L. (1985) *The Sex Which is Not One*. New York: Cornell University Press.

Isaacs, S. (1952) 'The Nature and Function of Phantasy'. In M. Klein, P. Heimann, S. Isaacs and J. Riviere, *Developments in Psychoanalysis*. London: Hogarth Press, pp. 67–121.

Jay, M. (1994) 'The Jews and the Frankfurt School: Critical Theory's Analysis of Anti-Semitism'. In J. Bernstein (ed.), *The Frankfurt School Critical Assessments*. London: Routledge, pp. 235–46.

Jenkins, R. (1986) *Racism and Recruitment*. Cambridge: Cambridge University Press.

Joffe, H. (1996) 'The Shock of the New: A Psycho-Dynamic Extension of Social Representational Theory', *Journal for the Theory of Social Behaviour*, **26**(2), pp. 197–219.

Jones, E. (1953) *Sigmund Freud: His Life and Work Volume One: The Young Freud 1856–1900*. London: Hogarth Press.

Joseph, B. (1989) 'Different Types of Anxiety'. In M. Feldman and E. Bott Spillius (eds), *Psychic Equilibrium and Psychic Change*. London: Tavistock/Routledge, pp. 106–15.

Joseph, B. (1989) 'On Understanding and Not Understanding'. In M. Feldman and E. Bott Spillius (eds), *Psychic Equilibrium and Psychic Change*. London: Tavistock/Routledge, pp. 139–50.

Joseph, B. (1989) 'Transference: The Total Situation'. In M. Feldman and E. Bott Spillius (eds), *Psychic Equilibrium and Psychic Change*. London: Tavistock/Routledge, pp. 156–67.

Joseph, B. (1989) 'Projective Identification: Some Clinical Aspects'. Feldman, M. and Bott Spillius, E. (eds), *Psychic Equilibrium and Psychic Change*. London: Tavistock/Routledge, pp. 168–80.

Khan, M. (1974) *The Privacy of the Self*. London: Karnac Books.

Klein, M. and Riviere, J. (1937) *Love, Hate and Reparation*. London: Hogarth Press.

Klein, M. (1946) 'Notes on Some Schizoid Mechanisms', *International Journal of Psycho-Analysis*, **26**, pp. 99–110.

Klein, M. (1936, 1975) 'Weaning'. In *Love, Guilt and Reparation and Other Works 1921–1945*. London: Karnac Books, pp. 290–305.

Klein, M. (1937, 1988) *Love, Guilt, and Reparation*. London: Virago.

Klein, M. (1946, 1997) 'Notes on Some Schizoid Mechanisms'. In *Envy and Gratitude and Other Works 1946–1963*. London: Vintage, pp. 1–24.

Klein, M. (1952a, 1997) 'The Mutual Influences in the development of the Ego and Id'. In *Envy and Gratitude and Other Works 1946–1963*. London: Vintage, pp. 57–60.

Klein, M. (1952b, 1997) 'Some Theoretical Conclusions Regarding the Emotional Life of the Infant'. In *Envy and Gratitude and Other Works 1946–1963*. London: Vintage, pp. 61–93.

Klein, M. (1957, 1997) 'Envy and Gratitude'. In *Envy and Gratitude and Other Works 1946–1963*. London: Vintage, pp. 176–235.

Klein, M. (1958, 1997) 'On the Development of Mental Functioning'. In *Envy and Gratitude and Other Works 1946–1943*. London: Vintage, pp. 236–46.

Klein, M. (1959, 1997) 'Our Adult World and its Roots in Infancy'. In *Envy and Gratitude and Other Works 1946–1963*. London: Vintage, pp. 247–63.

Kovel, J. (1970) *White Racism: A Psychohistory*. London: Penguin.

Kristeva, J. (1989) *Black Sun: Depression and Melancholia*. New York: Columbia University Press.

Kristeva, J. (1991) *Strangers to Ourselves*. New York: Harvester.

Kristeva, J. (2002) *Melanie Klein*. New York: Columbia University Press.

Lacan, J. (1977a) *The Four Fundamental Concepts of Psycho-Analysis*. London: Tavistock.

Lacan, J. (1977b) *Ecrits: A Selection*. London: Tavistock.

Laplanche, J. and Pontalis, J.-B. (1973) *The Language of Psychoanalysis*. London: Hogarth Press.

Lawrence, E. (1982) 'Just Plain Commonsense: "The Roots of Racism"'. *The Empire Strikes Back*. London: Hutchinson.

Lane, C. (ed.) (1998) *The Psychoanalysis of Race*. Columbia: Columbia University Press.

Leader, D. (2000) *Freud's Footnotes*. London: Faber & Faber.

Lechte, J. (1994) *Fifty Key Contemporary Thinkers: From Structuralism to Postmodernity*. London: Routledge.

Lifton, R.J. (1986) *The Nazi Doctors: Medical Killing and the Psychology of Genocide*. London: Macmillan.

Lyon, W. (1997) 'Defining Ethnicity'. In T. Modood and P. Werbner (eds), *The Politics of Multiculturalism in the New Europe: Racism, Identity and Community*. London: Zed Books, pp. 186–205.

Macey, D. (2000) *Frantz Fanon: A Life*. London: Granta Books.

Macey, D. (2001) 'Fanon, Politics and Psychiatry: The North African Syndrome', *Free Associations*, **8**(3), No 47, pp. 463–85.

Mannoni, O. (1964) *Prospero and Caliban: The Psychology of Colonization*. New York: Praeger.

Marcuse, H. (1972) *Eros and Civilisation*. London: Abacus.

Mason, D. (1995) *Race and Ethnicity in Modern Britain*. Oxford: Oxford University Press.

MacPherson, W. (1999) *The Stephen Lawrence Inquiry*. London: HMSO.

McCulloch, J. (1983) *Black Soul White Artifact: Fanon's Clinical Psychology and Social Theory*. London: Cambridge University Press.

McLelland, D. (1977) *Karl Marx: Selected Writings*. Oxford: Oxford University Press.

Mein Kampf (1973) London: Hutchinson.

Meltzer, D. (1978) *The Kleinian Development*. London: Karnac Books.

Menzies Lyth, I. (1988) *Containing Anxiety in Institutions*. London: Free Association Books.

Menzies Lyth, I. (1989) *The Dynamics of the Social*. London: Free Association Books.

Miles, R. (1990) 'Racism, Ideology and Disadvantage', *Social Studies Review*, 5(4), pp. 148–51.

Miles, R. (1993) *Racism After Race Relations*. London: Routledge.

Miles, R. (1995) *Racism*. London: Routledge.

Milgram, S. (1974) *Obedience to Authority: An Experimental View*. London: Tavistock.

Minsky, R. (1996) *Psychoanalysis and Gender*. London: Routledge.

Mirza, H.S. (1992) *Young, Female and Black*. London: Routledge.

Mitchell, J. (1974) *Psychoanalysis and Feminism*. London: Penguin.

Mitchell, J. (1986) *The Selected Melanie Klein*. London: Penguin.

Modood, T. (1997) *Ethnic Minorities on Britain: Diversity and Disadvantage*. London: Policy Studies Institute.

Modood, T. and Shiner, M. (1994) *Ethnic Minorities and Higher Education*. London: Policy Studies Institute.

Modood, T., Beishon, S. and Virdee, S. (1994) *Changing Ethnic Identities*. London: Policy Studies Institute.

Moran, A. (2002) 'The Psychodynamics of Australian Settler Nationalism: Assimilating or Reconciling with the Aborigines', *Political Psychology* 23. Forthcoming.

OFSTED (1995–6). *Exclusions From Secondary Schools*. London: HMSO.

Ogden, T.H. (1989) *The Primitive Edge of Experience*. London: Karnac Books.

Ogden, T.H. (1986) *The Matrix of the Mind: Object Relations and the Psychoanalytic Dialogue*. London: Karnac Books.

O'Prey, P. (1983) Introduction to J. Conrad, *Heart of Darkness*. London: Penguin.

Peukert, D. (1989) *The Genesis of the 'Final Soloution' From the Spirit of Science*. London: Vandenhoek & Ruprecht.

Phillips, J. and Stonebridge, L. (eds) (1998) *Reading Melanie Klein*. London: Routledge.

Popper, K. (1962) *The Open Society and its Enemies*. Princetown: Princetown University Press.

Pross, Chroust, and Gotz (1994) *Cleansing the Fatherland*. New York: Johns Hopkins University Press.

Pryce, K. (1979) *Endless Pressure*. London: Penguin.

Rex, J. (1970) *Race Relations in Sociological Theory*. London: Weidenfeld & Nicolson.

Rex, J. and Tomlinson, S. (1979) *Colonial Immigrants in a British City: A Class Analysis*. London: Routledge.

Rex, J. (1996) *Ethnic Minorities in the Modern State*. London: Macmillan.

Richards, B. (1989) *Images of Freud: Cultural Responses to Psychoanalysis*. London: Dent.

Rickert, J. (1994) 'The Fromm-Marcuse Debate Revisited'. In J. Bernstein (ed.), *The Frankfurt School Critical Assessments*. London: Routledge, pp. 278–319.

Ricoeur, P. (1970) *Freud and Philosophy: An Essay on Interpretation*. New Haven: Yale University Press.

Rosenfeld, H. (1988) 'Contribution to the Psychopathology of Psychotic States: The Importance of Projective Identification in the Ego Structure and the Object Relations of the Psychotic Patient'. In E. Bott Spillius (ed.), *Melanie Klein Today: Developments in Theory and Practice, Volume 1: Mainly Theory*. London: Routledge, pp. 117–37.

Roustang, F. (1990) *The Lacanian Delusion*. Oxford: Oxford University Press.

Rustin, M. (1991) 'Psychoanalysis, Racism and Anti-Racism'. In *The Good Society and the Inner World*. London: Verso, pp. 57–84.

Sabini, J. and Silver, M. (1986) 'Envy'. In R. Harre (ed.), *The Social Construction of Emotions*. London Blackwell, pp. 167–83.

Said, E. (1993) *Culture and Imperialism*. London: Vintage Books.

Said, E. (1995) *Orientalism*. London: Penguin.

Sandler, J. (1987) 'The Concept of Projective Identification'. In J. Sandler (ed.), *Projection, Identification and Projective Identification*. London: Karnac Books, pp. 13–26.

Sartre, J.-P. (1943, 1992) *Being and Nothingness*. New York: Washington Square Press.

Sartre, J.-P. (1968) 'On Genocide'. *Ramparts*, pp. 37–42.

Sartre, J.-P. (1976) *Anti-Semite and Jew: An Exploration of the Etiology of Hate*. New York: Schocken Books.

Sarup, M. (1992) *Jacques Lacan*. London: Harvester-Wheatsheaf.

Schwartz, J. (2000) *Cassandra's Daughter: A History of Psychoanalysis*. London: Penguin.

Seabrook, J. (1973) *City Close-up*. London: Penguin.

Segal, H. (1964) *Introduction to the Work of Melanie Klein*. London: Heinemann.

Segal, H. (1989) *Klein*. London: Karnac Books.

Segal, J. (1992) *Melanie Klein*. London: Sage.

Sekyi-Otu, A. (1996) *Fanon's Dialectic of Experience*. Harvard: Harvard University Press.

Seshadri-Crooks, K. (2000) *Desiring Whiteness: A Lacanian Analysis of Race*. London: Routledge.

Simmel, G. (1950) *The Sociology of Georg Simmel* (ed. and trans.) K. Wolff, New York: The Free Press.

Small, S. (1992) *Racialised Barriers*. London: Routledge.

Smith, A.M. (1992) *New Right Discourses on Race and Sexuality*. Cambridge: Cambridge University Press.

Smith, D. and Tomlinson, S. (1989) *The School Effect: A Study of Multicultural Comprehensives*. London: Policy Studies Institute.

Solomos, J. and Back, L. (1996) *Racism and Society*. London: Macmillan.

Spender, D. (1980) *Man Made Language*. London: Routledge.

Storr, A. (1996) *Freud*. Oxford: Oxford University Press.

Suttie, I. (1988) *The Origins of Love and Hate*. London: Free Association Books.

Symington, J. and N. (1996) *The Clinical Thinking of Wilfred Bion*. London: Routledge.

Theweleit, K. (1989) *Male Fantasies*. Vol 2. London: Polity Press.

Troyna, B. (1987) *Racial Inequality in Education*. London: Tavistock.

Troyna, B. and Carrington, B. (1990) *Education, Racism and Reform*. London: Routledge.

Troyna, B. (1992) 'Can you See the Join: An historical analysis of multicultural and antiracist education policies'. In D. Gill, B. Mayor and M. Blair (eds), *Racism and Education*. London: Sage, pp. 63–91.

Weber, M. (1949) *The Methodology of the Social Sciences*. New York: The Free Press.

Weber, M. (1978) *Economy and Society, Vol 1*. Berkeley: University of California Press.

Weber, M. (1993) *The Protestant Ethic and the Spirit of Capitalism*. London: Routledge.

Welch, D. (1993) *The Third Reich: Politics and Propaganda*. London: Routledge.

Werbner, P. and Modood, T. (eds) (1997) *Debating Cultural Hybridity: Multi-Cultural Identities and the Politics of Anti-Racism*. London: Zed Books.

Whitebrook, J. (1995) *Perversion and Utopia: A Study in Psychoanalysis and Critical Theory*. London: MIT Press.

Wieviorka, M. (1995) *The Arena of Racism*. London: Sage.

Wiggershaus, R. (1994) *The Frankfurt School*. London: Polity Press.

Williams, G. (1997) 'Reflections on Some Dynamics of Eating Disorders: "No Entry" Defences and Foreign Bodies', *International Journal of Psycho-Analysis*, **78**, pp. 927–41.

Winnicott, D.W. (1975) *Through Paediatrics to Psychoanalysis: Collected Papers*. London: Karnac Books.

Winnicott, D.W. (1971, 1991) *Playing and Reality*. London: Routledge.

Winnicott, D.W. (1992) *Human Nature*. London: Free Association Books.

Young, I.M. (1997) 'Asymmetrical Reciprocity: On Moral Respect, Wonder and Enlarged Thought', *Constellations*, **3**(3), pp. 340–63.

Young, R.M. (1994) *Mental Space*. London: Process Press.

Young, R. (1997) 'Phantasy and Psychotic Anxieties'. In B. Burgoyne and M. Sullivan (eds), *The Klein–Lacan Dialogues*. New York: Other Press, pp. 65–81.

Young-Bruehl, E. (1996) *The Anatomy of Prejudices*. Harvard: Harvard University Press.

Zizek, S. (1991) *Looking Awry: An introduction to Jacques Lacan through Popular Culture*. London: MIT Press.

Zizek, S. (1993) *Tarrying with the Negative*. Durham: Duke University Press.

Index